Military Lessons of the Falkland Islands War: Views from the United States

Also of Interest

The Armed Forces of the USSR, Second Edition, Revised and Updated, Harriet Fast Scott and William F. Scott

Red Navy at Sea: Soviet Naval Operations on the High Seas, 1956-1980, Bruce W. Watson

About the Book and Editors

Military Lessons of the Falkland Islands War:
Views from the United States
edited by Bruce W. Watson and Peter M. Dunn

The Falkland Islands war brought into sharp focus the historical essentials of victory: the valor of individual soldiers and of teams, on the one hand, and the imaginative and bold use of contemporary technology, on the other. This conflict, involving the commitment of superbly trained, professional soldiers by the British and the commitment of traditional and high-technology weapons by both sides, may offer more significant lessons than any other major war of recent years. This book contains analyses of the war by several prominent U.S. experts on national security affairs. Their observations reflect the continuing debate on such key issues in U.S. defense planning -- and in Soviet defense planning as well -- as the controversy over large versus small carriers, the advantages and disadvantages of a diesel- versus a nuclear-powered submarine fleet, the effectiveness of the Harrier-type airplane, the influence of high technology on amphibious warfare, and the ever-increasing use of "smart" weapons by all-purpose conventional armed forces.

Perhaps the most important lesson to be learned from the war is that there have been no quantum leaps in our knowledge of how to project power and how to fight a war far from home. Ultimately the foot soldier, well trained and capably commanded, was the key to victory. High-technology weapons, while important, were not the decisive factor. The V/STOL concept, as embodied in the Harrier plane and the use of small carriers, was vindicated, and the absolute necessity for different and separate management of naval and amphibious operations was again proven.

Intelligence provided by special troops augmented national intelligence systems and was also vital for victory. In the domestic arena, decisive action by the British government overcame an emotionally unified but otherwise deeply fractured Argentine political military leadership. And overall, Britain's management of the war, including the use of communications, was far superior to the Argentine performance.

BRUCE W. WATSON (Commander, U.S. Navy) is director of research at the Defense Intelligence School and is an adjunct professor in the Russian Area Studies Program at Georgetown University. Dr. Watson is the author of Red Navy at Sea (Westview/Arms and Armour Press, 1982).

PETER M. DUNN (Colonel, U.S. Air Force) is a veteran of three combat tours in Vietnam and is presently the assistant provost for research at the Defense Intelligence College. He is the author of the forthcoming book The First Vietnam War (Indochina 1945-46).

Military Lessons of the Falkland Islands War: Views from the United States

edited by Bruce W. Watson
and Peter M. Dunn

Foreword by F. Clifton Berry, Jr.

Westview Press • Boulder, Colorado
Arms and Armour Press • London, England

This book is included in Westview's Special Studies in Military Affairs.

The views expressed in this book are solely those of the authors and do not
represent the positions or policies of any agency or department of the United
States government.   The chapters in this book were derived from unclassified
publications and sources and are intended to neither confirm or deny,
officially or unofficially, the views of the United States government.

Published in the United States of America in 1984 by Westview Press, Inc.,
5500 Central Avenue, Boulder, Colorado 80301. Frederick A. Praeger, President
and Publisher.

Published in Great Britain in 1984 by Arms and Armour Press, 2-6 Hampstead
High Street, London NW3 1QQ.

Library of Congress Catalog Card Number: 83-51158
ISBN (U.S.): 0-86531-693-7
ISBN (U.K.): 0-85368-638-6

Composition for this book was provided by the editors
Printed and bound in the United States of America

5 4 3 2 1

Contents

Foreword

F. Clifton Berry, Jr.
Editor in Chief, *Air Force* Magazine

In this work, several of my colleagues discuss the major military lessons of the Falkland Islands War. Together they can be said to compose an American view of the conflict. My purpose is to present an overview of these lessons, which will serve as an introduction to the more detailed discussions that follow. In this respect, a recurring refrain runs through all the "lessons learned" that have so far come out of the conflict in the South Atlantic. It is this: these are not new lessons. Instead, they are replays of similar lessons from past wars.

Both sides relearned the obvious. A nation goes to war with what it has, not with what it would wish to have. For the British, add the lesson that war does not necessarily break out when and where you planned for it to occur. For the Argentine leaders, add the important lesson that one must be prepared to go all the way when one begins escalating a dispute from the diplomatic to the martial.

Cataloging the lessons learned from the Falklands conflict rapidly became a worldwide growth industry in mid-1982, with armed services planners and military thinkers in and out of governments on both sides of the Atlantic scrambling to develop useful data. For the military, it meant trying to derive, from the scant information available, lessons that might be applicable to their own equipment and organizations. For many of the civilians, the lessons included figuring out which ones supported their pet projects or theories. And for manufacturers, the lessons that validated their weapons could be turned into useful selling points with customers, present or prospective. In this context, the lessons that follow should be considered indicative rather than exhaustive, and tentative instead of conclusive.

PERSONNEL

One of the immutable lessons of any war is that the quality of the individual fighting man is paramount. In this case, the airmen on both sides can be proud of their record of individual skill, courage, and tenacity. The Argentine Air Force emerged from the war with high morale despite severe losses, and the Royal Air Force and Royal Navy aircrews returned from the conflict no less proud of their achievements. These accomplishments reflect the validity of rigorous selection and training policies in the air arms of both countries and the high quality of their leadership. They also show the importance of flexible thinking in aircrews that allows them to adapt to unforeseen or changing circumstances.

According to British sources, the Argentine ground forces were not of the same caliber as the airmen, either in individual qualities or in leadership. They cite the high incidence of cold injuries among the Stanley troops as an example of leaders who failed their soldiers.

INTELLIGENCE

Before the invasion, the Argentine political (and simultaneously, its military) leadership either lacked appropriate intelligence data or misread what it did have. It seemed to believe, on the basis of information held, that the British would not react as they did or that the US Government would support the Argentine case. They were wrong on both counts.

The British immediately reacted to oppose the invasion and retake the islands, and the US honored long-standing agreements with the British for exchange of information. As General T. R. Milton wrote after conversations with Argentine airmen, "They say the British could not have won that war without the considerable help of the United States, an ironic commentary on the American attempt to stay friends with both sides, since the general feeling in Britain is that we did not help enough. At any rate, in the Argentine view, American assistance at Ascension was vital to the British effort, and our satellite intelligence provided the British a great advantage."[1]

General Milton continued, "If the Argentines had received similar intelligence, they feel certain they would have sunk the Queen Elizabeth 2, a prize they badly wanted. As for Soviet satellite information, the Argentines deny receiving any, principally because they lacked the communication links. Evidently, the Soviets, always happy to take on a Latin American client, did offer their services."[2]

In the field of tactical intelligence, both sides relied heavily on pilot reports. These have the value of immediacy and an expert point of view, but are often defective because of the heat of battle and, in this case, the absence of cross-checks from other sources, human and technical. (On the ground, as the British brigade advanced toward Stanley, its leaders used the local telephone system for intelligence gathering. They phoned ahead and learned from citizens where the Argentine troops were or whether they had withdrawn.)

OPERATIONS AND TRAINING

For both sides, this was an air, land, and sea conflict requiring the best integration of all forces. For the British, it was conducted 8,000 miles from home. Although the Argentine forces fought closer to home, it was at the outer limits of their aircraft range. It was the sort of conflict that required

individual and unit initiative, as well as joint service integration.

In command arrangements, the British had the advantage. Once
Her Majesty's Government had decided to retake the islands, the
Prime Minister left the execution of the mission to the military,
supporting them in every possible way without micromanaging the
campaign. The Argentine side was afflicted by inter-service
tensions at home. Even with the best of will in the field, those
tensions inevitably affected adversely how the campaign was
fought.

Neither side had total air superiority over the battlefield.
This lack of superiority was a contributing factor to the loss of
five British ships. On their side, the British lost the same
number of Harrier aircraft as ships, all to ground fire. (That
was in the course of 1,650 sorties in all roles.) As noted, even
without air superiority, aircrews on both sides performed
admirably.

Airfield disablement proved difficult, raising questions about
its effectiveness in other conflicts in other theaters. The
Argentine Air Force continued to operate Pucara aircraft off the
Stanley airfield and British Harriers operated from a short
tactical strip at the San Carlos beachhead despite hits on both.

Neither side had complete night, all-weather capabilities in
their aircraft. Still, the aircrews pressed through marginal conditions to execute missions. This resulted in aircraft mishaps,
but also inflicted damage on both sides. Here again, the value of
realistic low-level flying training paid off.

Standoff weapons proved effective. The anti-ship Exocet fired
from Argentine Super Etendard aircraft was devastating, sinking
two British ships. Particularly deadly in the air-to-air role was
the AIM-9L all-aspect missile, which was credited with destroying
sixteen aircraft.

LOGISTICS

Argentina suffered from logistical shortfalls that might not
hamper a more affluent nation. These included lack of adequate
cargo aircraft, pierced metal planks (to lengthen the runway at
Stanley) and portable runway arresting gear for their higher performance aircraft.

The British forces had an 8,000-mile pipeline for logistics,
with the "forward" base at Ascension Island still 3,900 miles from
the fight. They were able to use merchant ships to carry much of
the needed bulk stocks and resupplied via helicopter from ship-
to-ship and ship-to-shore. The Argentines inflicted casualties on
the ships, but did not prevent accomplishment of their logistical
mission. In any case, both sides recognized the value of aerial
refueling.

For the British, Ascension Island was an essential depot and
staging base. As Frank Uhlig points out in his article, because
of the long distance it had to steam, the British fleet departed
Portsmouth immediately. As it sailed southward to Ascension,
stores and troops were airlifted to the island. When the fleet
arrived, personnel debarked for training on Ascension and then the

troops and equipment were loaded on the ships for the assaults on South Georgia and the Falklands. Thus, Ascension was a crucial logistical link throughout the Falklands War.

COMMUNICATIONS

The lack of secure communications hampered both sides in the conflict. The British reportedly exploited intercepted plane-to-plane conversations by Argentine aircrews, gaining a few minutes' early warning thereby. One British source said that late in the conflict, the Argentines had acquired a few sets of secure voice equipment from abroad, frustrating the British listeners.

For their part, the British aircrews practiced stringent communications discipline to deny information to Argentine eavesdroppers.

For communications back to the UK, the British reportedly augmented the limited existing capability on their ships with the addition of communication satellite terminals, taking advantage of leased capability on commercial satellites.

The paucity of extensive electronic warfare and electronic countermeasures capability on both sides meant that this conflict did not yield much in the way of "lessons learned" in that field. The main lesson is that both sides felt the absence.

AIRBORNE RECONNAISSANCE AND EARLY WARNING

As James George notes, both sides lacked an airborne early warning (AEW) capability and both sides had very little in the way of reconnaissance, although the Argentines believe the US assisted the British forces with satellite imagery. Consequently, the fighting in the air and on the sea continuously developed as a series of meeting engagements, and on land after British troops were ashore. This serious deficiency was partially overcome by fitting Sea King helicopters with the Searchwater radar. The Argentines, on the other hand, attempted to compensate for their deficiencies by using a Boeing 707 for long-range reconnaissance missions, with dubious results.

The British modified Victor tankers for reconnaissance, equipping them with radar, photo, and improved navigation equipment. Although the photography was on Ascension Island and not with the task force, this was better than nothing at all. British Nimrod aircraft, their primary long-range reconnaissance and anti-submarine planes, were modified for aerial refueling to be capable of nineteen-hour sorties. Nimrods were also fitted with Side-winders and had a capability for surface attack with bombs, Stingray torpedoes, and Harpoon missiles.

RESEARCH AND DEVELOPMENT

By the war's end, the Argentine pilots had developed a healthy respect for the Harrier, which proved to be a difficult opponent at low altitudes. Twenty Argentine aircraft were shot down by Sea Harriers in air-to-air combat, sixteen with the AIM-9L Sidewinder missile and the rest by the aircraft's 30-mm guns.

Concerning missiles, General Milton wrote that "it was the AIM-9L Sidewinder air-to-air missile that caused the most envy. In the opinion of the Argentines, almost any airplane becomes something to be taken seriously if it has the AIM-9L."[3] The wave-skimming Exocet anti-ship missile has already been cited. But as William Ruhe notes in his article, no air force has large stocks of "smart" weapons, and most must rely heavily on iron bombs and guns for much of their armament.

IMPROVISATION

Both sides improvised solutions to needs and problems. In the process they showed once again that the peacetime pace of development enjoys a luxury of layers of people who do little besides review and comment on other people's work.

More British than Argentine examples of improvisation have come to light. From sketchy reports, however, the military and industrial people on both sides were equally ingenious. One British source said that once the word came down, the bureaucracy was shifted aside, cutting to hours or days a process that normally takes months to years.

A few examples show the range of improvisation in airpower. Charles Corddry reported in Air Force Magazine that nine RAF Harrier GR3s, configured for close support in Europe, were fitted with all-aspect AIM-9L Sidewinders and Royal Navy two-inch rocket pods in a week's time. The first aircraft was modified within thirty-six hours.[4]

Aerial refueling modifications were done rapidly to a broad range of aircraft. The Nimrods have been mentioned. Vulcan bombers and C-130 transports were modified to receive fuel, and others were also converted to tankers.

LOOKING AHEAD

Both sides have begun to replace the losses from the campaign, and for both that is an expensive process. Peru, Israel, and Libya provided sorely needed replacements for Argentine aircraft that were destroyed and for other war supplies. Meanwhile, the British have lengthened the Stanley runway and added arresting gear to accommodate the F-4 Phantoms now based there. They have also installed surveillance radars and surface-to-air missiles to guard against airborne threats.

Whatever happens in the Falklands in the future, the following articles demonstrate that the lessons learned from this brief but sharp conflict are already being applied not only in the British and Argentine forces, but by other nations as well. For the major lesson is there for all armed forces to see: to avoid repeating one's own mistakes and those of others as well.

NOTES

1. General T.R. Milton, U.S. Air Force (Retired), "Too Many Missing Pieces," Air Force Magazine (December 1982): 48.

2. Ibid.

3. Ibid., p. 49.

4. Charles W. Corddry, "Britain's Near-Thing Victory," <u>Air Force</u> Magazine (December 1982): 51.

Acknowledgments

We wish to thank the following contributors for participating in this study: F. Clifton Berry, Jr., Norman Friedman, James L. George, Lawrence S. Germain, Gerald W. Hopple, Brad Roberts, William J. Ruhe, Harry G. Summers, Jr., William J. Taylor, Jr., Earl H. Tilford,Jr., and Frank Uhlig, Jr.

We are also indebted to Fred Praeger, Lynne Rienner, Barbara Ellington, Dean Birkenkamp, Miriam Gilbert, and the staff of Westview Press and to Lionel Leventhal of Arms and Armour Press for their advice, assistance, and encouragement.

Our appreciation goes to Colonel L. D. Badgett, Commandant, and Robert DeGross, Provost, of the Defense Intelligence College, for their support of this book; their steady enhancement of the College's intellectual horizons made this work--and will make others like it--possible.

Our thanks also go to that indispensable team whose patience and typing support contributed so much to this book: O. C. Moreland, Jr., Deborah J. Phillips, and Mary H. King.

Finally, we wish to thank Sue Watson and Jill Dunn, who (in addition to numerous other tasks) proofread, typed, and fed the editors during the completion of this book.

Bruce W. Watson
Peter M. Dunn

Introduction

William J. Taylor, Jr.
Brad Roberts

This volume is an important work, but its potential value can be derived only if digested in a strategic context. The nearly four decades of peace and prosperity enjoyed by the principal actors in the post-World War II era has obscured the fact that armed conflict remains an instrument of national policy in an international system of sovereign states. Contrary to the perceptions of many in the West, international violence is at an all time high, and is becoming increasingly frequent.

The spring 1982 war in the South Atlantic between Argentina and the United Kingdom over the Falkland Islands has had a special salience in the West. It assumed an importance for analysts in foreign and defense policy uncommon to the many other incidents of open international violence and nascent conflicts. The "lessons" of the conflict have been sought by many and sundry observers and participants. The primary analytical task has been to sort out from the many general and predictable verities the critical variables unique to this particular conflict. For the British, this introspection has led to lessons about military hardware, force structure, and the value of alliances, as well as to broader political-military lessons about the necessity of keeping the instruments of national power in rough parity with the political dictates of international commitment. For the Argentines, hard lessons were learned about the significance of professionalism in military manpower; similar political lessons about the capability-commitment dynamic probability were also drawn. NATO, the Soviet Union, Third World nations, arms manufacturers and other observers all have sought to identify lessons of their own.

Deriving lessons learned from various campaigns clearly has utility--as long as the lessons are learned in a strategic context.

A current concern, especially voiced on Capitol Hill, is that the United States is developing military forces without a clear scheme for their employment. The fear is that near-term defense budgets will determine long-range strategy--clearly the reverse of rational decision-making. US military leaders will state frankly in private that it is nearly impossible to develop capabilities without politico-military guidance--and that such guidance is woefully lacking. Simply put, the generals and admirals want to know what they are supposed to be preparing US armed forces to do. To have a capability without a strategy that envisions meaningful use of that capability is to break the fundamental link between war and policy. There is a basic truth in Clausewitz' dictum, "(War's) grammar, indeed may be its own, but not its logic." To raise issues of capability in the abstract is to establish a basic argument with no foundation. On the one hand, there will be those who advocate acquisition of capability to provide increased flexibility, to broaden the scope of options. On the other hand, there will be those who object that the acquisition of capability will encourage its use. Tragically, both are right, if irrelevant.

The role of strategy is to transform the total capabilities of a state into instruments of policy. In its simplest form, it is strategy that must tell the military planners what it is they must create capabilities to do and what they should plan to use those capabilities for once they are in hand. Strategy is the vital link in the transformation of national policy into objectives that may be stated in sufficient concrete detail to provide purpose. Thus, strategy is not abstract; rather, at the highest level, it may start with the abstract statement of policy, but it must apply the policy in the real environment of the world as it is today and as it is envisioned for the 1990s. Strategy must be refined and stated with increased specificity at each planning level, starting at the very highest and working down successively until it is stated most explicitly in the mission assigned a force.

In the absence of strategy and the guidance it supplies, the planners must turn to ad hoc substitutes. Practically this involves the preparation of contingency plans based on assumptions as to what the implementation of the plans might be expected to accomplish. In the absence of strategy, the assumed strategy will be inferred from the tactics, that is, from the specific uses of capabilities. Strategy at the highest level then becomes a restatement of successive aggregations of tactical goals. In the extreme, national decision-makers responsible for setting policy will become prisoners of events. There is an old saw in public policy analysis: "Show me your programs and I'll tell you your policies," and there is a certain element of truth in it. But, if this is in fact true, in some cases this will mean that program goals, contrived by the bureaucracies to permit "orderly" planning, will substitute for policy goals, and policy will be dictated from bottom to top. This is a danger in the "lessons learned" approach which we should always keep in mind.

The focus of the collection of essays which follows is on the lessons of the Falklands conflict; these lessons are primarily for the United States. No pretense is made of examining each of the issue areas for the possible implications for all interested parties; rather, each author has attempted to focus his analysis on the implications for the United States of the seventy-five days of war in the South Atlantic and the surrounding political-military environment.

The process of deriving lessons has been drawn out. The editors consciously have chosen to allow sufficient time to lapse since the conflict to ensure that pertinent data is available and salient aspects of the conflict are identifiable. With the benefit of well-informed hindsight, the analytical task has become easier.

The Falklands conflict is rich in lessons for the United States, richer than most other recent conflicts. British forces are similar to those of the US, and the conflict provided a test of machines, concepts, and manpower that simulation simply cannot provide (although some might argue this point). Certain aspects of the Argentine experience held lessons for US analysts for much of the same reason. The following essays treat each dimension by functional area. They highlight time-tested principles of warfare such as clearly defined objectives, battlefield surprise, economy of force, maneuver, and the application of mass at critical points. And they highlight aspects relevant to the US. For example, in discussing the so-called "electronic revolution," the focus is not on the avionics of the Exocet or Harrier, but on "smart-to-brilliant" technology on which the US is to rely heavily but which is not yet in hand. The analyses illuminate significant weaknesses in US armed forces. For example, the availability of civilian resources (a strong merchant marine and a defense industry with surge capacity) was critical for the British success; it is unclear that the US would be similarly able to draw on relevant domestic resources in time of crises.

There are other, more meaningful aspects of the Falklands conflict than those relating to technology and manpower, however. These pertain to strategy, and they raise one fundamental question: is the US preparing for the right kind of wars? It is an old truism that wars do not necessarily occur when or where expected or unfold according to the anticipated scenarios. Defense policy must, therefore, be flexible enough to meet the unexpected. Many in the US military are lulled into a false sense of confidence out of a sentiment that the US could have met the Argentine military threat to the Falklands without the difficulties encountered by the British. But that is to miss the point. The Falklands War was a test of the concepts that guide American engagement in the world and the ideas that dictate the character and posture of its armed forces. A conflict between the UK and Argentina in 1982 is likely to have only certain parallels to a future potential conflict between the US and some currently unknown adversary five or ten years down the road. The rough parallels must be the focus of our attention.

The strategy of American armed forces is determined by a perception of the nature of the international environment and of the political commitment to America's role in the environment. That strategy must take account of the changing nature of the world as well. The Falklands conflict points to a number of key forces that are shaping the character of the change.

First and foremost, the conflict highlights the growing technological competence of nations other than the traditional great powers. Powers traditionally conceived as "lesser" can now make military action by the great powers increasingly costly. The Falklands conflict highlighted the proliferation of high technology weapons, not merely the fact of their existence. This global proliferation of military power occurs at a time when great powers have come to depend for much of their security upon nuclear-tipped ballistic missiles (that have little utility today in most conceivable Third World conflicts). The traditional American response--to counter enemy technology with our own high technology--may no longer be adequate for Third World conflicts. Hardware must be tailored for specific purposes. The rapid proliferation of high technology weapons may have other negative effects--they could cause rapid and violent adjustment challenges to the international order with perverse implications for what stability exists today. The Argentine nuclear power program should also serve to raise the specter of future conflicts that are made far more complicated, and potentially much more destructive, by the proliferation of nuclear weapons and, more seriously, of Third World armed forces equipped and trained to employ limited numbers of nuclear weapons in pursuit of value-objectives.

Second, the Falklands War highlights the fact that some Third World conflicts have the potential to threaten fundamentally the interests of the West, and that American military resources are allocated inappropriately for this kind of future. Such threats are becoming more likely as military power diffuses internationally and troublesome domestic and regional trends progress. Yet the vast majority of US investment in its armed forces is in preparation for massive conventional and strategic conflict with the Soviet Union. In short, the conflict least likely to occur (at least in the coming decade or two) dominates the thinking, training, and resource allocation of America's military forces. An ability to cope with massive conflict in Europe does not imply an ability to deal effectively with small wars. The most probable conflicts in the coming years threatening US interests are likely to be "low-intensity," generally limited, at times unconventional wars. Examples are proxy operations, domestic wars of oppression or liberation, psychological warfare and terrorism. The Soviets, in the search for low cost, low risk operations with high strategic payoff, are likely to have incentive to foment or exploit these types of conflict.

Third, the Falklands conflict highlights the crucial importance of advance preparation to handle Third World conflicts. A failure to prepare for such a contingency on the part of the British unwittingly contributed to the seriousness of the conflict. British armed forces--like those of the US--have over-concentrated on one aspect of their missions, which was costly in terms of meeting the demands of the remainder of their missions. The absence of certain capabilities, such as shipboard missile defenses, long-range, high speed interceptors, and early warning aircraft nearly cost the British the conflict. The signalling of political will is also an aspect of preparation, and the British seemed to have neglected or relegated to very low priority the deterrent function of their token shipborne presence in the region which served as a symbol of British commitment to the defense of its presumed, but debatable, interests in the South Atlantic. Given a forecast that near term US defense budgets will be hit hard by the American Congress, decisions not taken by the US in the near future (even if taken in the late 1980s) to restructure and modernize its armed forces in such a way as to make their capabilities consonant with changing threat will leave the US in the early and mid-1990s with formidable conventional forces lacking in certain key capabilities to deal with Third World contingencies.

Fourth, the Falklands conflict highlighted the sometimes limited utility of armed conflict. Neither side gained. The Argentines sought a prize they were incapable of retaining, and have paid serious domestic and international costs. The British, in a defensive use of force, have served the broader cause of international stability and peace by denying gain from military aggression. But a solution to the underlying conflict that gave rise to violent manifestations in the Falkland Islands in the first place looks even more remote today. Those nations which perceive the current international order as illegitimate, or those who abet such nations, are likely to find new targets for their challenges to that order. In short, military power is a necessary but insufficient national policy instrument in the achievement of a peaceful and stable international order.

The essays that follow keep this analytical perspective in mind--technology and strategy. The lessons they spell out are useful in assessing how well oriented the US is toward future conflict and in providing a sense of direction for military planners. They cover a wide range of topics, though by no means all conceivable ones. In some cases, the lessons are clear-cut. In others, the lessons are more conjectural, treated primarily as implications of certain salient events or trends. Some of the issues treated in this text simply raise questions for US military planners, answers to which cannot be found in the experiences of the Falklands conflict itself. The authors are expert combat historians and tacticians with no particular stake in the conclusions which might filter their perceptions. They provide for the reader some major implications for the US of this most unexpected conflict. Their work may serve to turn American attention away from its preoccupations of the last decade to the future and its less well understood, more volatile possibilities.

1
Submarine Lessons

William J. Ruhe

In the Falklands War, submarines were engaged in wartime action for the first time since World War II. Although they were involved in only a few incidents, we can draw some important lessons from this experience. The best way to reveal the influence of submarines in the overall action would be a chronological examination of submarine participation in the Falklands War.

The sequence of submarine events begins with the landing on March 19, 1982, of an Argentine party of purported scrap metal workers on South Georgia Island, 800 miles to the east of the Falklands. On the 26th of March, the Argentines, in response to the British insistence that these illegal workers be removed from the island, evacuated these people but clandestinely left a shore party behind. It then became evident that the Argentine government was very much behind the incident. By the 29th, when a diplomatic solution to this occupation seemed to be stalled, Admiral Sir John Fieldhouse ordered the nuclear submarine HMS Spartan to leave the exercise in which she was engaged, embark stores and weapons at Gibraltar, and deploy to the South Atlantic. On March 30th, the nuclear submarine Splendid was ordered to deploy from Faslane in the UK and Conqueror sailed a few days later. Instructions to covertly prepare a task force for South Atlantic operations were received on March 31st. When the Argentines invaded the Falklands on April 2nd, further preparations were openly conducted.[1]

What is particularly significant about this sequence of prewar events is the fact that nuclear submarines were deployed rapidly and covertly toward a distant area of tension, with no effect on ongoing diplomatic negotiations. With their impressive speed and freedom from the impact of weather and sea conditions, nuclear submarines were also in the battle area well ahead of any surface forces, which were deployed at about the same time. And, if the political problem had been resolved satisfactorily prior to an outbreak of conflict, there was likely to be no evidence of pressure attributable to this threat from several nuclear submarines.

On April 12th, the British imposed a maritime exclusion zone of 200 miles around the Falklands, and on April 23rd they further

warned that any threatening approach by Argentine forces which
might interfere with the British mission in the South Atlantic
would be dealt with appropriately. Well before this time, the
British had revealed the presence of three nuclear submarines in
the war area. This threat had effectively stopped Argentine
reinforcement of the islands by sea since April 12th. However, it
was revealed that despite the British blockade one Argentine
resupply ship had arrived during this period.[2] The Argentines
then used the conventional submarine Santa Fe to haul relief
supplies to the shore party on South Georgia. The British nuclear
submarine Conqueror had been ordered to patrol off the island to
prevent any sealifted Argentine reinforcements, while a group of
Royal Marine commandos was covertly landed by helicopter on the
23rd. Thus, on April 25th, with the weather having cleared, a
British helicopter spotted the surfaced Santa Fe approaching the
main port of Grytviken. It would appear that the Santa Fe, which
did not know about British operations in the vicinity, had evaded
the Conqueror's patrol and was about to deliver its supplies when
she was attacked by British helicopters using AS12 missiles and
depth charges. The badly damaged Santa Fe limped to Grytviken and
was beached nearby. An AS12 wire-guided, six-kilometer range
missile with a sixty-three pound warhead, fired by a Lynx
helicopter, hit the Santa Fe's conning tower, inflicting serious
damage, while helicopter-launched depth charges apparently
destroyed the submarine's watertight integrity.[3]

The role of the submarine for emergency resupply of
beleaguered forces was reaffirmed. In addition, the conventional
submarine's ability to remain afloat long enough to be beached,
despite very close depth charges exploding at proper depth, was
demonstrated.

On May 2nd, the most profound submarine incident of the
Falklands War took place. The Conqueror located the Argentine
cruiser General Belgrano and its escort of two destroyers south of
the Falklands and slightly beyond the 200-mile exclusion zone.
The British felt that this small force, which was armed with
Exocet missiles, posed a clear threat to the British task force.
At the same time, other Argentine ships north of the zone were
apparently conducting the same sort of probing action. Since the
threat could not be ignored, Conqueror attacked the General
Belgrano with torpedoes.[4]

With her high submerged mobility, the Conqueror, in a periscope attack, gained an ideal attack position and, with a short
torpedo run, put two MK VIII torpedoes into the cruiser, which
subsequently sank. The MK VIIIs were pre-World War II, straight
running, forty-five-knot, 5,000-yard steam torpedoes. They were
evidently chosen in preference to the modern, wire-guided,
terminal homing Tigerfish torpedoes, which were also reported to
be aboard the Conqueror. Apparently, in the load-out of Conqueror
at the beginning of the war, there were not enough Tigerfish
torpedoes readily available, so she took on some of the older MK
VIIIs. Although the two destroyers dropped numerous depth charges
after Conqueror's attack, there was no evidence of their actually
having contact on Conqueror.

The decision of Conqueror's skipper to use these old torpedoes in preference to the Tigerfish attests to his appreciation of how a nuclear submarine's covert mobility relates to the weapons carried. The skipper recognized the proven reliability of the MK VIII; almost 4,000 of these torpedoes were used in World War II.[5] Their shortcomings were well ironed out by the end of that war. In addition, the MK VIIIs had 750-pound torpex warheads, approximating the destructive effects of the lighter Tigerfish torpedo warheads with their more efficient explosive. Although the MK VIII produces a good wake as opposed to the wakelessness of the electrically driven Tigerfish torpedo, the skipper evidently knew that he could approach undetected to close range and hit with the MK VIIIs, and the torpedo run would be so short that the cruiser would be unable to evade the torpedoes even if the wakes were promptly sighted.

The lesson illustrated by this selection of torpedoes seems to be that the high mobility of the nuclear submarine allows the use of simple, very low cost torpedoes in the anti-ship role--and even against warships under many circumstances. A second lesson is that a quiet nuclear submarine's speed and mobility allow it to make undetected approaches to targets which would be considered well escorted in the traditional sense, but which cannot begin to handle this new type of submarine threat.

After the sinking of the General Belgrano, Argentine naval surface forces stayed within twelve miles of the Argentine coast for the remainder of the war. The sinking of the cruiser was such a clear demonstration of nuclear submarine capability that no further attempt was made to risk any major Argentine warship outside of coastal waters. But at the same time, British nuclear submarines patrolled the coast to provide intelligence on aircraft sorties from Argentina which could mean likely air attacks on British forces. An examination of the waters in which the British nuclear submarines operated shows depths of twenty fathoms in spots and usually less than fifty fathoms where they could effectively use their periscopes for detecting aircraft.[6]

The British fleet's lack of an AEW aircraft capability was thus being remedied in part by stationing her nuclear submarines close to Argentine coastal airfields to provide early warning of large aircraft raids directed at the British forces in the Falklands area. But this was apparently a far from efficient operation, since a large-scale air raid caught the British with little warning and resulted in the loss of two landing ships which were in the process of being offloaded.

Another lesson from these forward operations is the need to ensure that today's submarines are efficient in shallow water operations and particularly at periscope depth. With waters under 100 fathoms all the way out to the Falklands from the Argentine coast, even the blockade against Argentine shipping had to be carried out in shallow waters.

Throughout the Falklands War, questions were continuously being asked about Argentine conventional submarines. What were they doing? Argentina started the war with four diesel-electric boats. Two were US fleet submarines transferred to the Argentine Navy, the Santa Fe (ex-USS Catfish) and the Santiago del Estero

(ex-USS Chivo), and two were German-built 209-type submarines.
The Santa Fe was quickly put out of action and virtually
destroyed. The Santiago del Estero was laid up at a naval base
and never saw action. But the two 209s which were in some sort of
refit status at the start of the war were buttoned up and quickly
deployed for sea operations. Little was reported about their
operations except that they claimed to have shot at the British
carrier Invincible and other targets but suffered torpedo trouble
and failed in their attacks.

These two ten-year old submarines have non-magnetic hulls, a
special feature of German submarines. They are of 1,285 submerged
tons and have eight torpedo tubes with a reload of eight more
torpedoes. They have a submerged speed of twenty-two knots and a
small complement of only thirty-two men.[7] They carry the German
twenty-one inch SST4 antiship torpedo, which has a 260-kilogram
warhead, is battery driven with a speed of about thirty-four
knots, and is wire-guided with both active and passive terminal
homing.[8] Interestingly, this torpedo has a three-dimensional sonar
for homing--which is particularly useful for submarine targets but
is a needless complication against surface ships.

What these two conventional submarines accomplished is summed
up in Sir John Fieldhouse's despatch to the Minister of Defence:

> Attacks on the Task Force by enemy submarines (the 209s)
> were a significant and ever present threat, which was
> recognized by the inclusion of anti-submarine Sea King
> helicopters in the air order of battle. A number of
> torpedo attacks were carried out by these aircraft against
> underwater contacts classified as possible submarines.
> Results of the actions are not known, but the high
> intensity flying rates of this helicopter force throughout
> the operations were an essential part of Fleet anti-
> submarine warfare defences.[9]

In his articles entitled "Navies in War and Peace," Admiral
Gorshkov observed that in World War II there were twenty-five
Allied ships and 100 aircraft involved in ASW operations for each
German submarine at sea. The same disparate use of ASW forces to
handle the threat of only two small conventional enemy submarines
seems to have taken place off the Falklands Islands. The
appalling weather, which created much surface noise, plus the high
density of marine life in the waters off the Falklands combined to
make ASW operations extremely difficult, resulting in a high
incidence of false contacts. The tiny shrimp-like krill which
breed in the cold Antarctic waters are found in huge tightly
packed schools which return convincing echos from action sonars--
and they reportedly make a lot of noise with their massed tiny
squeals. That the British warships expended large amounts of ASW
ordnance on false contacts in this environment is highly likely.
The magnetic anomaly detection (MAD) gear on British ASW aircraft
was apparently of little use for classifying the non-magnetic-
hulled 209s. The detectable magnetic signatures of these submarines were probably too weak to make a determination of sub or

non-sub in an environment where other masses of marine life could produce low magnetic signatures.

The experience of the Argentine 209s suggests that a highly complex antiship torpedo which requires a large number of electrical settings and a complex fire control system is difficult to use in war--particularly if there has been little or no opportunity to test out a torpedo's fire control system before going into war operations. Such torpedos are also almost impossible to use manually if there is a failure in the electrical firing sequence. The preference of the Conqueror's skipper for a torpedo which lends itself well to manual firing may also be an indication of this hazard in the use of today's sophisticated weapons.

That the 209 skippers were not certain whether the Invincible had been fired at would indicate the firing of their SST4s on sound bearings only (i.e., no periscope looks were involved; these would have made certain the nature of their target).

It is not clear why it would be advantageous to shoot on sound bearings from below periscope depth. The high seas experienced during the spring months in the Falklands area should have caused much water mixing with isothermal conditions down to considerable depths. Hence, the 209s would tend to be as susceptible to active echo ranging while operating deep as they would be up at periscope depth. At any rate, conventional submarines on both sides--the British had one in action in addition to the five nuclear submarines which eventually were present--accomplished little except for their nuisance value.

On the other hand, as summarized in the White Paper issued by the Secretary of State for Defence:

> Our nuclear-powered submarines (SSN) played a crucial role. After the sinking of the General Belgrano the Argentine surface fleet effectively took no further part in the Campaign. The SSNs were flexible and powerful instruments throughout the crisis, posing a ubiquitous threat which the Argentines could neither measure nor oppose. Their speed and independence of support meant that they were the first assets to arrive in the South Atlantic, enabling us to declare the maritime exclusion zone early. They also provided valuable intelligence to our forces in the total exclusion zone.[10]

In summary, nuclear submarines had totally dominated the operations of enemy surface ships. Conventional submarines, although ineffective, tied up a considerable number of ASW ships and caused a heavy expenditure of ASW ordnance. In another war, this might be an important way to dilute enemy ASW efforts against one's nuclear submarines.

NOTES

1. Despatch by Admiral Sir John Fieldhouse, G.C.B., G.B.E., Commander of the Task Force Operations in the South Atlantic: April to June 1982, to Ministry of Defence, 14 December 1982.

2. Ibid. It should be recognized that most of this submarine blockade would have to be conducted in shallow waters -- water of less than 100 fathoms. The great passive sonar detection ranges achievable by submarines against merchant ships is a deep sea capability. In shallow waters this capability is likely to be decreased considerably.

3. General Dynamics, Pomona, California Division, The World's Missile Systems, 7th ed., (April 1982).

4. The Falklands Campaign: The Lessons (London: Her Majesty's Stationery Office, 1982), p. 7.

5. G.J. Kirby, "A History of the Torpedo, Part I - The Early Days," JRNSS Journal, vol. 27, no. 2, p 53.

6. The Falklands Campaign: The Lessons, p. 7.

7. John Moore (ed.) Jane's Fighting Ships, 1980-1981 (New York: Jane's Publishing Inc., 1982), p. 25.

8. Ronald T. Pretty (ed.), Jane's Weapon Systems, 1977 (London: Macdonald and Jane's Publishers Ltd., 1976), p. 123.

9. Of interest was the use of Marconi's Stingray ASW torpedo on the British Sea King helicopters, "prior to final service tests for the new weapon, which were in progress in Britain when the conflict broke out." Aviation Week and Space Technology (7 June 1982).

10. The Falklands Campaign: The Lessons, p. 7.

2
Large Versus Small Carriers

James L. George

One of the most enduring naval debates since the mid-1960s has been the question of "large" vs "small" carriers. In those earlier years, with the development of the AV-8A vertical/short take-off and landing (V/STOL) plane (the US version of the Harrier) and the Soviet YAK-36 Forger, the debate revolved around the issue of V/STOL versus conventional takeoff and landing (CTOL) carriers. In this early debate, "small" essentially meant V/STOL while "large" meant CTOL.

Other arguments fueled this fire. One was the British decision to forego building expensive large-deck carriers in favor of the more affordable "through-deck" cruiser. Another was that after years of criticizing carriers as obsolete, the Soviet Union began to build carriers. Their first two classes were V/STOL carriers, the small Moskva class helicopter cruiser in the late 1960s, and then the larger Kiev, in the 1970s. Thus, as the old ruler of the seas was hauling down the Ensign from the last of her big-deck carriers, a new challenger was commissioning its first V/STOL ship. During this early V/STOL period, the United States Navy was still operating fifteen large-deck attack carriers as well as some smaller antisubmarine warfare (ASW) carriers; there was no interest in V/STOL.

The debate has evolved since that time. While the V/STOL versus CTOL question still pertains, today there is the additional question of large versus small CTOL carriers. With the retirement of American World War II carriers, and with the cost of the 90,000 ton, nuclear-powered Nimitz class carriers being $5 billion each, many argue that the navy should build small 40,000 to 60,000-ton CTOL carriers. Thus, small now includes both V/STOL and smaller CTOL carriers, while "large" usually indicates the nuclear-powered ships capable of carrying high performance Navy planes such as the F-14, A-6, and larger airborne early warning (AEW) and ASW planes. Presumably, the smaller CTOL carriers would not be able to carry these heavier planes, but could still have the multipurpose F-18, V/STOL and rotating wing planes. The Falkland Islands War, therefore, would be more applicable to the older "small versus large" (V/STOL vs CTOL) debate.

Before discussing the various points of view on the merits of each argument, a brief history is in order. The early carriers from the 1920s and 1930s, and those used throughout World War II, were, of course, small by later World War II standards. The American Essex class World War II carriers had from sixty to seventy planes, while the largest British carriers had about forty to fifty aircraft. The two French carriers built in the 1950s carry about forty planes each. The United States also built small, "jeep" carriers during World War II for ferry and ASW purposes. Finally, the nine helicopter landing platforms (LPHs) and five amphibious assault ships (LHAs) built in the 1960s and 1970s qualify as small V/STOL carriers.

The current debate derives from deployment of the V/STOL airplanes in the 1970s. The predecessor to the Harrier, the Kestrel, was tested in 1960, but the first operational plane, now called the Harrier, was not ordered until the late 1960s, with deliveries to the Royal Navy in 1970 and the United States Marine Corps in 1971.

It is important to understand the interest of both these services in a V/STOL plane. For the Royal Navy, it was born of necessity. In the mid-1960s, the British had planned to build a new class of large-deck CTOL carrier to replace their aging World War II era ships. In 1967 the Labour Government issued a White Paper which decreed that for budgetary reasons aircraft carriers would no longer be built. This coincided with the British decision to pull out from East of Suez. In other words, the Royal Navy was to forego an important mission of projecting power ashore.

The decision against building new carriers was a blow to the Royal Navy, and it is still debated in British Navy circles. However, it was also decided that some through-deck cruisers, not carriers, would be built. This was in keeping with the best traditions of doublespeak, but was necessary to circumvent the no carrier decision. This decision also meant Harrier would be built because a through-deck cruiser needed a V/STOL plane.

The original US Marine Corps mission was simple--it needed a close ground-support aircraft that could operate near front lines on short (or no) runways. This plane would also be able to operate off their larger amphibious ships such as Helicopter Landing Platforms (LPHs) and the new Amphibious Assault Ships (LHAs).

US naval interest in V/STOL or small carriers has been lukewarm at best, although it was once the top priority of a Chief of Naval Operations. In 1973, Admiral Zumwalt proposed a Sea Control Ship (SCS), which was to carry three to four V/STOLs and ten to fourteen helicopters, for use in convoy duties (like the old jeep carriers). The SCS would have been about 14,000 tons--a relatively small ship. Although proposed by a CNO, this ship was never accepted by the naval air community or Congress and eventually was quietly dropped. However, during the mid-1970s an LPH, the Guam, did operate as an experimental SCS and proved successful. The Marine Harriers were also used for an experimental period aboard the attack carrier Franklin D. Roosevelt, and again proved successful because of their flexibility.

The Carter Administration proposed two smaller carriers, a V/STOL and a CTOL. The V/STOL carrier (designated VSS) was to be about 22,000 tons with twenty-six aircraft of varied capability. In one configuration, it would have carried four V/STOL and sixteen large ASW aircraft, and six Light Airborne Multipurpose Systems (LAMPS) helicopters. The other carrier (designated CVV) would have displaced about 55,000 tons, would have had two catapults instead of the four on the larger nuclear carriers (CVNs), and carried about fifty airplanes. There was some debate whether the CVV could have had the capacity to carry all naval aircraft (including the F-14). Neither the VSS nor the CVV carrier was ever authorized.

Other attempts at smaller carriers have been made, to no avail. Congress actually authorized a modified DD-963 destroyer for a V/STOL role, but this was later reprogrammed as a regular destroyer. There have also been suggestions to recommission some of the smaller World War II carriers such as the Oriskany or the Bon Homme Richard. Although not capable of carrying the navy's latest planes, they could have been useful for smaller attack planes such as the A-7 or for ASW and V/STOL roles. Again, none of these proposals has been approved. The navy is still committed to the large nuclear carrier, but the cost is getting higher, and even advocates of large carriers are starting to have misgivings.

THE DEBATES

The arguments for each type of ship vary from the familiar "large carriers are sitting ducks" to advocates of V/STOL who see "every ship a carrier," with many in between. Most boil down to the question of vulnerability, then cost. Critics of large carriers see them as "sitting ducks" in conflicts with the Soviet Union or any enemy that can buy "smart" weapons such as the Exocet missile. Regarding cost, nuclear-powered carriers of the Nimitz class are approaching $5 billion without the airplanes and no country, not even the United States, can afford to build many of them.

Critics argue that the United States should not build CVNs, which are vulnerable and extremely expensive, but should opt for many smaller ships. The money spent on one CVN could buy five V/STOL or three small CTOL carriers, according to small carrier proponents. This would add to the flexibility and survivability of the carrier force.

Proponents of large carriers dispute these arguments, noting that pound for pound a carrier is one of the cheapest ships afloat. Also, while small V/STOL carriers might be relatively cheap at a billion dollars each, a small CTOL carrier with catapults would now cost at least $2-3 billion.

There is also the question of cost effectiveness. Proponents of large CVNs note that it would take three small CTOL carriers to match the capabilities and capacity of the larger ship. Even then, depending on the size of the small CTOL, it might not have the capacity to carry the best naval aircraft. As for V/STOL carriers, although five V/STOL carriers might equal a CTOL in quantity of planes, they would never equal the qualitative aspects of the large CTOL planes such as the F-14, AEW, and ASW planes (or attack planes such as the A-6 Intruder). Even advocates of V/STOL aircraft admit that it would be many years, (and perhaps never) before a V/STOL plane would ever have the capabilities of a CTOL plane.

THE CARRIER WAR IN THE FALKLANDS

There were no Coral Sea or Midway carrier battles in the Falklands War, but carriers did play a crucial role. Many have asked why the Argentines did not use their carrier the Veinticinco de Mayo--fear of attack by British nuclear powered submarines is the common assumption--but in fact they did use the carrier in one very important operation: the invasion. The Veinticinco de Mayo, with twenty planes and four other warships, supported the landing of the 2,000 troops who invaded the Falkland Islands on April 2nd. With no British warplanes present on the islands, the Argentines by default had absolute air superiority. Although not needed for the attack, the twenty planes could have wreaked havoc on the defenseless islanders.

This was the only involvement of Argentine sea-based air power during the war. Argentina had about 160 aircraft, including American A-4Q Skyhawks built in the 1950s and 1960s, French Mirages, and older British Canberra bombers. It also had some new Super Etendards that could have operated from its carrier plus some light Pucara attack aircraft which operated from grass fields on the Falklands. However, most planes flew from the Argentine mainland to the Falklands, a distance of about 425 miles. Even with inflight refueling, these planes had only limited time over their British targets, which limited their effectiveness signifi- cantly. For example, had the Super Etendards been operating from the carrier only 200 miles away, they would have had more time for their Exocet attacks and might have inflicted even greater damage on British forces.

On May 7th, when the British extended their sea and air blockade from 200 miles around the Falklands to within twelve miles of Argentina, the Argentine carrier was effectively bottled up in home waters. This ended the participation of Argentine naval air power in the war.

British carrier operations began on April 5th, when a thirty- six ship British task force under the command of a submariner, Admiral J. F. "Sandy" Woodward, set sail. (It is noteworthy that the US Navy would never allow a submariner to command a carrier task force.) While the force consisted of two light cruisers, four destroyers, and five frigates plus some amphibious craft, the main body comprised the new V/STOL ASW carrier HMS Invincible and the older light carrier (now called a Commando ship) HMS Hermes. Their air complement was twenty Harriers and forty helicopters of various types. The fact that the Invincible had been sold to Australia, and was to have been delivered that summer, raises the question of whether the British would have dared to retaliate with only one carrier. The navy also used a cargo ship, Atlantic Conveyor, to ferry twenty more Harriers. During the fighting about twelve RAF Harriers were flown from the United Kingdom to the Falklands in a seventeen-hour, 8,000-mile record-setting flight with multiple air refuelings. However, because of other losses, the total Harrier strength in the war zone remained at about forty during the conflict.

British sea-based air power was first used in combat on April 25th, when Her Majesty's forces captured South Georgia Island in a two-hour battle. Royal Navy helicopters played a key role with an attack on the Argentine submarine Sante Fe, which was caught on the surface and attacked by rockets and machine gun fire.

The carrier air war began on April 30th, when Harriers attacked Port Stanley and Goose Green airfields, and additional strikes were made on the following days. Recognizing their lack of an airborne early warning system, the British asked the United States for long-range AEW aircraft, but one reason these were not given concerned the long time needed to train British crews.

The British continued their air attacks against Argentine forces and supply ships. Although attacks on Argentine ships continued throughout the war, the supply lines were never completely interdicted.

While British casualties were significant, involving several ships sunk and aircraft lost, and while the British never established complete air superiority, they were able to project impressive sea-based air power, and this was the decisive factor in the British victory.

THE MILITARY LESSONS

While there are many different lessons with differing arguments for both the large and small carrier advocates, there is one general lesson that pertained to the Falklands conflict just as it pertained to any battle during World War II: air superiority is an absolute necessity.   If the Royal Navy had lacked even the limited V/STOL carriers the British would not have been able to attack the islands.   Conversely, had the Argentines stationed some of their planes on the Falklands, they might have won.   Air superiority is as vital today as it was during any battle of World War II.   While this might at first seem an obvious lesson, it was one ignored by the Soviet Navy for almost thirty years, and it will not be corrected until they start commissioning their CTOL carriers or build better V/STOL planes.

At first glance, it might appear that since the V/STOL planes were able to maintain air superiority, they would be adequate. However, tactical considerations and geography favored their use here.   As noted, had the Argentine Super Etendards and A-4s flown from the Falklands the story may have had a different ending. Thus the British Harriers had nearly a free ride in their role. Would twenty Harriers have been able to maintain air superiority over the Argentine mainland?   More important, these numbers of V/STOL planes may not have been a match for the air forces of some developing nations.   To maintain air superiority for anything other than isolated islands or extremely small countries would require the large numbers of sophisticated aircraft found only on CTOL carriers.

A second general lesson relevant to the large versus small carrier debate centers around an airborne early warning or AEW capability. This lesson is emphasized repeatedly in The Falklands Campaign: The Lessons, which was sent to Parliament by the Secretary of State for Defence in December 1982. Without an AEW capability, the British fleet had virtually no warning of enemy air attack. This, coupled with the limited capabilities of the Harriers, meant that warning time was restricted to the ship's radar range. The Harriers did a marvelous job in reacting rapidly, with pilots stationed in cockpits and being airborne in minutes after notice; but even this could not adequately compensate for the lack of an early warning system. Thus the navy operated as it did in World War II.

The question then arises, can a small and/or V/STOL carrier ever have the AEW planes equivalent to the CTOL planes on board large CTOL carriers? The answer for V/STOL carriers is: not for the foreseeable future.

Since the Falklands, the Royal Navy has jury-rigged a helicopter with radar for an AEW capability, but helicopters, although versatile, have limited capability for two reasons--range and time on station. The US Navy's E-2 Hawkeye AEW aircraft has a 200-mile range with six hours on station. The best the helicopter could do would be 100 miles range with one hour on station. The US Navy's newest helicopter, the ASW Seahawk (LAMP III), for example, has a fifty-mile radius with three hours on station. In other words, several helicopters would not match the performance of a Single E-2. The E-2 has a radar range of 240 miles and a flying range of 200 miles; thus one Hawkeye patrolling between the Falklands and the mainland could have simultaneously covered both Argentine planes flying off their runways and the British fleet off the Falklands.

An AEW helicopter is better than nothing and would suffice for short periods of time. The US Navy is experimenting with "tilt-rotor" V/STOL planes, where propellers are tilted horizontally for helicopter-like takeoffs and rotated vertically for normal flight. This has some potential for longer range and more time on station, but these planes are still in the experimental stage. However, since these are V/STOL planes, they would probably always be lighter than similar aircraft found on CTOL. In short, there is simply no V/STOL craft--whether helicopter, tilt-wing, or modified Harrier--that would have the capability and endurance of the current CTOL AEW planes.

Regarding a small CTOL carrier, since the E-2 is a propeller plane which does not need a catapult for launching, it conceivably could be used on small CTOL carriers.

CONCLUSIONS

Based on the evidence one must conclude that the Falklands War does not provide a satisfactory answer to the large versus small carrier debate. Certainly a large carrier could have provided the British or Argentines with an airborne early warning capability and the ability to launch the most modern naval aircraft, and either of these would have been critically important. Conversely, one should keep in mind that the roles and missions of a nation's navy must be taken into account. Nuclear powered attack aircraft carriers are terribly expensive and are simply beyond the defense budgets of all but two superpowers. Furthermore, one should consider the most likely uses for the carrier. Here a CVN in the naval inventory of a small nation is just as inappropriate as its absence in the US Navy, which is faced with a significant and growing Soviet naval threat. Thus, if there is a message in the Falklands War, it is that there is a place in the spectrum of naval warfare for both large and small carriers and that a nation's defense needs, naval missions, and national finances are among the factors which will influence its decision for a large or a small carrier.

3
Surface Combatant Lessons[1]

Norman Friedman

The Falkland Islands War was the first time a Western fleet had encountered mass air opposition in the jet age. For the defense analyst, it was one more example of the age old problem that the wars never match the popular scenarios, and that the old bipolar image of the world no longer exists. For the student of politics, this is a cautionary tale. Most Western scenarios for the outbreak of war emphasize the NATO-Warsaw Pact confrontation. Yet most of the world's states are, at least nominally, nonaligned. Almost every one of them harbors some grievance against its neighbors, and that issue, however old, is often used as a rallying cry.

British forces, nominally impressive, seemed ill-suited to war in the South Altantic. Specifically since their withdrawal from East of Suez, Britain's naval evolution was influenced by the antisubmarine warfare mission in the eastern North Atlantic. Here the navy would enjoy the support of large land-based air forces, including radar early warning aircraft. Organic air cover had been reduced to two V/STOL carriers (Hermes and Invincible) with small fixed-wing air groups, perhaps nine to twelve Sea Harriers each. On the positive side, the Royal Navy is a highly sophisticated force enjoying an excellent reputation not only for bad-weather seamanship but also for command and control. Like the US Navy, it had long experience with distant operations requiring logistical support at great distances.

Many of the weapons the Royal Navy would bring to the Falklands--the Sea Harrier V/STOL fighter, the array of anti-aircraft and antimissile missiles--had never been used in combat. Missing was the massed gun firepower of the past. Nor were the Sea Harriers a very promising replacement, carrying no more than 3,000 pounds of bombs each. Thus the British destroyers and frigates, each armed with no more than two 4.5-inch guns, had to provide shore support fire, at least until artillery had been landed. The number of ships per gun, or per independently-aimable gun, was high, causing congestion in the landing area and exposure to air attack. This problem afflicts all Western navies, but it is unpleasant to recall that a post-World War II Daring class destroyer (one or two of which are still afloat) provided three twin 4.5 inch guns on the same displacement as a frigate with one such gun. The frigate, of course, is adapted to an ASW and, to a lesser extent, an AAW environment in which the destroyer could not survive, but the loss of naval gunfire remains an important issue, highlighted by the British experience.

The fleet steaming to the Falklands included the two V/STOL carriers; the Type 22 frigates, Broadsword and Brilliant, armed with the Sea Wolf anti-missile system; the Type 42 missile destroyers Cardiff, Exeter, Liverpool, Coventry, Glasgow, and Sheffield, armed with Sea Dart air defense missiles; the County class missile destroyers Antrim and Glamorgan, armed with the elderly Sea Slug area defense missile and with the Sea Cat point defense missile; the Type 21 frigates Active, Avenger, Ambuscade, Antelope, Ardent, and Alacrity, all armed with Sea Cat; the Rothesay class frigates Yarmouth and Plymouth, armed with Sea Cat; and the modified Leander class frigates Minerva, Argonaut, Andromeda, and Penelope (of which Andromeda had Sea Wolf).

Observers familiar with it considered the Argentine Navy one of the best in Latin America, operating its ships at sea a large percentage of the time. Primarily antiship in orientation, it had bought Exocet missiles. And because of the longstanding naval dispute with Chile, Argentine Air Force pilots had been trained for antiship attacks. The principal strike aircraft was the American A-4 Skyhawk. The Argentine Navy had just taken delivery of six French Super Etendard fighters designed to carry the AM-39 air-launched version of the Exocet missile. Argentina also possessed French Mirage and Israeli Dagger supersonic fighters, as well as a few Canberra bombers and some domestically-built Pucara counterinsurgency aircraft. Finally, there were a few Macchi MB-326 trainers with light fighter-bomber capability. About 400 miles from Argentine bases, the Falklands were at the maximum range of many of these aircraft. For example, loaded with three bombs, a Skyhawk has a combat radius of only about 130 miles; with one bomb and two drop tanks this increased to about 450 miles, just sufficient to reach the islands. Two Hercules tankers could extend fighter and fighter-bomber range, but they could refuel only about four aircraft at a time. This was a significant limitation because most modern shipboard antiaircraft systems, such as those aboard the British fleet, suffer from saturation at relatively low levels of attack. Once Argentine forces were on the Falklands, the Pucaras and MB-326s could be based there.

Range limits in Argentine aircraft initially focused attention on the Argentine carrier Veinticinco de Mayo, which could bring her Skyhawks closer to the target area. Furthermore, she had been refitted to operate the Super Etendard. However, the Veinticinco de Mayo stayed close to the Argentine coast throughout the war, and the Super Etendards appeared to have flown from shore bases.

These comparisons do not explain the performance of the British and Argentine forces in battle. Indeed, one of the main lessons of the war was just how misleading hardware comparisons can be. To the analyst, it is important to emphasize specifically Argentine circumstances, as opposed to conditions which might confront any Western force intervening in the Third World. Argentina was typical of many potential intervention sites in that its forces were heavily armed with modern weapons. Moreover, that armament was weighted towards firepower more than in the case in Western navies, which invested in global electronic and in command and control systems. Thus, to some extent, the issue was whether that Western investment had been worthwhile or whether, as some have suspected, it was merely a means of sinking vast sums without a trace. Here the evidence is mixed. The British Task Force was reportedly unable to achieve a sufficient level of air defense coordination (a command and control issue) to prevent a high degree of saturation by attacking Argentine aircraft. Command and control (C^2) deficiencies contributed to the loss of the Sheffield, since she was said to have been unable to operate her electronic surveillance measures (ESM) suit while communicating via her satellite terminal. Ironically, she was probably using the terminal rather than high frequency (HF) in view of the direction finding (DF) danger the latter presents.

From the Argentine perspective, a lack of ECM aboard attacking aircraft presumably contributed to very heavy losses and thus to the Argentine defeat. The Argentines were able to locate the Task Force once it entered their sea area; this suggests that they made a reasonable choice between investments in surveillance and fire-power. In the end, their most severe lack in C^2 was in inter-service coordination; as in other nations this was more of a political problem. The Argentines were able to detect British naval movements and to direct air attacks, reportedly because of the presence of two mobile Westinghouse TPS-43 three-dimensional air defense radars on the Falklands.

The next question is whether the relative competence of the Argentine Air Force is typical of the Third World. It may be easier to train a few fighter or fighter-bomber pilots than to train an army; certainly, the pilots also come closest in peace-time to simulating wartime conditions. In the Middle East there have often been claims that Soviet-trained pilots do not approach Western-trained ones (such as the Israelis and even the Iranians) in competence, and it is possible that the Western (much of it British) training of the Argentine Air Force was responsible for some of its effectiveness. However, the Argentines also achieved a very high level of elan, reflected in their willingness to keep flying despite extraordinary casualties, and probably despite operational strains due to the long sortie ranges.

Moreover, the Argentine successes must buoy any Third World country facing a prospective Western naval air attack. In Vietnam, the North Vietnamese made a few attempts to attack carriers and cruisers and enjoyed only one success, a 250-kilogram bomb hit on the destroyer Higbee; the bomb destroyed only one gun mount and did not sink the ship. Now, however, Third World air-crews have the Argentine example: ships can be sunk by aircraft. Whether that would be possible against a more effective air defense, such as one the United States would put up around a carrier battle group, is hard to say.

As for the Argentine Navy, it appears that there was some attempt to sail after the loss of the General Belgrano. Admiral Anaya apparently tried to use his carrier, but was restrained by his Junta colleagues, who realized that the fleet was too important a national asset to place at risk. However, he must at some point have considered the postwar implications of a defeat in which the navy had made few or no sacrifices. One must suspect, then, that problems of maintaining an elderly and varied fleet would have prevented its use. Throughout the Third World, navies rely on foreign-built ships, often equipped with weapons, sensors, and spare parts no longer in production.

The submarine problem may have been more acute. In peacetime, surface ships have a value in the foreign relations of states. Submarines have virtually none; if they are effective at all, they must be nearly undetectable and are therefore useless for showing the flag. Moreover, submarines are much more expensive to maintain. Thus it is likely that a high proportion of Third World submarines are at a lower state of readiness than are their accompanying surface ships. If so, it may be that the submarine threat to Western seaborne intervention in the Third World has been overstated.

But the British were not willing to assume that the Argentine submarines were in port. One actually penetrated the Task Force ASW screen, but her effort was negated by a faulty fire control system. In the absence of some long-range detection system, the British could not hunt submarines, and they did not have the numbers of escorts necessary to establish a tight screen.[2] The announced large expenditure of ASW ammunition suggests a high false alarm rate. Nor does it seem likely that the few British nuclear submarines were able to restrict the Argentine submarines to their bases. On balance, then, the Argentine submarines were able to affect British operations by their existence, even if they could not achieve any spectacular results. This suggests that ASW combat operations in the Persian Gulf or the Indian Ocean, where acoustic conditions are poor, would be difficult. The rate of expenditure suggests that current war stocks of torpedoes and other ASW munitions may be too small, since peacetime planners could underestimate the level of false alarms--which ran at a ratio of nine false to one real contact late in World War II.

The first British ships to reach the war zone were nuclear attack submarines, which demonstrated their strategic mobility. Their publicized presence sufficed to justify the British proclamation (on April 7th, effective April 12th) of a 200-mile maritime exclusion zone centered on the Falkland Islands. In effect, this became a free-fire zone, simplifying any identification problems that the submarines may have encountered.

While there were never enough British submarines to enforce a total blockade, the Argentines preferred not to test them. That was evident after the HMS Conqueror sank the cruiser General Belgrano with torpedoes on May 2nd, as the latter, with two escorts, approached the 200-mile zone. It now appears that the General Belgrano group was the vanguard of a major Argentine sortie, and the destruction of the ship aborted the operation. The Argentines did, however, manage to pass a large container ship through the blockade after the British landing at San Carlos; bad weather and a high sea state can still degrade modern submarine and other electronic sensors.

The sinking of the General Belgrano showed how rapidly underwater warfare has evolved. Her two escorts were former US destroyers equipped with the first of the long-range sonars, the SQS-4 or its equivalent, with a nominal range of 5,000 yards. The Conqueror could detect the surface ships at a much greater range, and apparently her attack was a surprise. The Captain of the General Belgrano said later that his ship was not even closed up at action stations, even though the British had proclaimed all Argentine warships prospective targets. It appears, too, that the Cabinet in London may have attempted to fine-tune the operation by ordering the ship damaged rather than sunk, and her escort spared. Thus the cruiser was hit twice, but she did not suffer the typical back-breaking damage of a modern torpedo.[3] The submarine left before the cruiser foundered, and photographs of the sinking suggest that progressive flooding from the hit aft eventually caused the cruiser's loss.

Once the British surface fleet arrived off the Falklands, a conventional air-sea battle developed. With a limited number of fighter aircraft and without airborne early warning aircraft, the fleet should have had to rely heavily on its array of surface-to-air missiles. The entire range of operational British weapons of this type was represented in the South Atlantic, from the obsolescent Sea Slug aboard County class destroyers through the Sea Cat and Sea Wolf point-defense weapons, and up to the current Sea Dart.[4] Only Sea Wolf is effective against a sea-skimming missile like the Exocet. All had been designed to counter conventional air raids and attacks by large (Soviet-type) air-to-surface missiles, which approach at higher altitudes.

The Argentines possessed a substantial force of obsolescent jet fighter-bombers. They had little or no ECM capability on board, and, like nearly everyone else, had never faced the array of modern defensive missiles which the British fleet possessed. Their standoff weapons were the French Exocet radar-guided sea skimmer and the older US command-guided Bullpup. Exocet is a fire-and-forget weapon, which (like all radar-guided missiles) is subject to active countermeasures and deception, and requires a contrast between the radar returns of the target and its surroundings. Thus it is most useful in the open sea, and least so in enclosed waters. The Bullpup requires pilot guidance all the way to its target; this increases the vulnerability of the launching aircraft. There were also the conventional bombs and rockets. Thus the great strength of the Argentines was their numbers, which may saturate the defense, and the possible technical surprise of the Exocet.

Given the limited number of Sea Harriers on hand, the British force would rely heavily on its surface-to-air missiles. This reality reflected the logic behind the steady shrinkage of the Fleet Air Arm. For example, until quite late the Invincible and her sisters had not been intended to operate fixed-wing aircraft at all. In fact, however, the Sea Harriers, few as they were, proved very important.

The British missile systems were vulnerable to saturation. This is a common problem since a ship usually has to devote one guidance channel to each incoming target, and that channel remains occupied throughout the engagement with the target. Both Type 22 (Sea Wolf ships) and Type 42 (Sea Dart destroyers) have only two

channels. This was the case of HMS Coventry. She first detected
two fast, low-flying incoming aircraft and locked on with her two
Type 909 guidance radars. Two more aircraft then approached from
her other side, hitting her with three bombs, which destroyed
most of her port side and sank her. It is significant that she
never had time to actually engage the first two aircraft. The
Type 42 has a manually-operated combat system, which first detects
the target on the air search radar, then re-detects it on a target
indication radar, and finally passes it to one of two guidance
radars. The Sea Dart missile involved further delays, since it
requires two minutes while its gyros are aligned. Since missiles
cannot be maintained warmed-up indefinitely on the launcher, this
was a continual problem.

This system is best adapted to the scenario of the 1950s, when
these missile systems were first designed. Aircraft would
generally approach at relatively high altitudes, and would be
detected by the search radar several minutes before coming into
missile range. However, the Argentines often chose low-level
approaches, where detection would be at much shorter ranges,
making the built-in operational delays in the Sea Dart system
potentially fatal. It should be noted that Coventry had been
quite successful earlier in the same day, shooting down three
Skyhawks. However, she was later struck by four attackers.

In theory, a long-range missile system can overcome saturation
by engaging enemy aircraft sequentially, before they can come
close enough to strike. That requires long-range detection and a
fast missile. In theory, too, a good command and control system
for a fleet will partially overcome saturation by dividing
incoming aircraft between various ships, so that none is overloaded. Long missile and detection ranges are necessary here, and
in the Falklands case both detection and numbers of ships were
deficient. Detection was an acute problem because, given its wave
length, the standard Type 965 air search radar is rather
ineffective against low-flying aircraft. These aircraft could be
detected at short-range by radars such as 992Q; but long-range
detection would have required airborne early warning, which the
British lacked. The only other possibility was a short-range,
fast-reaction weapon, such as Sea Wolf. However, a Sea Wolf
installation, particularly the radar and the command and control
elements, was a sufficiently major task, precluding emergency
installation aboard existing ships. Presumably the recent British
decision to buy the American "Phalanx" close-in defensive system
for the British carriers reflects the gravity of this problem.

Sea Wolf was also problematic. Designed for a very different
threat, the sea-skimming anti-ship missile such as the Exocet, it
is vulnerable to saturation, since it has only two directors.
Moreover, it cannot deal sequentially with weapons approaching
simultaneously, because it appears to have a very short range.
Nor is it capable of sustained firing since each Type 22 has only
two six-round launchers, and must be reloaded manually. Because
there is very little warning time, the system must be largely
automated, with a high-data-rate radar feeding directly into the
combat system. Indeed, Sea Wolf is sometimes described as auto-
matically-triggered by threats approaching the ship. In the

Falklands, the Royal Navy tried to use this effective point-defense system as an area-defense weapon, with Type 22 frigates screening larger ships. The results of such screening are unclear, but in some films the Type 22s appeared to be extremely close to the carriers they were protecting.

There is no inexpensive escape from this dilemma. In the United States the horrendously expensive Aegis system is the only proposed solution. As of this writing, it seems that the Royal Navy has decided to abandon area defense missile development; Sea Dart Mark 2 has been cancelled. It seems unlikely that Britain will soon build a Ticonderoga-size cruiser required to support an effective area defense system. What the Falklands experience suggests is that even under relatively low (or unsophisticated) threat conditions, an inexpensive fleet air defense system may be unattainable. It is true that fighters might have made up for the absence of area missile defense, but they would have been required in much greater numbers, and they may have required airborne control.

Saturation affects virtually all naval systems, including guns. HMS Ardent, a Type 21, was credited with three air defense channels (Sea Cat, 4.5-inch and 20-mm guns) and was reportedly sunk by a simultaneous strike by four aircraft. Even so, the experience of the ships in Falkland Sound suggests that providing as many short-range air defense channels as possible is well worthwhile, especially if these remain inexpensive. In US terms, this favors both the Phalanx and the stillborn infrared homing 5-inch shell. The latter is particularly interesting because it is, in theory, a fire-and-forget weapon with a very high rate of fire.

ECM is the other major shipboard counter to missile attack. Understandably, the Royal Navy has not been forthcoming with information concerning its doctrine. There are some indications that it much prefers passive operations. For example, the Sheffield was on a "silent" picket station trying to avoid any emission except that of her satellite transmitter. Questions have been raised about the standard British ESM systems, which reportedly are not fully capable of detecting the Exocet search radar.

This illustrates a more general and significant problem. Western forces have been designed against the severe threat of the Soviets. In some cases Soviet equipment is so different from Western types (e.g., in radar cross section, mission profile, and radar emitting band) that this Western investment is wasted in combat against Third World countries which have been armed by the West. Thus a major lesson of the war is that the enemy is not always a Soviet proxy. In the case of the Sheffield, there have been suggestions that the Abbey Hill system installed might have picked up the radio chatter of the Super Etendard pilots but not the Exocet seeker.

British policy appears to favor the use of decoys rather than jammers, since reports emphasize both chaff and novel forms of deception. For example, Plymouth, in company with Sheffield, reportedly fired clouds of chaff almost continuously during daylight hours, without any reference to ESM. Helicopters carrying radar warning receivers and, in the case of the Lynx, radar reflectors, may have been used to decoy missiles. The helicopters were said to have dipped low to simulate a ship, then climbed to break lock. Given the limited number of Exocets available to the Argentines, the number of missiles successfully decoyed is unknown; but at least four hit targets.

Given the limitations of its shipborne defensive missiles, the Task Force had to rely on its aircraft for cover. By all accounts the Sea Harriers performed splendidly, and none was lost to enemy air action. Armed with the newer AIM-9L Sidewinder, the Sea Harriers accounted for more Argentine aircraft than did any other single system. Moreover, the ski-jumps fitted to the carriers permitted the Sea Harriers to remain airborne significantly longer, and at least in theory, they might have maintained air patrol stations at considerable distances from the force.

Here the Task Force's limitations became evident. Combat Air Patrols (CAPs) can also be overwhelmed or avoided. Each aircraft can be in only one place at a time, and its weapons have range limits. That the AIM-9L could home on the forward aspect on an incoming airplane helped enormously, since the Harrier did not have to get on the target's tail, and could thus remain in place as the targets approached. That it was a fire-and-forget weapon also helped, since the Harrier could operate on the basis of one target per missile, rather than dedicating itself to a single engagement at a time, as in the case, for example, of a Sparrow-equipped Phantom (which must maintain radar lock on the target until missile impact). Again, US Task Force operational experience since the mid-1950s has emphasized the need for numbers of radars supporting a massive CAP, and the radars had to include airborne ones if the low-flying attackers were to be detected in time. In the absence of airborne radars and airborne fighter control, CAP fighters cannot themselves be expected to acquire and attack all incoming enemy aircraft.

This may explain why, during the first major air battle between the Royal Navy and the Argentine Air Force, intercepts were carried out over the fleet itself. Although the Sea Harriers could maintain a CAP about one hundred miles out, this was impractical because there simply were not enough Sea Harriers to cover the perimeter. It appears that the Task Force employed a mixture of CAP and deck-launch interceptor (DLI) tactics, the latter exploiting the short take-off run of the fighter.

The lack of airborne radar warning aircraft was felt in several ways. First, the Sheffield had little or no effective warning of aircraft which probably approached at low altitude and then popped up suddenly to shoot. Second, she was required to stand on picket duty precisely because there were no airborne pickets, which would not have been vulnerable to missile attack. It is noteworthy that Sheffield and Coventry were apparently sunk and Glasgow hit while on picket stations. All three ships were worthwhile targets which had to be destroyed before the Argentines could hope to neutralize the larger ships. Any survivor of the destroyer picket line off Okinawa would know this. Third, the lack of airborne radar proved particularly costly once the British entered San Carlos Sound. Again, their problem was not new; it was similar to the German attacks in Norway in 1940, when ships were unable to maneuver and were denied effective early warning because incoming aircraft could not be detected easily over land. A radar airplane such as the Grumman E-2C can detect low-flying aircraft even over land, and it can direct both shipboard and airborne countermeasures.

It has been reported that the Ministry of Defence has accepted a helicopter-radar combination (Sea King AEW-1) to provide the V/STOL carriers with effective radar warning. The principal liability is the poor fuel economy of the helicopter, and since the British carriers have only limited fuel capacity, they may be unable to support the almost continuous surveillance required. That was certainly the case with US proposals to use the LAMPS helicopters of American destroyers and frigates to form continuous patrol lines in support of convoys and naval formations; there was just not enough fuel aboard the ships. Too, AEW radars require extensive maintenance. If the United States finds four a bare minimum to maintain coverage over a battle group, then six helicopters may be required aboard an Invincible. Unfortunately, space aboard the latter is critical; there is not that margin for "overhead" such as the AEW which Americans take for granted. Nor is there a great margin for unserviceability, in terms of number of aircraft or of ASW helicopters.

The issue of serviceability becomes more critical as the total number of aircraft is reduced. In the Falklands, the Harriers showed an enviable rate of availability.

Another major issue which remains generally unresolved is the vulnerability of modern ships to air attack. While Exocet received much publicity for destroying the Sheffield it failed to disable the larger Glamorgan; this was less widely reported. In the latter case the missile hit near the hanger and blew off the hanger door, demolishing the Wessex helicopter inside. There was a blast and a fireball, and the resulting fire was not brought under control for 3½ hours. However, the ship never lost way, and was steaming at twenty-three knots within fifteen minutes after the attack. Although she suffered thirteen killed and fourteen wounded, Glamorgan was never placed out of action because the missile struck high and in a relatively unimportant part of the ship. Reportedly her navigator was able to save her by turning his ship as the missile approached.

The other three major British naval casualties fell victim to conventional "iron" bombs and the Argentines reportedly damaged twelve surface combatants, six of them by unexploded bombs.

Ships varied in their ability to survive bomb damage. In general, ships were hit close to the waterline by skip-bombing, so that even unexploded bombs, such as that which hit the Glasgow, caused considerable flooding. In the case of the frigate Ardent, the bomb struck below the waterline, passed through a fuel oil tank, and destroyed a Sea Cat magazine but did not explode; the inrush first of fuel oil and then of sea water extinguished any fire. One, and possibly two, County class destroyers were struck by unexploded bombs, with more limited damage. On the other hand, Ardent was destroyed when she took a bomb in an engine room; the bomb exploded while it was being disarmed and started a devastating fire. Bombs, and perhaps rockets, also touched off the fire which sank the other Type 21 frigate, HMS Antelope.

Fire was responsible for three of the four combatant warship losses. For example, the captain of the Sheffield described pungent black smoke filling much of the ship within seconds of the impact of the Exocet missile. Subsequent photographs showed only a relatively small hole where the missile had struck and it was later reported that its warhead never exploded; although there is some disagreement about this, many reports stated that the fire damage was caused by the burning missile fuel (propellant). The Exocet's motor may have continued to burn for a minute after the weapon struck. The hit in the galley started an oil fire which spread along cable runs and piping, causing spontaneous combustion. Plastic partitions and furniture also burned. It is said that the heat of this fire caused the PVC insulation around cable runs in the machinery spaces to smolder, releasing toxic fumes. The fire could also have been fed by fuel oil in piping and perhaps in header tanks in the machinery spaces. Paradoxically, had the missile exploded, it would have been easier for the smoke to escape from the ship. It should be noted that PVC insulation is usually described as fire resistant (it does not ignite easily), and should not emit dangerous fumes unless it is heated to a high temperature for a certain time--as in a raging fire. It appears, too, that the crew of the Sheffield found it difficult to fight the fire effectively because their polyester overalls were themselves flammable. If so, this would be a shocking defect in crew protection procedures.

Accounts of the loss of the ship suggest other problems as well. A Type 42 destroyer has four machinery spaces: two engine rooms with two auxiliary (diesel generator) machinery spaces at the ends. In theory, then, no single hit should have been able to disable the ship. In fact, it appears that the Sheffield was operating on only one set of her gas turbines, a consequence of her COGOG (cruiser or boost) machinery arrangement. That engine room was hit, and the adjacent diesel generators were also put out of action. However, the other set of generators was never brought into action. Furthermore, the Exocet so damaged the fire main of the ship that effective fire fighting became difficult in any case, and the crew was reportedly reduced to dipping buckets in the sea to attack the flames.

Most of the celebrated ship losses of World War II can be retraced not to glaring errors of design, but rather to quite minor and unsuspected items: the twisted propeller shaft in the Prince of Wales; the flooded uptake in the Ark Royal; the pyrotechnics magazine in the Arizona. What World War II also showed was that ships the size of the Sheffield, properly designed, could survive extremely heavy damage, including fire damage, if their damage-control equipment was sufficiently duplicated and sufficiently well separated. Perhaps those lessons are being disregarded because they drive up the cost of a ship without adding to her firepower or other capabilities.

The losses of the two Type 21 frigates, Ardent and Antelope, are puzzling. Both reportedly burned intensely, and both had aluminum superstructures, which at first were blamed for their loss. But Sheffield had been built entirely of steel, and all three ships had steel hulls. This issue was of particular interest to the US Navy because nearly all modern US surface combatants have aluminum superstructures (which reduce the topweight associated with extensive radar arrays and with large topside combat control spaces). Indeed, in 1975 the US Navy had had a sobering experience when the missile cruiser Belknap burned after a collision with the carrier John F. Kennedy. Reports of that incident suggested that the aluminum tended to melt, not burn, causing the control of the ship to be degraded. There had also been the 1972 Worden incident, in which a Shrike anti-radiation missile caused considerable damage through the spalling of aluminum superstructure plates struck by missile fragments.

News photographs of the sinking of the Ardent seem to show that the ship structure was intact, but burning brightly, which suggests that the material in the structure was itself flammable, perhaps with some magnesium in it.[5] There have also been suggestions that the melting or collapse of the superstructures of the Type 21s tended to contain and concentrate the heat of the fire, causing the ignition of normally heat-resistant materials in the ships. Bomb hits, but no sinking, on all-steel frigates in San Carlos Sound were also reported. Alternatively, it might be noted that the Type 21s were among the few gas turbine ships present, and that peculiarities of the gas turbine, such as its massive open uptake and its fuel line configuration, might bear some blame.

Again, this is a most serious issue from an American point of view, and one which has received attention since the Belknap fire. The improvements now reported included kevlar covering for the inner sides of aluminum structures to reduce or prevent spalling, insulation to delay or prevent melting of the structures, and automatic halon sprinkler systems to fight fires. The Royal Navy experienced such fire damage in 1977 aboard a Type 21 frigate in dockyard and reportedly took its own countermeasures. Either these were insufficient, or they had not yet been implemented in the ships which were lost. Although there were no reports of ships surviving the type of damage which claimed the Sheffield and the two Type 21s, that remains an open question at this time.

To date the experience of the Falklands has been applied primarily to the air-sea battle; the principal issues are the continuing viability of large surface warships and the efficacy of modern air defense systems. Strategically, the issue is the rising technical sophistication of Third World powers as it affects Western (particularly US) capabilities to intervene far from home, coupled with the question of bases. From a British point of view, there is also the vital question of the future structure of British forces. Although clearly Britain will not drastically realign her forces to enable her to fight another Falklands War, it is possible that the war will have brought into question fundamental assumptions of British doctrine and materiel.

In each case feelings already run so high that quite opposite "lessons" have been extracted from the very limited evidence. For example, the Secretary of the US Navy, John Lehman, maintains that the battles show that only large carriers can be viable in a future war, since only such ships can support adequate airborne early warning and interceptor aircraft. In his view, the war shows that the areas of the world susceptible to a "low-threat, low-mix" approach are both limited and rapidly shrinking. On the other hand, advocates of "low-mix" such as Senator Gary Hart and Admiral Elmo Zumwalt have claimed that the destruction of the Sheffield proves exactly the opposite point: even the best defense leaks, and even expensive surface warships are extremely vulnerable. Exponents of weapons such as the Exocet will point out that, although they are small, one could suffice to wipe out a warship costing hundreds of millions of dollars.

This last "lesson" may well come under the mis-learned category. There were exactly four Exocet missile hits in the Falklands, one on the Sheffield, two on the Atlantic Conveyor, and one on the Glamorgan. Of the two warships, the smaller and newer one was lost, albeit to fire days after the initial hit. Moreover, the fact that much of the ship remained intact to the end suggests strongly that better design (such as better decentralization of power and command and control) would have enabled her to keep fighting. That was certainly the lesson of much of World War II. As for the Glamorgan, it was probably not merely the cleverness of her navigator which saved her. She was, after all, much larger that the Sheffield, so that any hit would affect a smaller percentage of her length. It is also likely that, constructed in a more affluent era of British warship design, she was better adapted to damage control. She was, after all, about a decade closer to the lessons of World War II. Perhaps the chief lesson of the Sheffield (and of the two Type 21s) is that there is no substitute for size and for careful design against battle damage.

For an American, the Sheffield case is particularly misleading. In many ways the most comparable US warship would be the Perry class frigate. Both ships have a single missile launcher and two fire control channels. However, the Perry has twice as many missiles aboard, and she has a much more highly automated combat system as well as a Phalanx last-ditch defense system aft. If the latter works as advertised, a Perry in the position of the Sheffield might well have survived by shooting down the one Exocet coming at her. In any case, where the Royal Navy considered the Type 42 a large and sophisticated ship, for the United States it is at the "low" end of Admiral Zumwalt's "high-low" mix. In the case of the Perry, survivability might have been assured by the sheer bulk of the ship, which would have limited the extent of damage. This suggests that the potential survivability of the larger ships is greater, a point often overlooked.

As for the carriers, the greatest liability of the British air operation was the limited number of aircraft available. Even given the magnificent qualities ascribed to the Harrier, there is no substitute for numbers. Numbers are a cushion against all sorts of surprises, and the operational loss of about a tenth of the air group on the Hermes, in one mid-air collision, was just such a surprise. Nor were aircraft the only limit. Hermes steamed to the Falklands with munitions piled topside because her magazines were not large enough for the sustained operation the

British knew they would have to mount. Even large carriers suffer from limited internal volume, but volume becomes more expensive as overall ship size is decreased. Any sustained operation expends ammunition at a very high rate, and at a great distance from home, the rate of underway replenishment, at least at first, will be limited.

One of the misfortunes of the current carrier debate in the United States is that many of those involved do not appreciate that ship size is the least expensive item. Electronics and air-craft cause the greatest expenses. The former are almost standard. Every carrier needs air search radars and equipment for directing aircraft in to land in bad weather. As for aircraft, it is unfortunately customary to include their cost with that of the carrier, as though somehow a ship with sixty aircraft provides a similar capability to one with ninety, at a bargain price. Since neither of the British carriers was damaged, the adage that a large ship has markedly better survivability than a smaller one was not tested. However, past experience suggests that it is a very real issue. It was obscured by the apparent giantkilling capability of the Exocet. In fact, the only giant killed was a big merchant ship, and no one has ever claimed very great surviv-ability there. Incidentally, it is noteworthy that the Atlantic Conveyor took a long time to sink after the two Exocet hits.

Very much as in the case of the Styx which sank the Eilat in 1967, the Exocet has about it the aura of a weapon whose time has come. There is something attractive about an inexpensive weapon which appears to make investment in large warships unnecessary. Alas, the Falklands battles prove nothing of the sort. What they do show is that surface ships are necessary to project power at a great distance, and that those same surface ships can be sunk by a determined enemy. That is not exactly a new lesson, but it is one too often forgotten: the surface Navy exists, not merely to float, but to accomplish missions which no other platform or set of platforms can accomplish. The issue is not whether the surface ship remains viable, but rather what sort of surface ship represents the best combination of survivability and mission effectiveness.

All of these lessons bear on the fate of the US Rapid Deployment Force (now named CENTCOM, or Central Command), and on the continuing US mission of power projection abroad. British spokemen have argued that the Falklands is irrelevant to their requirements, since the Royal Navy and British defense policy reflect the realities in Northwest Europe. Traditionally that has meant a concentration on ASW, with the AAW-oriented carrier fleet increasingly dismissed as expensive and unnecessary. After all, there will be effective land-based air forces in the vicinity, ready to come to the aid of convoys in distress.

World War II experience suggests that no such use of land-based aircraft will be entirely successful; it is difficult to have them on the scene when they are needed, and standing patrols are far too costly. As for the Western European scenario, it is impossible to imagine that the most important task in the opening phase of a war would be to support a NATO landing on the Northern flank. Such a landing would have some points of similarity to the operation in Falkland Sound: the ships would have to operate close to land, with degraded radar performance (even in the absence of massive Soviet-style jamming), and against very stiff air opposition. Point defense systems such as Sea Wolf would help, but not enough.

Nor could a naval commander in such circumstances hope for much in the way of land-based air support. Even at a distance of 300 miles, such support is very expensive in terms of dedicated aircraft, and it is hard to imagine that the limited resources of the RAF would not be heavily taxed in a major war. Any convoy headed for the Northern flank would have to provide its own air defense. Possibly standard NATO doctrine is for US warships to carry out this mission, with British carriers in an ASW support role, in which case the limited capabilities of the British carriers will not be a liability. However, one cannot but shrink from the prospect of having to rely on such a limited resource as the thirteen (or even fifteen) US carriers in a worldwide conflict. The limitation on size and capability imposed on the Invincible class (for what seems to have been political reasons) does not seem any more justifiable than when they were built.

Another traditional British mission is convoy escort, which until recently meant ASW. Now it means AAW, both against submarine-launched missiles and against Soviet long-range aircraft. Again, when the Invincible-Sea Harrier combination was first conceived, it was enough to destroy the Bear D targeting aircraft to break up a Soviet anti-ship missile attack. Now the Backfires (which can confirm their own targets) can range over the prospective convoy routes. The Falklands experience suggests that the current British fleet is ill-designed to counter raids of twenty or more Backfires, which are very much within Soviet capabilities.

Tactically, the Exocet raids show that it is poor economy to destroy a missile after it is launched. Had the British been able to intercept the Super Etendards, they would have wiped out the missile threat and would not have had to devote large resources to it. That, however, would have required a combination of more efficient interceptors and airborne early warning. The only alternative, a raid on the Argentine mainland, was politically infeasible. That it was even mentioned suggests the gravity of the problem.

There is a danger that the British victory will blind Britain to the real defects in current and prospective weapons and probably in current defense policy, just as, in 1915, the sinking of the German armored cruiser Blucher blinded the British public to the greater failure of the British battle cruisers to achieve sufficient tactical coordination to defeat the other German ships that day. There are, after all, enormous industrial and financial stakes; the arms export market is a vast one, and "combat proven" is a valuable endorsement. There are already glowing accounts of the performances of Sea Wolf and Sea Harrier, and surely Sea Dart will soon be rehabilitated. That is why it is so important to seek the underlying lessons of the conflict; the experience is far too valuable, far too dearly bought, to be ignored.

NOTES

1. Condensed and reprinted from Orbis: A Journal of World Affairs, Winter 1983, by permission of the publisher. Copyright 1983 by the Foreign Policy Research Institute, Philadelphia, Pennsylvania.

2. Like the US Navy, the Royal Navy employs task force protection tactics which depend to some extent on maintaining a substantial speed of advance--which was impossible in the restricted operational area off the Falklands.

3. Note that the General Belgrano was sunk by MK VIII topedoes designed in the 1930s, rather than by modern homing torpedoes-- which the British apparently rightly distrusted. It was not all very modern technology!

4. Sea Slug apparently was not used against aircraft; Glamorgan was hit after using hers against Argentine shore positions.

5. More recent reports, however, attribute the apparent spattering in the photographs to the film itself; the British reported no aluminum fires at all, and the entire issue appears to have been blown out of proportion.

4
Air Power Lessons

Earl H. Tilford, Jr.

The war in the South Atlantic over the Falklands was a
surprise. The British, including the Royal Navy and the Royal Air
Force, oriented to and prepared for a war in the North Atlantic or
Europe in support of their North Atlantic Treaty Organization
(NATO) commitments against Warsaw Pact and Soviet forces, were
unprepared for a fight so far from home and against so unlikely an
enemy as Argentina. The Argentines were equally unprepared for a
conflict of the magnitude of the one they provoked with their
invasion on the Falkland and South Georgia islands on April 2,
1982.
At the time of the invasion the Argentines seemed to have all
the advantages. The islands are much closer to Argentina than
they are to Britain. Nevertheless, the distance was far enough
from Argentina to complicate the employment of air power. At
about 400 nautical miles from the nearest bases, the skies over
the Falklands proved to be at the extreme end of the combat radii
of the jet aircraft in the Argentine inventory.
When the war began the Fuerza Aerea Argentina (FAA) was among
the finest in Latin America. It contained about 225 combat aircraft, including sixty-eight Douglas A-4 Skyhawk single-engine jet
fighter-bombers, twenty-six Israeli-built copies of Dassault-
Breguet Mirage IIIs called "Neshers" in Israel and "Daggers" in
Argentina, twenty-one French-built Mirage IIIs, and a number of
Argentine-built IA-58 "Pucara" counter-insurgency aircraft. Two
KC-130s provided a limited aerial refueling capability. The Naval
Air Force included eleven A-4Q Skyhawks and five of the fourteen
Dassault-Breguet Super Etendards ordered in November 1981.[1]

During the war Argentine pilots earned the respect of their enemies and most of the world with their skill and bravery. They were good and obviously well trained. In fact, many of them had been trained by the Israeli Air Force, which is regarded as one of the world's best combat forces.[2] Despite its training and the courage of its crews, the FAA was not prepared for the kind of sophisticated air defense system use by the Royal Navy. Furthermore, the Argentines had never been in combat with a foreign power. Their air crews had no combat experience except for a few members who may have flown in counter-insurgency operations against guerrilla forces. The military tradition of the FAA and Naval Air Force was limited to domestic strife.

The Royal Navy and Royal Air Force, on the other hand, have a rich military tradition. Like most Argentine pilots, British crews have had virtually no opportunities to fight for the last quarter of a century. However, they have maintained a high level of proficiency by training in NATO exercises, participating in US Air Force "Red Flag" exercises in Nevada, and flying against "aggressor squadrons" at home. The process of staying ready to fight Soviet and Warsaw Pact forces demands a high level of what has come to be called "readiness."

In April 1982, the Fleet Air Arm consisted of thirty-four Sea Harriers and ninety or so helicopters of various types.[3] The Royal Air Force, one of the world's largest and finest, numbered 700 combat aircraft, most of which were committed to NATO or the defense of the British Isles.[4] However, the potential represented by the size and capabilities of British air power was largely irrelevant in that most of this force was not suited to nor available for a war 8,000 miles from Europe.

Britain, like many Western nations, had reduced the size, and some would argue the capability, of its military forces in the late 1960s and through the 1970s. For instance, the British Aerospace (BAe) Vulcan bombers, long the backbone of Britain's manned nuclear delivery capability, were to be phased out of the RAF in 1982.[5] The more sophisticated Panavia Tornado GR.1s which are replacing them would not be suitable for the kinds of missions flown in the South Atlantic by the Vulcans. Ironically, in February 1982, the Argentine government inquired at the Ministry of Defence about purchasing the Vulcan bombers.[6] Acquisition of such a long-range bomber force would have made Argentina the only Latin American nation with a strategic bombing capability and it would have changed the entire complexion of the balance of forces in the South Atlantic.

Budget cuts had their impact on the Royal Navy as well. In an economy move the Royal Navy retired its last carrier at the end of the 1970s. Fleet defense now rests with two V/STOL (Vertical/Short Take-Off and Landing) carriers, the HMS _Hermes_ and HMS _Invincible_.[7]

Despite cutbacks in procurement and reductions in force, the British naval and air forces possessed some of the finest weaponry available. The surface-to-air missiles, fire control systems, and BAe Harriers were all of the latest variety and quite capable.

The crews had been trained well. In short, the British were ready
to fight and proved able to perform well in a war which no one
seriously imagined would happen. Since they had been preparing to
fight the much more challenging and dangerous Soviet/Warsaw Pact
forces, the war with Argentina, fought in an inhospitable climate
so far from the normal area of operations, presented unique and
unforeseen problems.

Britain's great advantages then were in its equipment and in
the training of its troops, airmen and sailors. Argentina had
advantages of its own. Among these was that the Argentines were
fighting for something in which they firmly believed, namely that
the Malvinas were theirs. Napoleon Bonaparte noted that in war
the moral is to the physical as three is to one. For generations,
Argentines had been told, "Las Malvinas son nuestros!"[8] The conviction that their cause was just plus the excellent training of
the aircrews combined to make the Argentine airmen a spirited and
tenacious force.

In addition to the nationalistic aspiration to lay claim to
territory most Argentines felt to be justly their own, the FAA
would seem to have the advantage of being closer to the area of
conflict. That proved to be illusive because the Argentine Air
Force was pushed to its limit in conducting operations at a
distance of 400 miles.[9] Furthermore, the Argentine Navy, a force
which paled in comparison with the Royal Navy, proved to be little
help, the contribution of its air squadrons notwithstanding.
Nevertheless, the FAA assembled a considerable force of A-4s,
Mirages, Daggers, Mk 62 Canberra twin-engine jet bombers, and IA-
58 Pucaras for the fight over the South Atlantic.[10]

Distance was not the only problem for the FAA. Maintenance
had become a nagging irritant. In 1978, President Jimmy Carter
"punished" Argentina for human rights infractions by placing an
embargo on shipments of military items (including aircraft spare
parts). For instance, some ejection seats on the A-4s flown by
both the FAA and the navy reportedly were inoperable because they
lacked explosive canisters.[11] There were undoubtedly other
shortages in spare parts for the Skyhawks, but the mechanics who
worked on that particular aircraft were well trained and knew how
to overcome many of the problems. Those working on the newer
French and Israeli-built aircraft were somewhat less
experienced.[12]

For the British the task of retaking the islands was
formidable. The scope of the operations was tremendous owing to
the distance from the islands and the fact that the Argentines
were already entrenched. There were many problems and challenges
for air power. Even as the task force sailed the problems of
logistics and supply came into focus. Helicopters had to ferry
supplies to ships while they sailed away from the British Isles on
their way to Ascension Island 4,000 miles to the south.
Meanwhile, RAF four-engine C-130 (Hercules) transports and VC-10
jet transports hauled supplies and personnel to Ascension to prepare for the arrival of the task force.[13]

As the British task force steamed south, Argentina waited for what might develop in the South Atlantic. In fact, the Argentines seem to have done too much waiting and not enough preparation. While the Argentine military did move a relatively large number of troops to the islands, the high command did not develop a coherent strategy for defending the newly acquired possessions. For instance, only a few, specific reserve units were called to arms.[14]

Prior to April 1982, the British maintained only a token force on the Falklands and had never built military installations of any consequence. The runway at Port Stanley, suited only for light transports, could not accommodate heavy military aircraft or jet fighters which require a longer runway. Accordingly, the Argentines stationed only one squadron of IA-58 Pucaras, and a handful of T-34 and Aeromacchi MB-339 light jet strike fighters, on the islands.[15] The only paved runway, the one of Port Stanley, at 4,000 feet in length, was barely long enough for C-130s. The light jet fighters stationed there could take off and land with a minimum margin of safety. In an emergency they could use the grass field at Pebble/Burbon Island, but would have to take off without armament.[16]

No one believed that these light jets and the Pucaras would be very useful against the approaching British fleet. Certainly the Argentines were aware that the A-4s, Mirages, and Daggers would be fighting at the end of their combat radii when flying from mainland bases. Why then did they not lengthen the runway outside Port Stanley? According to one Argentine source, aluminum runway material was "available" but there was no time to ship it to the islands. This source claimed that the size and weight of the materials required a large vessel which was not available.[17] Whatever the reason for not lengthening the runway, the absence of A-4s and other combat jets put the Argentines at an extreme disadvantage by limiting their flexibility and proscribing their scope of operations. One must assume that the planning for this operation was less than complete and might have resulted from a miscalculation of British resolve.

By the end of April the British task force was in the South Atlantic. Realizing that they would be fighting not only at a numerical disadvantage, but fighting far from their normal area of operations, the British enhanced their strengths to meet the challenges posed in employing force under these circumstances. The possession of weapons of greater sophistication than those used by the Argentines proved key to giving the British their victory. Among these weapons was the Harrier.

Conceived in the mid-fifties, the Harrier was then, as it is today, a bold departure in aerodynamic theory and design. In the 1950s jet combat aircraft were designed and built for speed. The Lockheed F-104, billed as "the missile with a man in it" and called the "Starfighter," was typical of designs that called for high speed. Its thin wings, long fuselage, high rate of fuel consumption, and limited maneuverability typified the kind of aircraft visionaries of the 1950s designed to fight wars in the

1960s. Typically these aircraft handled poorly at low altitude and often stalled a low speeds. The concept of using vectored thrust to direct the blast of the jet engine downward to allow for near vertical take-offs and landings offered the possibility of designing a wing without flaps and other high-lift devices. Such a wing would provide additional space for carrying armament. Furthermore, the plane theoretically would be very maneuverable at high and low altitudes. Another advantage would be that such an aircraft could operate from landing pads, open fields, and other confined areas.[18]

In 1957 Hawker-Siddeley began work on project P.1127 as a private and joint venture between Hawker Aircraft and Bristol Siddeley.[19] The chief designer was Sir Sydney Camm, whose previous designs included the Hawker Hurricane, Tempest, Typhoon, and the classic Hawker Hunter jet fighter-bomber.[20] Work on the P.1127 proceeded rapidly, considering the novelty of the design, with the first prototype beginning tethered hovering tests on October 21, 1960, some seventeen months after initial construction began. Its first untethered flight occurred a month later and in March 1961, the first flight trials began.[21] In early 1963 the "Kestrel," as it was known, landed on the aircraft carrier Ark Royal. The event drew little attention, though members of the Royal Air Force, Royal Navy, Luftwaffe, as well as the US Air Force, Army, and Navy witnessed it. In the early 1960s, the Royal Air Force still officially acquiesced in the notorious 1957 White Paper that held that combat aircraft were obsolete and would be surpassed by missiles. Thus official interest in the P.1127 was subdued.[22]

The development of the Harrier continued despite its radical design and the uncertain political climate. The aircraft grew in size and became more refined. It gained a larger engine which increased the thrust from 12,500 pounds to 21,500 pounds.[23] After the British decided to modernize their air forces to meet the projected threat through the seventies and eighties, the decision was made on August 31, 1966 to procure the Harrier.[24] Three years later, in July 1969, Number 1 Squadron of the Royal Air Force became the first unit to operate the Harrier.[25]

The Royal Navy did not show much interest in the Harrier until fiscal cuts forced the standard size aircraft out of the fleet. Faced with the prospect of having a fleet without air power, in 1975, the Royal Navy decided to develop the Sea Harrier from the model already in service with the RAF. While the RAF version of the Harrier was designed for the air-to-ground role, the navy needed a point defense aircraft with a primary air-to-air mission. Changes made to the Harrier included raising the cockpit to enhance visibility and the addition of a Ferranti Blue Fox air-intercept radar.[26]

Ordinarily, at sea the only air threat posed to the Royal Navy would be from long-range Soviet bombers like the Tu-95/Bear or the Backfire. Sea Harriers could contend with the subsonic Tu-95s and, with greater difficulty, could be used against the more capable Backfires. When operating near coastal areas the projected threat includes an array of fighter-bombers and land-based bombers and would be more formidable.

Neither the Sea Harriers nor the RAF version of the Harrier are supersonic. Argentine Mirages and Daggers are capable of speeds nearing mach 2. In numerous engagements over the Sinai, Syrian countryside, and Mediterranean, Israeli pilots flying Mirages have bested MiG-21s. Mirages and Daggers are generally rated among the better combat aircraft in the world and super-ficially they seem to have many advantages over the slower Harriers.

One of the big surprises of the Falkland Islands War would be the performance of the Harriers. Besides their unique maneuvering characteristics, the Harriers had another surprise waiting for the Argentines, their AIM-9L Sidewinder missiles. These advanced heat-seeking missiles proved more capable than the earlier models used by the US Air Force over Southeast Asia. In addition to homing on the exhaust of the enemy aircraft, these advanced Sidewinders have an "all aspect" attack capability which means the pilot need not get on the enemy's tail before firing but can fire at approaching targets.[27]

The British deployed twenty-eight Sea Harriers and fourteen RAF GR-3s to the South Atlantic. The latter were primarily equipped for ground attack missions. Royal Air Force GR-3s were scheduled for modifications to arm them with the AIM-9Ls in 1983. Those modifications were accelerated so that the RAF Harriers used in the South Atlantic were able to use the advanced Sidewinders.[28] Argentine jets operating at the limit of their combat radii did not attempt to engage the British in dogfights. Air-to-air combat consisted of Harrier pilots firing their AIM-9Ls or shooting their 30mm cannon at Mirages, Daggers, and Skyhawks as they flashed by en route to their targets. No Harriers were lost in air-to-air combat.

Aerial action began before the task force reached the Falklands. While the British task force steamed southward from Ascension Island, an Argentine Boeing 707, the longest range air-craft in the FAA, flew to within a few miles of the ships. Sea Harriers were scrambled to intercept the flight. The Harriers regularly intercepted the reconnaissance flights over the next several days and the Argentine B-707 crews began referring to the British interceptors as "our old acquaintances."[29] Sea Harrier pilot Simon Hargreaves recalled his first encounter with an Argentine Boeing 707, "I had live Sidewinders locked on him. If I had fired he would have been dead, but I wouldn't like to have been responsible for starting a war."[30]

It was not Harriers, Vulcans, or Skyhawks that first became involved in aerial combat. Helicopters were in action from April 24th when a British helicopter was reported down on the Argentine-Chilean border. Exactly why it crashed in the mountains of southern Argentina is not known, but there is speculation that it had dropped off a Special Air Service team engaged in intelligence operations.[31] The following day, about 1,500 miles to the east, a British helicopter struck the first blows when it machine-gunned and fired rockets at the Argentine submarine <u>Santa Fe</u> as it attempted to unload reinforcements at Grytviken Harbor on South Georgia Island. The captain of the damaged submarine ran the vessel aground. The crew and their passangers were captured by British troops later that afternoon when Royal Marines invaded South Georgia Island.[32]

By April 29th, the fleet was off the Falklands. On May 1st, air action began when a BAe Vulcan flew from Ascension Island to drop twenty-one 1,000-pound bombs on the airfield outside Port Stanley. A few hours later Sea Harriers followed up with a bombing and strafing attack.[33] The Argentine Air Force and Naval Air Force struck their first blows on the same day. Mirages, Skyhawks, and Canberra bombers raided the fleet to inflict minor damage on two vessels. In those first raids two Mirages and a Canberra were downed.[34]

The Falklands War provided the first opportunity for Vulcan bombers to get into combat. Throughout the campaign the Vulcans flew five sorties against the airfield at Port Stanley. These refueled missions from Ascension Island represented the longest combat bombing sorties in the history of aerial warfare. Of the fifty-five 1,000-pound bombs dropped by the Vulcans on the airfield only one hit the runway.[35] While the Vulcans accomplished little tactically, they did have an important psychological affect because the Argentines were made to believe that Prime Minister Margaret Thatcher could lose her patience and order the bomber strikes against mainland targets. This possibility added another dimension to Argentine defense problems.[36]

Additionally, the British used the Vulcans for defense suppression missions. A single Westinghouse radar set located on a hill outside Port Stanley was the target of these raids. The Vulcans had been modified to carry AGM-45 Shrike missiles which home in on electronic emmissions.[37] At least one Shrike was fired and the Argentines claimed that it destroyed a fire control radar belonging to an antiaircraft artillery battery. The Argentines repaired it quickly. An aircraft that fired a missile made an emergency landing in Brazil where the authorities confiscated an anti-radiation missile.[38] Whether the British fired more Shrikes and hit the Westinghouse radar is unclear.

The British used air power to accomplish two objectives. Their first priority was to protect the fleet from Argentine air attack. The second objective was to provide close air support for the Army and Royal Marines when they went ashore. To protect the fleet the British attacked Argentine aircraft on the island, using helicopters to ferry SAS troops in raids and using Harriers in direct attacks on airfields and aircraft at Port Stanley and at the Pebble Island airfield on West Falkland Island. As the fighting evolved, the protection of the fleet became the main concern for the British because its destruction became the primary objective of the Argentine Air Force and Naval Air Force.

To provide an adequate defense for the fleet the British devised a coordinated strategy. Sea Harriers, while integral to the fleet's defense, could not suffice on their own because of their limited speed and because they could not operate far from the fleet away from radar cover provided by their own ships. Ideally, a fleet would be defended by long-range interceptors flying far from their carriers, under the control of airborne early warning aircraft. But, as is known, the British had given up that option when they scrapped their heavy carriers, delivered their naval F-4 Phantoms and Buccanneers to the RAF, and mothballed the Fairey Gannet airborne early warning aircraft.[39]

To defend the fleet the British had to employ a mix of systems, including electronics, Harriers, surface-to-air missiles (SAMs), anti-aircraft guns, and at close range, small arms and hand-held Blowpipe missiles. The result was a defense in depth that worked fairly well. According to British sources, seventy-two Argentine aircraft were confirmed shot down and there were fourteen probable kills.[40] Sea Dart, Sea Wolf, Sea Cat, and Rapier surface-to-air missiles accounted for thirty-five confirmed and eight probable kills. The threat of early detection by British radar and being blown out of the air by SAMs long before reaching the objective forced the Argentine pilots to fly at low altitude. Down low the Mirages and Skyhawks lost the advantage of speed that they would have had at higher altitudes. The Harriers, on the other hand, armed with AIM-9L Sidewinders, were in their element at low altitude where they accounted for twenty confirmed and three probable kills.[41]

Argentina adopted a simple air strategy: destroy British ships. Bombing and strafing troops after they came ashore would seem appealing given the lack of natural cover on the islands. However, because the Argentine aircraft were operating at the extreme end of their combat radii they did not have the fuel to search for troops on the move. The best way to stop the invasion was to sink the ships in the hope of either killing the troops before they went ashore or making the cost to Britain so high that Whitehall would opt to withdraw or negotiate. Again, for Argentina, strategy was determined by limitations.

The attacks on the fleet proved costly. Argentine pilots have been incorrectly and unfairly compared to Japanese kamikazes of World War II. They were not committing suicide by attacking the fleet. Indeed, the FAA made provisions for search and rescue forces to be deployed whenever possible.[42]

The Argentine Air Force and Navy scored some impressive victories in their attacks on the fleet. Perhaps the most impressive were registered by the Navy's Etendard squadron. In November 1979, the Argentine government ordered French Dassault-Breguet Super Etendards when the Carter Administration refused to sell Argentina additional A-4 Skyhawks.[43] Between November 1980 and August 1981, Argentine pilots trained in Brittany, France. At about the same time five Super Etendards, along with five AM-39 Exocet anti-ship missiles, were delivered to Argentina. Two days before Argentine forces moved on the Falklands the navy declared the missiles "operational."[44]

On May 4th, the Super Etendards went into action. An Argentine Navy P-2 electronic surveillance aircraft directed the Etendards to their target, a Type 42 destroyer. At a range of between twenty and thirty miles each of the Etendards fired an Exocet. One hit the HMS Sheffield, eventually sending it to the bottom.[45] Three weeks later the Etendards attacked the fleet again and once again fired their Exocets beyond visual range of the targets. Because of the size of the radar return on their cockpit scopes the Argentine pilots believed they were stalking one of the two light aircraft carriers operating off the Falklands. They were correct. After firing their Exocets, the Argentines turned for home. Both missiles streaked toward the target. However, a British Lynx helicopter used a combination of chaff and electronic jamming to turn the missiles from their intended target. The missiles locked on another large return, this one coming from the Atlantic Conveyor, a cargo ship, hitting it with devastating results.[46]

The ease with which the Etendard squadron chalked up two impressive kills stands in contrast with the tortuous experiences endured by most Argentine pilots flying against the British fleet. Mirage, Dagger, and Skyhawk pilots flew so low en route to their targets that salt water drops evaporated on their windshields, obscuring vision. After the trying experience of flying just above the waves for fairly long distances, the Argentine pilots had to run the gauntlet of Harriers, missiles, and antiaircraft fire presented by the British defense in depth. When they reached the fleet, the Argentine pilots were at their mental and physical limits.[47]

Besides the perilous nature of flying en route to the battle area and the intensity of the British defensive screen, the Argentine crews had to contend with ordnance that did not always detonate. Some have speculated that Argentine pilots pressed their attacks so low that the bombs did not have time to arm before hitting their targets. The bombs dropped from Argentine Navy A-4s seem to have had a higher rate of explosion than those used by the FAA, possibly because the Navy used "snake eye" (500-pound Mark 82) bombs with extendable tails that acted as air brakes to slow their descent.[48]

According to a British source, many bombs hit the water just aft of the ships suggesting that the Argentine pilots aimed for the middle of their targets without compensating for the vessel's forward speed. Air Force crews might be more prone to this kind of mistake since they do not normally practice against naval targets. However, one Argentine Navy pilot indicated that he lined up his aircraft on the stern of the British ship as he made his bomb run.[49]

The British used air power effectively to support their troops after they went ashore. Laser target marking from the ground was used to enable Harriers to score direct hits on entrenched Argentine troops.[50] As the British closed in on Port Stanley, Harriers dropped 1,000-pound bombs with fuses set to go off fifty feet above the ground. These air blasts proved more efficient at killing Argentine troops in fox holes and they also tended to be more terrifying than ground detonations.[51]

Helicopters were indispensable in supporting ground operations. Sea King and Wessex helicopters hauled ammunition, tents, spare parts, and other essentials to the British troops as they advanced from San Carlos to Darwin and Port Stanley. On one occasion, a helicopter lifted a 5,000-pound artillery piece to the top of Mount Kent overlooking Port Stanley.[52]

The air war in the South Atlantic demonstrated both the power of the defense and the continuing need for an articulate strategy. The high attrition rates, particularly among Argentine aircraft, showed that the defense tends to predominate over the offense in aerial warfare when the defense is well equipped with technologically sophisticated weaponry operated by skilled technicians employing a coherent strategy. Harriers using AIM-9Ls and 30mm Aden cannons accounted for twenty confirmed and three probable kills. Antiaircraft guns and small arms kills totaled seven confirmed and one probable.[53] Clearly the high-tech weaponry of the British demonstrated its usefulness.

While Argentina possessed less sophisticated defensive weapons, they still performed well; Argentine antiaircraft fire and surface-to-air missiles downed five Harriers and four helicopters. Furthermore, high-tech weaponry, (a pair of Exocets) accounted for the loss of ten helicopters that went down with the Atlantic Conveyor. Three other helicopters were lost when bombs and an Exocet hit the Ardent, Conventry, and Glamorgan.[54]

The Argentines achieved partial air denial with their intense antiaircraft fire. That is to say that they prevented the British from continually doing whatever they wanted to in the skies over the Falkland Islands. For instance, the British never closed the runway at Port Stanley. While one might claim that Vulcan crews flying at higher altitudes might not be practiced in the delivery of conventional iron bombs, Harriers appeared to have been only a little more successful in closing the runway. This was due in large part to the intensity of Argentine antiaircraft fire which prevented the Harriers from pressing their attacks too closely.

Bravery and spirit were common on both sides. British troops demonstrated tremendous courage and competence in their march across the island from San Carlos to Darwin and on to Port Stanley. British pilots eagerly sought combat with the Argentine Mirages, Daggers, and Skyhawks as they pressed toward their targets. The Argentine Air Force and Navy crews wrote a new and gallant page in the history of aerial warfare. Their courage drew praise and admiration from around the world and they earned the respect of their enemies. However, as demonstrated in countless encounters between colonial powers and native forces, at Pickett's Charge during the Battle of Gettysburg, on the Western Front in World War I, and in the last days of the Pacific campaign in the Second World War, courage and valor are no match for superior weaponry effectively employed.

Argentina never developed an appropriate strategy for this war. They placed too much of a burden on their air forces and their air strategy relied too heavily on frontal attacks and the courage of the air crews. Attacks on the fleet played to the strengths of the British, their defense in depth made effective by the possession and skillful employment of a variety of sophisticated weapons.

In conclusion, the war in the South Atlantic confirmed already established principles of aerial warfare. All things being equal, in the age of high-tech weaponry the defense will predominate unless an innovative offensive strategy can be devised (as the Israelis did against the Syrian SAMs in the Bekaa Valley in 1982). Neither side employed innovative offensive air strategies. Courage and spirit are important for air crews, but cannot in themselves overcome the effects of highly sophisticated weaponry. Finally, air power played a large role in the fighting in the South Atlantic, but it did not play the decisive role. For the British, air power was part of a total force employment that resulted in victory.

Neither Britain nor Argentina gained very much from this war. The British lost aircraft and helicopters and expended lives and money that could have been used elsewhere. Argentina sacrificed a good part of its air and naval forces and shed the blood of its fine air crews. The British retained the Falklands and demonstrated that the West still has some courage and resolution. The Argentines provided martyrs for future generations to emulate. Both sides would do well to heed Abraham Lincoln's admonition: "Suppose you go to war, you cannot fight always; and when, after much loss on both sides, and no gain on either, you cease fighting, the identical old questions as to terms of intercourse are again upon you."

NOTES

1. "The Military Balance," Air Force Magazine (December 1981): 108.

2. John Laffin, Fight for the Falklands (New York: St. Martin's Press, 1982), p. 95.

3. "Britain Reacts Swiftly to Falklands Takeover," Aviation Week and Space Technology (12 April 1982): 25; and Derek Wood and Mark Hewish, "The Falklands Conflict, Part 1: The Air War," International Defense Review, vol. 15, no. 8 (1982): 978.

4. "The Military Balance," p. 70.

5. Bill Gunston and Ray Bonds (eds.), An Illustrated Guide to NATO Fighters and Attack Aircraft (New York: ARCO Books, 1983), p. 142.

6. Laffin, p. 11.

7. Wood and Hewish, p. 978.

8. Malvinas: An Unlawful Colonalism (pamphlet) (Buenos Aires: Publisher unnamed, 1982), 15 pages. Argentine literature abounds with emphatic claims to ownership of the Malvinas. This pamphlet is but one example of the feelings the Argentines have about their rights to these islands.

9. John W.R. Taylor, ed., Jane's All the World's Aircraft, 1982-83 (London: Jane's Publishing Company, Ltd., 1983), p. 51.

10. "La Fuerza Aerea Argentina y La Fuerza Terea," Aerospacio, (Septiembre-Octubre 1982): 41.

11. Robert L. Scheina, "The Malvinas Campaign," Proceedings (May 1983): 113.

12. Laffin, p. 78.

13. Charles W. Corddry, "Britain's Near-Thing Victory," Air Force Magazine (December 1982): 52.

14. "La Fuerza Aera Argentina y La Fuerza Terea," p. 37.

15. "Las Operaciones de Ataque," Aerospacio, (Septiembre-Octubre, 1982): 51; and Scheina, p. 104.

16. Scheina, p. 105; and "El Teatro de Operaciones," Aerospacio (Septiembre-Octubre 1982): 25.

17. Ibid., p. 26.

18. John F. Guilmartin, Jr., "The Harrier: V/STOL Vindicated," Air University Review (September-October 1982): 74.

19. John W.R. Taylor, ed., Jane's All the World's Aircraft, 1964-65 (London: Sampson, Row, Marston, & Co., 1965), p. 153.

20. Guilmartin, p. 72.

21. Taylor, Jane's All the World's Aircraft, 1964-65, p. 153.

22. Gunston, ed., NATO Fighters, p. 36.

23. Guilmartin, "V/STOL Vindicated," p. 76.

24. Gunston and Bonds, p. 44.

25. Francis K. Mason, Harrier (Annapolis: Naval Institute Press, 1983), p. 78.

26. Ibid., pp 129-130.

27. The Falklands Campaign: The Lessons, (London: Her Majesty's Stationery Office, 1982), p. 9.

28. Ibid., pp 19-20; and Mason, pp. 142-143.

29. "La Exploracion," Aerospacio (Septiembre-Octubre 1982): 67.

30. Hargreaves, quoted in Laffin, pp. 37-38.

31. Samuel L. Morison, "Falklands (Malvinas) Campaign: A Chronology," Proceedings (June 1983): 120.

32. Laffin, pp. 41-42.

33. Wood and Hewish, p. 981.

34. Morison, p. 121.

35. Wood and Hewish, p. 981; and Christian Eliot and Gerd W. Gossler, "The White Paper on the Falklands," Naval Forces, vol. IV, no. 1, p. 42.

36. "La FAA y la Fuera de Tereas" Aerospacio (Septiembre-Octubre 1982): 36.

37. Eduardo H. D'Odorico, "Misiles en las Malvinas," Aerospacio (Noviembre-Diciembre 1982): 56.

38. Wood and Hewish, p. 980.

39. Taylor, Jane's All the World's Aircraft, 1982-83, p. 49.

40. The Falklands Campaign: The Lessons, p. 20. British sources indicate that throughout the war an estimated 117 Argentine aircraft were destroyed. This figure includes those destroyed in air-to-ground attacks and SAS raids.

41. Ibid.

42. "Busqueda y Salvamento," Aerospacio (Septiembre-Octubre 1982): 72.

43. Scheina, p. 107.

44. Robert L. Scheina, "Super Etendard: Super Squadron," Proceedings (March 1983): 135.

45. Scheina, "The Malvinas Campaign," p. 107.

46. Wood and Hewish, p. 978.

47. "La FAA y la Fuerza de Tereas," pp. 46-48.

48. Scheina, "The Malvinas Campaign," p. 112.

49. Captain De Corbeta Alberto Jorge Philippi, "Odyssey of a Skyhawk Pilot," Proceedings (May 1983): 111.

50. Eliot and Gossler, "The White Paper on the Falklands," p. 44.

51. Laffin, p. 68.

52. Ibid., pp. 120-121.

53. See Annex B, Weapons Systems Performance Against Enemy Aircraft," The Falklands Campaign: The Lessons, p. 45.

54. Ibid., Annex C "Ship and Aircraft Losses," p. 46.

5
Amphibious Lessons

Frank Uhlig, Jr.

BACKGROUND

Two men stood in the rain on a steep Norwegian hillside one autumn day in 1972. They were part of a small crowd watching British and Dutch Marines land on a small beach at the head of a fjord. The first man asked, "Why are you decommissioning one of your modern amphibious ships and turning the other into a school ship?" The second man replied, "We don't have money for everything and we think we need frigates more than we need amphibious ships." That man was Lord Carrington who, at the time, was Britain's Minister of Defence. I was the man with the question.

That brief conversation captures the essence of the main and really only issue about amphibious warfare. The question is, is it essential that a maritime power's armed forces be skillful in and well equipped for amphibious warfare?

The answer generally given now, in the past, and probably in the future, is no.

Since the landing of troops on a hostile shore is one of the four most likely events in most naval wars (the others being the acquisition of advanced bases, the strategic movement of troops, and the establishment of a blockade, all practiced in the Falklands episode),[1] one must ask why people turn away from amphibious warfare. That they do is clear. Although the British had earlier made many amphibious landings, establishing landing a quarter of a million troops on the hotly-defended shore of Gallipoli in 1915 was a daunting task for which there was little contemporary precedent. And while with difficulty the British and French managed to get a large army ashore against a well-entrenched and inspired Turkish Army on the heights over the narrow beaches, the Allies failed in their months-long campaign--forced by the Turkish mining of the Dardanelles--to reach Istanbul and remove Turkey from the war. It was an ineptly planned and poorly commanded campaign, and finally the troops were withdrawn by sea. The lessons of this major campaign remained relatively dormant until the late 1930s, when a small group of military and naval officers were ordered to study amphibious issues. But when war began in 1939 the group was disbanded; with national survival

51

at stake, few could see a need for amphibious operations in the war just beginning.[2]

Hardly anyone in the German armed forces could either and, when they arrived at the Channel coast in the spring of 1940, the Wehrmacht's legions could do little more than look at the narrow strip of sea which barred them forever from England's shore.[3]

In the United States things were better, for by 1939 the US Navy and Marines had been at work for six years developing a doctrine for amphibious warfare and a destroyer--the oldest one in commission--was being converted into a high-speed transport, chiefly by substituting four landing craft and their davits for twelve torpedo tubes.[4]

The Japanese, who had immediate problems to solve on the China coast and ambitions farther down the line, had done more than any of the other great naval powers; they had developed both an impressive landing ship and practical landing craft. American officers on duty with the Asiatic Fleet noted and photographed these craft, which they saw in some numbers, but their reports to Washington went no further than the nearest file drawer.

The major lessons of World War II are well enough known, with Guadalcanal, Normandy, and many other important events including development of the atomic bomb. It was the bomb, according to many, which would put an end to amphibious warfare. Inchon in Korea came shortly after that, but Inchon, in the nuclear age, was considered an aberration; such a large number of ships anchored close to one another, just as they had been off Normandy and Iwo Jima, would be a splendid target for a nuclear weapon.

However, although there have been many wars since 1945, in none has a nuclear weapon been exploded. Yet there is a problem. Partly there is the fear that in "the big war" nuclear weapons would be fired. There is no avoiding that fear. Moreover, many people, civilian and military alike, believe that no matter what the nature of the weapons fired, a war between NATO and the Warsaw Pact would be brief, perhaps lasting no more than a week or two. Amphibious forces could not be brought to bear in so short a time.

But there is also an emotional thing, and sometimes the ghost of a doctrinal thing. Soldiers are uncomfortable near the sea, and are especially uncomfortable when they are on it in a small ship or craft over which they have no control. Sailors are uncomfortable near the shore, and especially uncomfortable when they have to anchor the ship, or worse yet, run her onto the beach where the enemy controls the shore. Both soldiers and sailors get especially uncomfortable when they are in a large, slow target which is being fired at but from which they cannot shoot back.

Within the US Navy, most surface warfare officers would prefer to be in a fast, heavily armed cruiser, destroyer, or frigate which would likely seek out the foe, than in a slow, poorly armed amphibious ship which would try to avoid the enemy. Neither carrier pilots nor submariners are likely to have, or to want, amphibious experience, though some of the former must endure it (or even come to like it) en route to command of a carrier.

For a long time the Air Force, as is known, found it hard to see value in support operations on the surface of the land, and harder yet to see value in operations on the surface of the sea.

Much of that has changed. Still, the Air Force has yet to show any interest in those operations where sea and land meet. (This, however, is also a doctrinal issue with the Navy and Marines.)

Chiefly, then, it is the Marines who have an interest in advancing their skill and improving the equipment used in amphibious warfare. Indeed, without their interest, amphibious skill and power in this country would have withered long ago. But in Vietnam, where there were few amphibious operations, many junior members of the Corps let their professional thoughts drift far from the borderline between land and sea.

In Britain there have been many defense reviews (or rationalizations) since World War II; induced by reduction in its overseas responsibilities and a desperate need to save money. These have hit the services hard. No service has been more injured by them than the Royal Navy. Over the years that service had been required to assume that never again would the British fight without allies, that in the future the fleet would operate largely within range of fighters flying from fields on the British Isles or some other NATO territory (and therefore big carriers would not be necessary), and that opposed amphibious landings were a thing of the past.

Despite these conditions the Royal Marines survived as a force of seven or eight thousand men and amphibious ships never quite disappeared. But in 1981 the new defense minister, John Nott, faced with trying to ensure that Britain carried its share of NATO's defense burden despite an ever-shrinking economy, followed the example of many of his predecessors, and examined the Armed Forces anew. He saw four main roles for them: deterrence (which meant Polaris for now and Trident for later); protection of the British Isles (which meant RAF interceptors and air-defense missiles); the central front in Europe (the British Army of the Rhine); and protection of shipping (that is, all the Navy except the Polaris and Trident submarines). The Navy's role was seen as the least urgent of the four and, if Soviet submarines were the main threat at sea, it would largely be up to British submarines and frigates to deal with them.

While it is true that following Nott's review the Navy had some small carriers and they could fly Sea Harrier V/STOL fighters, there were fewer than three dozen such aircraft in the inventory. Their intended role was not to fight for air superiority over a fleet or a beachhead, but (because it had to be acknowledged that shore-based fighters had their limits) to fend off or shoot down long-range Soviet aircraft far at sea. In any event, both such carriers possessed by the British, the old Hermes and the new Invincible, were scheduled to be sold and the future of the two under construction was doubtful.

The Royal Marines survived again, though cut from four commandos (light infantry battalions) to three, but the two remaining amphibious assault ships and the handful of amphibious craft still afloat were scheduled to be sold or scrapped. Happily for Britain, however, in the autumn of 1981, Mr. Nott spent a day aboard the lone active amphibious assault ship, the Fearless, found out what such ships could do, and reprieved them for a few years. That was the situation in Britain in April 1982.

THE ARGENTINE INVASIONS

One thing to keep in mind is that in the seventy-five day Falkland Islands War there was not just one amphibious landing; there were four. There were the two Argentine landings which resulted in the seizure early in April of both South Georgia and the Falklands, and the two British landings, the first late in April, the other late in May, which led to British recovery of those islands. Let us first examine the Argentine operations.

On the 19th of March 1982, the Argentine Navy's 5,000-ton troop ship Bahia Buen Suceso entered the harbor of Leith, in South Georgia. South Georgia is an almost uninhabited British island 800 miles east southeast of the Falklands. The transport carried civilian workmen hired to scrap some long-abandoned whaling ships and equipment at South Georgia. The island's only human inhabitants that March were thirty-five British Antarctic Service scientists whose headquarters were at Grytviken, a few miles from Leith, and two English women making a television film. It is very cold, so mountainous that not enough flat space has ever been found for an airstrip, and almost continually buffeted by very high winds and seas.

The Argentines did not inform the British base commander of their presence as they ought to have done. What they did do was to raise their flag at Leith. The British discovered them the day after their arrival and ordered them out until they had gotten the base commander's permission to land. The Argentines departed, leaving some of their men behind.

The British ice patrol ship Endurance sailed from Port Stanley on the 20th, shortly after receiving word of the intrusion, arrived at Grytviken on the 23rd, and disembarked her thirteen-man Marine detachment (reinforced by nine from the Falklands garrison). These twenty-two men set up their defenses at the entrance to King Edward Cove, behind which lay Grytviken.

According to the London Sunday Times Insight Team, another Argentine naval transport, the 9,200-ton Bahia Paraiso, entered Leith harbor after dark on March 25th and disembarked Marines by boat.

Be that as it may, about noon on April 2nd, the Bahia Paraiso appeared outside Grytviken but, as the wind was blowing Force 10-- which creates "very high waves, long overhanging crests, and surface of sea white with foam" according to the internationally used Beaufort Scale--she left. The next morning she and an Argentine corvette were reported by British scouts to be near Leith. At 10:30 a.m. the Bahia Paraiso informed the British at Grytviken that the Falklands had been surrendered to Argentina and suggested that South Georgia should also be surrendered "to prevent any further loss of life." The transport, with a helicopter, some landing craft; and about fifty Argentine Marines, was accompanied by a small warship, the corvette Guerrico, which also carried a helicopter.

The Argentines, apparently unaware of the presence of the twenty-two Royal Marines, expected no resistance. They launched both helicopters, the larger of which landed fifteen Marines on the shore of King Edward Cove. The battle began when the British shot down the troop-filled helicopter on its second run, killing two Argentines. The Guerrico, armed with a 100-mm and a 40-mm gun, opened fire. The British responded with rifles and machine guns. They hit the Guerrico more than 1,000 times, while an 84-mm antitank rocket reportedly hit her once below the waterline and once on her 100-mm gun. One Argentine sailor was killed. The remaining Argentine Marines went ashore by helicopter and by boat, worked their way behind the British defenders, and caused the latter to surrender.[5] Meanwhile the major Argentine landing had taken place on East Falkland Island.

About the 28th of March the Second Marine Battalion (700 men) and nineteen of Argentina's twenty tracked landing vehicles (LVTs) were loaded aboard the country's only LST, the Cabo San Antonio. After they were aboard, the Cabo San Antonio sailed south from Puerto Belgrano. The rest of the task force--the guided missile destroyers Santisima Trinidad and Hercules, the corvettes Granville and Drummond, the transport Isla de los Estados, and the icebreaker Almirante Irizar--sailed independently. They formed up later. The submarine Sante Fe, with ten frogmen embarked, had already departed. Leaving port at the same time was the covering force, consisting of the small carrier Veinticinco de Mayo (with seventeen or eighteen aircraft aboard), an oiler, a tug, and four destroyers.

The invasion force, feigning a course for Ushuaia in Southern Argentina, soon ran into heavy weather and their speed of fourteen knots fell to eight knots, and then to six.

The plan was to sail southward to the west of the islands, and then northward on their eastern side. H-hour was 6:00 a.m. on April 1st. But on March 29th the heavy seas forced the invasion force to change course and sail north of the islands. They also caused D-day to slip to April 2nd. On the 31st the Argentines intercepted a message from the islands' governor forecasting their coming.

Once again the invasion commanders changed their plan. H-hour for the main landing was now set for after dawn, rather than in the dark. The Santa Fe was to have landed the frogmen to take the lighthouse at the entrance to Port Stanley. However, since the Argentines now believed the lighthouse was fortified, this landing was cancelled. Rather, at 2:00 a.m. the frogmen went ashore to secure the main landing beach.

When the frogmen hit the beach, the Santisima Trinidad had already been anchored for five hours at Port Harriet just below Port Stanley. Under moonlight she landed eighty commando-trained marines, using rubber boats. This force was to isolate the Royal Marine barracks from everything else at Port Stanley. The Argentines say their troops were ordered to use force only defensively and, if possible, were to accomplish their mission without destruction or death.

While some of the Argentine Marines marched inland to the British barracks at about 2:00 a.m. and found it empty, others went to Government House. At about 5:00 a.m. those at the barracks heard shooting at Government House.

At about 6:15 a.m. the Cabo San Antonio landed her troops via LVT at York Beach in Port Stanley's outer harbor. The LVTs were fired on, returned the fire, and moved inland. While they advanced on Port Stanley, a helicopter-borne detachment from one of the ships took the airfield. The LVTs met more light resistance on the way to the center of town, but shortly thereafter the defenders surrendered.

The first C-130 with army troops from Comodoro Rivadavia landed shortly after the runway was cleared.

The next day two S-2 antisubmarine aircraft flew into the airport from the carrier. For ten days these aircraft flew reconnaissance flights out of Port Stanley. Chiefly they were seeking sites for auxiliary airfields. Soon after the seizure, the Second Marine Battalion, which had specialized in amphibious warfare, was returned to the mainland. They were replaced by other marines and a large number of soldiers.[6]

COUNTERATTACK

The British government had been slow before the invasions to recognize that their worst fears were likely to be realized. Once the invasions occurred, however, they reacted rapidly.

On April 2nd Major General Jeremy Moore, Royal Marines, was told to sail the 3 Commando Brigade (Reinforced) as soon as possible. The brigade's main elements were the Marines' three remaining major combat formations (40 Commando, 42 Commando, and 45 Commando, totalling about 2,000 riflemen). Had this been a NATO war, Dutch marines would have been included. For this war, their place was taken by the Second and Third Battalions of the British Army's Parachute Regiment, to which were added (also from the Army) a field artillery battery (six 105-mm howitzers) and a Rapier SAM battery (four multiple launchers).

Some of the Marines were quite distant. One company, for example, was in Borneo. Others were on leave after just having come back from three months of exercises in Northern Norway.[7] Much of the Army and Navy were also scattered. Ships in home ports were about to send their men off on Easter leave.

Nevertheless, it was essential that a force capable of waging war be seen to have sailed. Both of the Royal Navy's small carriers had arrived recently at Portsmouth and both sailed on April 5th.[8] Rear Admiral John Woodward, commander of the carrier task group, was embarked in the Hermes, the larger carrier. Supplies were still being lifted to the ships by helicopter as they sailed from Portsmouth.

The Fearless, which three weeks earlier had been off the Lofoten Islands north of the Arctic Circle, was also at Portsmouth. She sailed on April 6th with her landing craft, boat crews, vehicles, and Headquarters 3 Commando Brigade embarked. The brigade headquarters, along with embarked staff of the Navy's Amphibious Warfare Command, began to plan for landings at places about which few people knew much and without the time to get the necessary information. The Fearless's sister, the Intrepid, had been decommissioned pending disposal. With hard work she was brought back into service and, filled with landing craft and the goods of war, sailed south on April 26th.[9] But she would have room for few of the Marines and parachute troops.

So on April 5th the cruise liner Canberra, then approaching Southampton, and the roll-on roll-off freighter Elk were requisitioned in accordance with existing contingency plans. They were the first of about sixty British commercial ships to be requisitioned or chartered. As soon as the ships reached port they were made ready for war. In the case of the Canberra, British industry began fabricating two helicopter decks for her while she was still at sea. When she arrived in port early on the 7th these, and the gear she would need to refuel while at sea, were added. On the 9th she sailed southward carrying 2,000 men (40 and 42 Commandos and 3 Battalion of the Parachute Regiment). The Elk, loaded with arms, ammunition, and light armored vehicles, sailed the same day. Altogether the Brigade numbered 4,820 men, some of whom sailed southward in other ships and some of whom flew to Ascension Island in RAF troop and cargo transports.[10]

Ascension, a barren speck seven miles by seven, eight degrees south of the equator, lacked a harbor, but it did have a 10,000-foot runway. It was here, in mid-April, that the ships gathered. The troops were able to get out of the ships and practice amphibious landings. They marched, practiced marksmanship, and regained that edge of fitness they had lost in the 3,700-mile voyage south. Supplies which had been flown down from Britain while the ships were en route were carried out to the ships in helicopters and boats.[11]

When the ships departed England they went in haste, with whoever and whatever was available. For political effect that was good, but for landing troops on a hostile shore that was bad. So while they lay in the tropical waters off Ascension, halfway between springlike London and wintry Port Stanley, their passengers and cargo were removed and then put back in a way that would be more useful at the landing beach. Most importantly, battalions were reconstituted.[12]

The senior commanders, joined by the overall task force commander, Admiral Sir John Fieldhouse, who ran the whole operation from Northwood near London, made plans on the basis of newly arrived information, including word that the Argentine garrison in the Falklands had been increased from 3,000 soldiers to 10,000.

The first British action, however, was not at the Falklands, but at South Georgia. This island is about 1,200 miles from South America and therefore much beyond the effective range of the Argentine Air Force. Its recapture would provide a quick victory, make a useful political statement about British intentions, and provide the British with an anchorage much closer to the Falklands than Ascension.

The recovery of South Georgia was entrusted to a troop of the Army's Special Air Service (SAS), some of the Marines' Special Boat Squadron (SBS), a company of Marines, the guided missile destroyer Antrim, the ice patrol ship Endurance, the oiler Tidespring, and two frigates. On April 21st the Antrim approached to within about ten miles of South Georgia and launched two helicopters bearing between them about a dozen SAS troopers who were to reconnoiter the Argentines' positions. Although the weather foiled the first effort to land the men, the Antrim's pilots succeeded on the second try. The wind and the cold worsened and the next day the SAS troops, now likely to perish on the glacier where they had landed, had to be rescued. Three helicopters were sent; two crashed. The third, bearing all the SAS troops and the crews of the crashed aircraft, made it back to the ship. The SBS force, which had landed in rubber boats from the Endurance, had a similar experience, and was returned to its ship by helicopter. Another effort by rubber boat, this time by the SAS, also came close to disaster.

At this point the old Argentine submarine Santa Fe entered Grytviken with supplies for the garrison. As she departed on the surface early on April 25th, helicopters from several of the ships attacked her with depth charges and missiles. The damaged submarine managed to turn around and reach King Edward Cove, where she beached herself in shallow water.

Though the Tidespring (with the main body of the landing party) was still 200 miles to the north, the landing force commander, Major J.M.G. Sheridan, formed a pick-up company of those marines and army elements in the Antrim, as well as a couple of naval gunfire support parties, about seventy-five men in all. That afternoon helicopters bore the men ashore near Grytviken while the Antrim and the frigate Plymouth fired on the Argentines. As Sheridan's party neared Grytviken, he asked the warships to steam closer and show themselves to the garrison. But before the Antrim could appear, the 137-man garrison, under Lieutenant Commander Alfredo Astiz, surrendered.[13] The British now had their important victory, a useful anchorage, and a battered Argentine submarine.

In the meantime, perhaps partly because of an amphibious landing near Port Stanley simulated by the carrier group on May 1st,[14] it was becoming evident that the invasion force, less than 5,000 strong, would not be sufficient against an entrenched foe of twice their number. It was evident that the British would need reinforcements; the obvious solution was to call on the British Army's emergency out-of-area force, 5 Brigade. But two of that force's three infantry battalions, those of the Parachute Regiment, were already en route to the war with the Marines. All that remained was a battalion of Gurkhas. So a battalion each from the Scots and Welsh Guards were added to 5 Brigade.[15] While this was occurring, more merchant ships were being taken up from trade, among them the passenger liner Queen Elizabeth 2. That ship, bearing the 3,000 men of 5 Brigade, sailed on May 12th, en route to South Georgia. There, using some deep-sea trawlers that had been requisitioned for service as minesweepers, the QE2 transferred the men of 5 Brigade to the Canberra and Norland, the latter a requisitioned North Sea passenger ferry. But as the QE2 sailed from England, that was still a couple of weeks in the future.

The British commanders at Ascension planned for a wide range of contingencies, but were unable to work on a single plan since the British government had not yet made its intentions clear. What was clear was that against as powerful a force as the Argentines had assembled at Port Stanley, an assault landing there would be impossible. It might be that the British political leaders would be content with raids, or with a landing on West

Falkland where there were few Argentines, so the British could announce to General Galtieri, "We're here, try and push us off." But that was not what Margaret Thatcher had in mind. It was the Argentines who were to be pushed off, so West Falkland Island was ignored.

Nonetheless, raids could be useful, and on the night of May 14th-15th a party of Special Air Service troops was lifted by helicopter from the carrier Hermes to Pebble Island (at the north end of West Falkland). There, with the assistance of gunfire from one of the destroyers, they blew up six Argentine light attack planes and five other aircraft before flying back to the carrier.[16] Some of these raiders were later lost when their helicopter collided with an albatross and crashed into the sea.

If the Argentines were to be defeated, then East Falkland had to be invaded. The nearer the landing site to Port Stanley, where the captive civilians, the harbor, and the airstrip were, the better. But that was where most of the 10,000 Argentines were, too, with their communications, radar, and artillery.

The major problem with landing anywhere in the Falklands was that the ships and troops would be just within range of land-based aircraft from Argentina. The Skyhawks and other aircraft possessed by the Argentine Navy and Air Force outnumbered the Harriers on the Hermes and Invincible by five to one.

The invasion site chosen was Port San Carlos, on the northwestern coast of East Falkland Island. The harbor opened up on Falkland Sound, the strip of water between East and West Falkland, and offered some protection against attack by submarines. Falkland Sound was unmined and Port San Carlos was only lightly guarded.[17] The terrain between Port San Carlos and Port Stanley was so boggy that most wheeled vehicles could not pass. Since the British forces about to be landed had few vehicles and planned on traveling overland by foot and by helicopter, this was no handicap. To the truck-heavy Argentines, it was.

Because of the high hills and short over-water distances, Port San Carlos offered protection to ships from Argentine missiles such as the Exocet, for antiship missiles need long, open stretches of water and can be distracted by such things as hills. To bombs, however, hills and short stretches of water mean little, and bombs are what the Argentine Skyhawks would deliver.

Not only would the Harriers be vastly outnumbered by their foes, they could not take advantage of being close to the ships of the amphibious force under their protection. If the carriers were not to be risked unduly they would have to be at such a distance from the amphibious force that the Harriers could stay on station only briefly. So both attacking and defending aircraft would be fighting at the far edges of their combat radii.

Just a day before the landing, there was another transfer at sea, this time only about 200 miles from the objective. One of the three battalions in the Canberra was moved to the Fearless and a second to the Intrepid, thus reducing greatly the danger of losing the major part of the landing force if the Canberra were sunk.[18] The probable reason for delaying this transfer until just before the landing is that while there was plenty of room in the Canberra, the other two ships were much smaller than the liner and already fully loaded. Eventually there were 1,500 in the Fearless alone. The newcomers had to find space for themselves where they could, but they would not be aboard for long. Happily for the British, there was a calm sea on the day the transfers took place. Such weather could not be predicted or counted upon and the fleet had expected the transfer to take two or three days.

Despite the anticipated Argentine superiority in the air, at last light on the cloudy evening of May 20th the British amphibious task group, screened by destroyers and frigates, began the 200-mile run to Port San Carlos. It was late autumn and, at 50° south latitude, the opposite end of the Atlantic from Newfoundland, last light came early. So the ships were hidden for many hours from Argentina's day fighter-bombers. Keeping radio silence, they steamed northward around East Falkland and into Falkland Sound, arriving off Port San Carlos at about 3:00 a.m. Although the clouds had now vanished and the skies were clear, the ships remained undiscovered as they began to land the invasion force by landing craft. There was a small fight ashore when the Special Boat Squadron encountered an Argentine outpost, but that soon ended,[19] with the Argentines dead or dispersed.

At dawn the amphibious ships were moved in to San Carlos Water, an arm of the Sound protected by hills on both sides, and the invasion continued, using both landing craft and helicopters. Destroyers and frigates stood poised to provide gunfire support and to defend the invaders and their transports from the expected Argentine air attacks. Those attacks began at about 10:00 a.m. Some of the ships had medium-range SAMs, some had short-range SAMs; hardly any had what all needed, which was both. For a day the ships and the aircraft battled it out. There was a day's pause and then two more days of attacks, this time met by British missiles fired from shore as well as from ships. There were heavy casualties on both sides, with two frigates going down, and six other combatants damaged. But according to the British, the defenders (surface ships, SAMs ashore, and Harriers) had shot down forty-three of the attackers. More importantly, all the British amphibious ships and transports remained unharmed. More such battles followed on the next day as the Argentines sank a destroyer (which shot down three attackers before being fatally wounded). At high cost to themselves the ships had shielded the land forces while the latter were establishing themselves ashore.[20]

The Canberra and Norland, after disembarking their troops (42 Commando and 2 Para Battalion), steamed off on May 21st for South Georgia, where they picked up the QE2's passengers, the troops of 5 Brigade. They arrived back at Port San Carlos on May 31st and the next day these troops were moved ashore in helicopters, landing craft, and even large rafts called Mexiflotes.

Thereafter the battle was conducted mainly on the ground, with support from surface ships' gunfire and carrier aviation. As some troops moved on foot through vile weather to Douglas and Teal Inlet they were met by amphibious ships and craft which carried their supplies and equipment. Other units made substantial tactical advances in landing ships, landing craft, and helicopters. An effort to speed the advance still further led to the Welsh Guards being moved to Bluff Cove, below Port Stanley, in two unarmed logistic landing ships, the Sir Tristram and Sir Galahad. On June 8th the foul weather which had both impeded and protected the British began to clear. The Sir Tristram had largely unloaded her passengers when the Argentine Air Force struck after a week's respite, but the Sir Galahad was still filled with troops. The low-level attackers hit both ships and caused over 100 casualties, fifty of them deaths. The Sir Galahad was a total loss.[21]

By now the campaign was nearing its end. Argentine forces were in Port Stanley while British troops were storming the heights on the town's landward side. At sea on the 12th the guided missile destroyer Glamorgan was shooting in support of the troops ashore when an Exocet missile fired from a hastily rigged trailer near Port Stanley hit her in the helicopter hangar. The ship survived and was ready to continue her job, but she was lucky.[22]

Two days later, on June 14th, Major General Mario Menendez, the governor of the Malvinas Islands, surrendered to Major General Moore and the fighting over the Falkland Islands was at an end.

SIGNIFICANCE

One should not make too much of a small war. Neither should one ignore what it has to tell us simply because it was small. Here are some thoughts perhaps worth considering.

The center of British effort was the amphibious landing with which the recapture of the Falklands began. The blockade by submarines, surface ships, and aircraft was a useful part of the British effort, but by itself it could not have won the war. The bombing of the airfield at Port Stanley, especially the long-range bombing, was difficult, expensive, and on the whole ineffective. The recapture of South Georgia, while effective, was important only because of the contribution it made to later operations.

The Falklands War added to already substantial evidence that, in general, if a power wishes to be sure it can achieve a military purpose across the sea, it must have forces skillful in and well equipped for amphibious warfare. It did not show us whether in the special case of a NATO conflict with the Warsaw Pact over Europe such forces are useless, essential, or anything in between.

For a long time the US Marines, the world's chief proponents of amphibious readiness and skill, have argued the case for more specialized amphibious shipping. This war showed that many non-specialized ships, both naval and commercial, can be put to use in amphibious warfare. The main requirement was that they have a deck upon which they could launch and recover a helicopter. Some landings were even made in rubber boats from ordinary ships, though they were all small landings and made in great secrecy. Unfortunately, the number of "ordinary" commercial ships under the British, US, and other NATO flags is far smaller than formerly. In any event, except for relatively light expeditions, such as that to the Falklands, more than a helicopter deck will be needed. Cranes will be needed to move heavy or bulky equipment, or containers, from the ship to boats alongside. Roll-on roll-off ships will need special ramps. Any surviving break-bulk freighters, all of which carry their own cargo booms, should be treasured. As it happens, in preparing to support the Rapid Deployment Force in the Indian Ocean, the US Navy and Marines have taken the steps necessary with several ships, and that may be enough.

Clearly, the war showed there must be some naval-manned specialized amphibious ships. There must be ships in which amphibious staffs can be established. They must provide working spaces, sensors, communications, and means of transportation to and from the ship. And they must be ready when needed. There must be other ships able to carry, launch, and maintain enough landing craft of sufficient size to carry troops and their heavy equipment and supplies to the beaches. And there must be ships able to do the same things with helicopters. With only two such ships, the British had to take appalling risks, such as redistributing the troops at sea just before the invasion and allowing such valuable ships as the Canberra and Norland to come under fire. They got by, but theirs was a landing of a fairly small force, unburdened with any heavy armor, upon a beach not defended from ashore. Even so, had the British not had the Fearless and Intrepid, with their command facilities, well decks, landing craft, helicopter decks, helicopters, stores, and maintenance shops, they probably could not have recaptured the Falklands. Interestingly, those ships, lightly armed as they were, were better armed than many US amphibious ships are and they were able to do something to defend themselves against enemy aircraft.

The war also showed how modern arms and equipment affect where and when you can, or must, make your landing. Because of helicopters, one can land at many places not practical for landing craft. Yet, without landing craft, one cannot land to stay. (Curiously the British, who had invented the air cushion vehicle, a type which easily passes from sea to land and which might have been very useful in crossing the bogs ashore, took none of these with them. The main reason may have been that there was no room for them in either the Intrepid or the Fearless.) Modern, easily moved weapons, such as the anti-tank rocket which holed the Argentine corvette Guerrico at South Georgia and the Exocet missile on a trailer at Port Stanley which damaged the British destroyer Glamorgan, show clearly that one's landing must be where the enemy forces are not. To keep the enemy absent for as long as possible, landings should be made at night. The successful landing at Port San Carlos met those criteria.

This tells us something else we knew long ago. It was Nelson who is credited with saying "a ship's a fool to fight a fort." And in World War II, whenever it was possible, invaders avoided landing on a fortified coast. Tarawa, Normandy, and Iwo Jima were simply occasions when it was not possible. Still, as at Normandy and Iwo, in the future there could be times when if one wished to lodge an army ashore, he could only do it in the face of fire. The modern solution to that condition is not clear.

The stories so far available are not clear on this point, either, but it looks as if the Argentine garrison at South Georgia surrendered as a result of the fire from the British destroyer Antrim. If that is so, it is the first time, to the writer's knowledge, since the American Civil War that naval gunfire deserved the chief credit for an amphibious success.

Though the Royal Navy's guns were few in number and small in caliber, they appeared to have been useful not only at South Georgia but also in support of troops ashore in East Falkland. The official British account said that "the infantry would not have been able to carry their objectives without the support they received from artillery and naval bombardment." Unfortunately, no evidence is given to support that statement.

If naval fire support for troops is needed, it will have to be provided by guns. Shipborne missiles, which are useful against airplanes, other ships, other missiles, and obvious targets ashore, are not suited for engaging a suddenly discovered battery of antiship missiles in the hills, for digging out a machine gun nest in a well-hidden bunker, or for stopping an attack by enemy infantry. The United States should not be surprised if the big guns of the New Jersey and Iowa prove to be even more useful than their modern long-range missiles. This country should also not be surprised if our amphibious ships are sunk because they lack modern weapons with which to defend themselves.

The unwillingness of the Royal Navy to risk its two carriers close to the landing site probably would be matched by the US Navy if the latter had to conduct an amphibious landing on a hostile coast. But the coming of a practical combat airplane which can take off from a very short runway with a useful load of fuel and ammunition and return vertically means that a partial solution is at hand to the problems of air defense of the amphibious task force and close air support for the landing force. The practical combat airplane is, of course, the Harrier. Had there been more Harriers, some could have been flown from amphibious ships' helicopter flight decks, or even from container ships such as the Atlantic Conveyor, until a short runway could have been made for them ashore. In fact, as soon as such a runway, or forward operating base, was made ready, the RAF's Harriers, a few of which had been flying from the Hermes, did go ashore. The development of such aircraft and techniques is to be encouraged in the US armed forces.

Further, the Falklands War tells us how useful it is to ally oneself with the weather and the environment. The most heavily engaged Argentine invaders of the Falklands, the eighty from the Santisima Trinidad, came at night and suffered no losses on the beaches from the small but determined band of defenders. The force making the South Georgia invasion carried it out by day and did suffer casualties. The British invasion at Port San Carlos took advantage of the long night and, while they lasted, the low clouds. As a result, many hours passed between the time the ships began their run in towards the amphibious objective area and the time the Argentine air forces, equipped only with day aircraft, were able to respond. Day aircraft, it should be added, equip most of the world's tactical combat squadrons. The vile weather and the boggy ground of the Falklands, impassable to most vehicles, meant that the Argentine Army did not even attempt to meet the British invaders when they were at their most vulnerable, that is, when the British were establishing their beachhead.

When the Argentine air forces finally attacked the British at Port San Carlos they engaged the defending surface combatants, sinking three and damaging many others. They hit none of the amphibious ships or transports laden with troops and the goods of war.

Thus, though the Argentine air forces can count their successes, they missed the targets that counted. The frigates went down, but the landing of the force which ejected Argentina from the islands she coveted went forward. Had the hits which devastated the frigates been made instead upon the Fearless, Intrepid, Canberra, and Norland, there is a good chance that the islands would still be flying the Argentine flag.

Whether it was the sailors in the frigates or the aviators in the Skyhawks who chiefly were responsible for this circumstance is not yet clear. But the disposition of the ships, with the amphibious ships and troopers inside and the frigates outside, certainly contributed. In any event, both contestants and all bystanders had best think about whether the glamorous targets are also the important ones.

Finally, though it is not one of the issues dealt with here, the war tells us how important it is for warriors to be both physically and mentally ready for war. The British were and the Argentines were not. That, more than their differences in arms and equipment, was why the British won and the Argentines lost.[23]

NOTES

1. This is one of the tentative findings I have arrived at as a result of a study I have been conducting on the activities of the US Navy and its allies in war since 1775.

2. A brief description of this period can be found in Chapter 1 of L.E.H. Maund, Assault from the Sea (London: Methuen, 1949).

3. The Germans had carried out a successful amphibious operation against the Russians in the Gulf of Riga in 1917. And in April 1940, only a few weeks before their army's arrival at the English Channel, they had conducted a highly successful amphibious assault upon the unready Danes and Norwegians, using conventional naval and commercial ships. But they had given no thought, or at least no effective thought, to amphibious operations as a distinct form of warfare requiring its own doctrine, ships, equipment, and skills. Thus they were unprepared for an assault across a contested sea upon the shore of an alert and implacable foe.

4. The best discussion of the period known to me is in the opening chapters of Jeter A. Isely and Philip A Crowl, The U.S. Marines and Amphibious War, Its Theory, and Its Practice in the Pacific (Princeton: Princeton University Press, 1951). The destroyer was the Manley (DD-74), completed in 1917.

5. This account is derived from (a) Robert Scheina's "The Malvinas Campaign," Naval Review 1983 (U.S. Naval Institute

Proceedings (May 1983): 98-117; (b) a conversation with Dr. Scheina in October 1982; (c) "The Invasion of South Georgia" in The Globe and Laurel, The Journal of the Royal Marines, (May/June 1982): 148-151; and (d) The Sunday Times (London) Insight Team: War in the Falklands, The Full Story (N.Y.: Harper & Row, 1982), pp. 66-75, 92-94. Dr. Scheina, who called on various officers of the Argentine Navy a short time after the war, is one of the few North American historians knowledgeable about the Latin American armed forces. His forthcoming history of Latin American navies is to be published by the U.S. Naval Institute.

6. Scheina, cited above. Accounts from British sources differ in details.

7. Good accounts of these early events are in Globe and Laurel (May/June 1982): 141-143, 158-159, 162-167; and in Globe and Laurel (July/August 1982): 220.

8. Nick Kerr, "The Falklands Campaign," in Naval War College Review (November/December 1982): 14-21. Kerr, a Commander in the Royal Navy, served in the Operations Centre, Ministry of Defence, during the war. Another good source is the series of articles in the monthly Navy International for the issues May through September 1982. Early events are covered under the general heading, "The Falkland Islands" in the May issue, with "Political Considerations" on pp. 1029-1034, and "Military Operations" on pp. 1035-1039. Tables on pp. 1040-1042 describe the opposing naval and air forces.

9. Globe and Laurel (May/June 1982): 168 (on the Intrepid) and 176-177 (on the Fearless).

10. On the Canberra and other merchant ships; see A.J. Ambrose, "Logistics - The Involvement of the Merchant Navy" in Navy International (May 1982): 1043-1045. See also Kerr and Globe and Laurel. An official list of merchant ships taken up from trade is printed in The Falklands Campaign: The Lessons (Her Majesty's Stationery Office, London: 1982), p. 40.

11. Globe and Laurel (May/June 1982): 156-157.

12. D.V. Nicholls, "Amphibious Victory," Globe and Laurel (July/August 1982): 220.

13. Globe and Laurel (July/August 1982); "Retaking of South Georgia," pp. 234-235; War in the Falklands, The Full Story, pp. 148-154.

14. The Falklands Campaign: The Lessons, p. 7.

15. "The Falklands Crisis, Operations, and Progress after April 13," Navy International (June 1982): 1097.

16. "The Falklands Crisis, Operations and Progress after May 7,"

Navy International (July 1982): 1160.

17. The Falklands Campaign: The Lessons, p. 7.

18. Nicholls, pp. 221-222.

19. Ibid., pp. 222-223.

20. The Falklands Campaign: The Lessons, p. 9.

21. Ibid., pp. 10-12.

22. Ibid., p. 12. War in the Falklands, The Full Story, p. 268. See also Scheina, pp. 114-116.

23. This paper's virtues, whatever they are, reflect the degree to which I took advantage of the generously given assistance of many people of whom Dr. Robert L. Scheina must be mentioned first. Others to whom I am indebted are US Navy Captains Hugh Lynch, Robert Prehn, and Edward Colbert, and Commander K.R. Mc Gruther; Commander Brian Needham Royal Navy; Lieutenant General Philip Shutler, US Marine Corps (Ret.), Colonels Edward Fitzgerald and Joseph Ruane, USMC; Lieutenant Colonel John Wetter, USMC; Major James Stefan, US Army (Armor); and Professor Mike Blouin, Naval War College.

6
Ground Warfare Lessons

Harry G. Summers, Jr.

> The original means of strategy is victory--that is,
> tactical success....Yet insofar as a tactical success
> is not the one that will lead directly to peace, it
> remains subsidiary...

Clausewitz, On War[1]

INTRODUCTION

One of the most striking features of the Falkland Islands War was that in this modern age of electronic warfare, missiles, high performance aircraft and nuclear submarines, the decisive battles that, as Clausewitz put it, "led directly to peace" were won with rifle and bayonet, were won by the age-old infantry tactic of "closing with the enemy and destroying him by fire and maneuver."

What makes this even more ironic is that those who carried the day--the infantry foot-soldiers of the Army and the Marines-- have always been the poor relations of the military family. They are rarely held up as symbols of military prowess. Rather, it has been those who fly planes, sail ships, maneuver tanks, manipulate exotic electronic equipment, and fight wars at a gentlemanly distance with cannons and missiles who supposedly represent war-fighting ability in our modern age.

We think of this as peculiar to our own time, but over a hundred years ago Richard J. Gatling, the inventor of the Gatling gun (an early machine gun), said that his invention was designed "to save men." He said, "The thought occurred to me that if I could get up a gun with which one man would do the work of a hundred, that would to a great extent supercede the necessity of large armies."[2] In his analysis of war-making in America from the Civil War to World War I, Berkeley Professor Thomas C. Leonard found a prevalent American belief that "technology would shorten wars; modern weapons would ensure less bloodshed."[3] This belief has flourished in our own time when whole military strategies were built on the premise that nuclear weapons would be a substitute for battlefield manpower. (It is instructive to note that,

67

according to the US Army Chief of Staff General Edward C. Meyer, the Soviet Union saw nuclear weapons not as a <u>substitute</u> for their large conventional forces but, by achieving <u>nuclear parity at all levels</u>--strategic, theater and tactical--as a means of <u>validating those forces.</u>)[4] As we will see in the Falkland <u>Islands War,</u> modern technology was useful in getting the infantry to the point of decision, and it was helpful in preparing their way and supporting their efforts; in the final analysis, however, it was the men who "slogged up to Port Stanley with rifle and pack" that ultimately carried the day.

THE BEACHHEAD AT SAN CARLOS WATER

But for a while it looked like they would never have that opportunity.   Operation SUTTON, the plan for the amphibious invasion, suffered from one grievous fault.   It was designed to get the land forces ashore, but was remarkably silent on what they were to do once the beachhead had been established.   This was a predictable (and hence avoidable) failing, for as the eminent military historian Russell F. Weigley has detailed, the same error was made at the Normandy invasion in 1944, where too great an emphasis on just getting the troops ashore almost cancelled their ability to execute the missions for which they were put there in the first place--i.e., the destruction of the enemy's army and his will to fight.[5] In the Falklands this shortcoming was especially frustrating to the senior British officer ashore, Brigadier Julian Thompson, the Commander of the Royal Marine 3rd Commando Brigade. His brigade staff had been given the responsibility of planning the amphibious invasion, but had specifically been directed by Rear Admiral John Woodward, the Amphibious Force Commander, to plan no further than the beachhead.   Marine Major General Jeremy Moore, the designated land force commander, would complete the campaign plan when he arrived with the Army's 5th Infantry Brigade.   But no sooner had the beachhead been established on May 21st than the strategic headquarters for the entire campaign, the Commander-in-Chief Fleet (located at Northwood, near London, and referred to by the British simply as "Northwood" much as we would call the Department of Defense "the Pentagon") began to pester Brigadier Thompson for signs of movement.[6]

Modern communications are at one and the same time a great blessing and a great curse.   Because orders can be instantaneously transmitted around the world, and the home-based strategic decisionmaker thousands of miles from the battle scene can speak directly to the tactical commander, the illusion is created that one is just as knowledgeable about battlefield conditions as the other.   Brigadier Thompson was in daily contact with Northwood and daily they pressured him to move against the enemy.   What they could not appreciate at such a great distance was the enormity of the problems he faced.   Two of the critical assumptions of Thompson's plan had gone awry--the assumption that the Navy would maintain decisive air superiority, and the assumption that sufficient helicopters would be available to airlift forces and supplies.   The failure of the first assumption caused the failure of the second.   When Argentine air attacks sank the <u>Atlantic</u>

Conveyor on May 25th, ten Wessex and four Chinook helicopters, upon which British movement outside the beachhead had hinged, were lost. Further, lack of air superiority limited the time supply ships could be off-loaded to only a few nighttime hours, for before daybreak they had to make for the safety of the open sea. Logistics problems on the beachhead were enormous, and there was difficulty in even getting food to the troops.[7]

But Brigadier Thompson's problems with air defense and logistics were overshadowed by a problem he had not counted on-- political pressure for "good news" from the front. Such conflicts between political and military priorities are not new. For many years, the American military took as an article of faith the proposition advanced by Brevet Major General Emory Upton in the late 19th century that military operations and politics were radically and fundamentally things apart. A 1936 Command and General Staff School manual warned of the danger of violating this precept. "In most of the great wars of history, there can be found military exploits calculated to feed the press rather than to beat the enemy," it complained. "Statesmen at times become unduly impatient in regard to the inevitable slowness with which the obstacles to success are overcome in the field. This feeling frequently arouses a desire for a change of plans."[8] This is precisely what happened to Brigadier Thompson. Less than a week after he secured the beachhead, he was ordered by Northwood to immediately engage the enemy. Not only did they order him into battle, they also selected the precise location: the Argentine base at Goose Green, some thirteen miles south of the beachhead. As one account put it, "London needed a tangible victory. If there ever was a politician's battle, then Goose Green was to be it."[9] It was apparent that the battle philosopher for the Falkland Islands Campaign was to be Clausewitz, not Upton. Since war is part of policy, policy will determine its character, Clausewitz wrote. "Political considerations do not determine the posting of guards or the employment of patrols," he said, "but they are the more influential in planning of war, of the campaign, and often even of the battle."[10]

Not only were political considerations to be paramount, Brigadier Thompson was ordered to do what most tactical rules and regulations specifically warn against. He was ordered to split his forces in the face of a numerically superior enemy. The 2nd Paras (2d Battalion, The Parachute Regiment) were to attack the Argentine force at Goose Green. The 45 Commando (45th Battalion, The Royal Marine Commando Regiment) and 3 Para were to shoulder 120-pound packs and move on foot some fifty miles overland to begin the investment of Port Stanley. The 40 and 42 Commando were kept in reserve at the beachhead. On May 27th, the movement to contact began.

THE BATTLE AT GOOSE GREEN

The 2nd Battalion, The Parachute Regiment, under the command of Lieutenant Colonel Herbert Jones, was organized into four ninety-man rifle companies and a support company. The entire battalion would make the attack on Goose Green, but the absence of transport caused them to cut their heavy weapons to two manpacked 81mm mortars. This organic firepower deficiency was compensated for by direct artillery support from a three-gun (105mm) section from the 8th Battery, 29th Regiment, Royal Artillery, and by naval gunfire support from the frigate _Arrow_. Harrier air-strikes would also be available.

Colonel Jones planned to move out of the beachhead on the night of May 27th, and make an approach march under the cover of darkness to an attack position at Camilla Creek House, some eleven miles to the south. After resting during the day, the battalion would again move out during the night of May 28th to begin the actual attack. One rifle company would reconnoiter the four miles to the line of departure ("start line" to the British) which Jones had established across the head of the approximately two-mile wide isthmus which linked the two main parts of East Falkland Island. He would then attack down the isthmus with two companies abreast to seize Darwin, some six miles farther south.

At first, things went according to plan. Although some enemy harrassing and interdiction fire fell to their flank, the attack position was secured by 3 a.m. on May 28th. But while they prepared for their forthcoming assault, they were startled to hear a BBC World Service News Bulletin announced that "2 Para was within five miles of Darwin." Colonel Jones was so enraged that he told the BBC correspondent accompanying the unit that he would sue the Secretary of State for Defence if any of his men died in the forthcoming battle.[11] As a result of this leak, tactical surprise had been lost and the enemy was forewarned and forearmed.

But although they had been fired on earlier in the day, 2 Para's lead elements met no resistance when they began their advance at 6 p.m. on May 28th. Led by sappers of the 59th Independent Commando Squadron, Royal Engineers, the line of departure at the head of the isthmus was soon secured. At 2:35 a.m. on May 29th, the left flank company crossed the line of departure. Meeting light resistance, they advanced some four miles to their intermediate objective overlooking the town of Darwin, halfway down the isthmus. For some unexplained reason, the attack was not coordinated, and the right flank unit was forty-five minutes late in crossing the line of departure. They began meeting heavy resistance immediately. Although the Paras attempted to clear the enemy as they advanced, some Argentine strongpoints were inadvertently bypassed, requiring the follow-on company to eliminate these pockets of resistance instead of leapfrogging through the lead company as had been planned.

As dawn broke, the tide of battle swung to the Argentines, for British troops in the open were pinned down by a well-armed enemy in prepared positions supported by machine guns, artillery (including direct fire from 35mm antiaircraft guns), and close air support by Argentine Pucaras and Skyhawks. To add to their problems, British close air support was absent due to the fog and, just when they needed it most, the frigate _Arrow_ was compelled in the face of threatened Argentine air attack to retire to the safety of the San Carlos anchorage. The momentum of attack had been lost. In order to get his battalion moving again, Colonel Jones, in an action that would win him British's highest award,

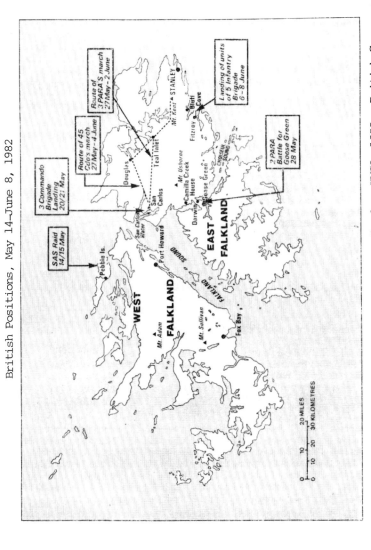

71

British Positions, May 14–June 8, 1982

SAS Raid
14/15 May

3 Commando
Brigade
Landing
20/21 May

Route of 45
Cdo's march
27 May–4 June

Route of
3 PARA's march
27 May–2 June

Landing of units
of 5 Infantry
Brigade
6–8 June

2 PARA
Battle for
Goose Green
28 May

Pebble Is.

WEST
FALKLAND

Mt. Adam

Mt. Sullivan

Fox Bay

Port Howard

San Carlos
Water

San Carlos

Douglas

Teal Inlet

Mt. Usborne

Camilla Creek
House

Darwin

Goose Green

Mt. Kent

STANLEY

Fitzroy

Bluff
Cove

CHOISEUL
SOUND

EAST
FALKLAND

FALKLAND
SOUND

0   10   20 MILES
0   10   20   30 KILOMETRES

Reprinted from the Falklands Campaign: The Lessons, London: HMSO, 1982. British Crown copyright; reproduced by permission of the Controller of Her Britannic Majesty's Stationery Office.

the Victoria Cross, led an attack on an Argentine machine gun position but fell mortally wounded before he could reach it. The command of the battalion passed to the second-in-command, Major Chris Keeble. Major Keeble ordered his reserve company up along the shoreline on the right to launch an attack on the Argentine flank.

This successful attack, combined with close air support from the Harriers, which had joined the action as soon as the weather cleared, recaptured British battlefield initiative. The Argentines began to withdraw and by nightfall Goose Green had been invested.

Reinforced by J Company of 42 Commando, Major Keeble planned to make his final attack on the morning of May 29th. Before he did so, however, he sent two Argentine prisoners into Goose Green under a white flag to invite the Argentines to surrender. To his surprise, the Argentines immediately accepted. Intelligence had told the British that there was less than an enemy battalion in the entire Goose Green-Darwin area and 2 Para expected about eighty Argentines to surrender. Instead, some one hundred and fifty men in Air Force uniforms marched out of the town, followed closely by a column of some nine hundred Argentine soldiers. In remarkable similarity to the American experience in Vietnam, it later developed that national-level British signal intelligence (SIGINT) had intercepted the entire Argentine order-of-battle and the Ministry of Defence in London had known the magnitude of enemy forces at Goose Green. The high security classification of this information, however, prevented it being passed to the commanders in the field.[12] Such gross bureaucratic dereliction could have caused a battlefield disaster, as similar dereliction did in Vietnam when the Special Forces camp outside Khe Sanh was overrun by enemy armor that SIGINT (but not the camp commander) knew was there. Fortunately, in the Falklands this disaster was averted by the shock and ferocity of 2 Para's attack.

The four hundred and fifty soldiers of 2 Para had done what no computer-driven warfighting model could ever have predicted-- beaten a well-entrenched, well-armed defender four times their strength. At a cost of seventeen men killed and thirty-five wounded, they killed some two hundred and fifty Argentine soldiers and took over twelve hundred prisoners of war.

Emory Upton would cynically have said that the politicians in London finally had the battlefield victory they so desperately needed. But there was more to it than that. Clausewitz had warned that war is a remarkable trinity of the people, their government, and their army. As the United States found to its sorrow in Vietnam, this interrelationship causes public opinion at home to be an even more crucial military center of gravity than destruction of an enemy in the field.[13] From a tactical point of view, Brigadier Thompson was correct in opposing the Goose Green operation as a diversion from the decisive objective at Port Stanley. But at the strategic level, what was overriding was the need for an immediate battlefield victory to compensate for the gloom caused by the sinking of the frigates Ardent and Antelope, the destroyer Coventry, and the Atlantic Conveyor container ship. In restoring public morale, the victory of 2 Para at Goose Green guaranteed the continuation of public support that made further prosecution of the war possible.

YOMPING TO PORT STANLEY

After Goose Green, all attention could be focused on the re-capture of Port Stanley, not only the capital of the Falkland Islands but also the location of the bulk of the Argentine military forces. Port Stanley was located at the tip of a fifteen-mile peninsula on the opposite side of East Falkland Island from the beachhead at San Carlos Water. Across the five-mile base of this peninsula between Teal Inlet to the north and Bluff Cove to the south lay a chain of mountains, Mount Estancia to the north, Mount Kent in the center, and Mount Challenger in the south. Midway down the peninsula, about half-way to Port Stanley, was another range of mountains, Mount Longdon in the north, Two Sisters in the center, and Mount Harriet to the south. Three miles ahead stood yet another range, Wireless Ridge to the north, Tumbledown Mountain in the center, and Mount William to the south. Overlooking Port Stanley itself was the eastern portion of Wireless Ridge across Stanley Harbor to the north, and Sapper Hill to the south. These mountain chains were selected as a series of successive intermediate objectives for the British assault on Port Stanley.

From the beachhead at San Carlos Water on the west side of East Falkland Island, it was some forty miles to the first inter-mediate objectives, Mounts Estancia, Kent, and Challenger. The problem was how to get there. As we have seen, helicopter lift capability had been severely limited by the sinking of the Atlantic Conveyor. Argentine air attack made amphibious movement extremely hazardous. Land transport was restricted to the limited number of BV202s (arctic warfare tracked transport vehicles) organic to the Commando unit and two troops (platoons) of the Blues and Royals with a combined total of eight Scimitar (30mm gun) and Scorpion (76mm gun) light reconnaissance tanks. While these vehicles were to prove to have great cross-country mobility and subsequently provided excellent support for the marching columns, there were not enough of them to transport forces. The only alternative left was to move the combat units by what the Royal Marine Commandos called "yomping"--a term originally coined to describe cross-country movement on skis, but now used to describe cross-country foot marches with full pack.[14] While the battle at Goose Green was still underway, 3 Para was marching on Mount Estancia, reaching there on May 31st without encountering enemy opposition; 45 Commando was close on their heels, reaching its initial objective at Teal Inlet to the north of Mount Estancia. The two left flank battalions were now in place.

While this was going on, D Squadron of the Special Air Service (SAS) had been patrolling Mount Kent. Noting that this mountain dominated the first intermediate objective line, Brigadier Thompson decided to use his limited helicopter assets to occupy it in force and air-landed a company of 42 Commando on Mount Kent on May 31st. On June 1st the rest of the battalion was lifted in to occupy Mount Challenger further to the south. "Yomping" overland,

45 Commando reached Mount Kent on June 4th. Now, with the excep-
tion of 2 Para at Goose Green, and 40 Commando at San Carlos
Water, 3 Commando Brigade was in position across the base of the
Port Stanley peninsula. The assault of Port Stanley had begun.

ARRIVAL OF THE ARMY 5TH INFANTRY BRIGADE

As 3 Commando Brigade closed on its first intermediate
objective, the Army's 5th Infantry Brigade began disembarking at
San Carlos Water. Commanded by Brigadier Tony Wilson, the Brigade
had officially been designated Britain's "out-of-area" force for
operations outside NATO. As with the early days of our own Rapid
Deployment Force, however, it had not been given the organic
logistics and fire support necessary for such operations, and
since its organization five months earlier, it had little training
in brigade team operations. To make matters worse, two of their
organic battalions, 2 and 3 Paras, had been detached to the 3rd
Commando Brigade at the beginning of the crisis and replaced by
two battalions withdrawn from "public duties" (i.e., guard and
ceremony). These battalions--the 1st Battalion Welsh Guards and
the 2nd Scots Guards--had been trained as mechanized infantry to
fight from armored personnel carriers. Only the Brigade's third
battalion, the 1st Battalion, 7th Duke of Edinburgh's Own Gurkha
Rifles (7th Gurkhas), were trained as regular infantry. These
deficiencies were not considered critical by the Ministry of
Defence, for 5 Brigade was initially considered merely to be a
reserve for 3 Commando Brigade.

With the Brigade came the designated land force commander,
Royal Marine Major General Jeremy Moore, and his eighty-man staff.
They had joined 5 Brigade on board the Queen Elizabeth 2 at
Ascension Island, and had been virtually incommunicado while the
events at Goose Green and the march on Port Stanley had been
unfolding. When General Moore finally came ashore at San Carlos
Water on May 30th and assumed operational command of the land
campaign from Brigadier Thompson, he was faced with an immediate
tactical problem. The issue at hand was whether to hold 3
Commando Brigade in reserve, or whether to attack with 3 Commando
and 5 Brigade abreast. Brigadier Wilson quite naturally favored
the latter course of action, which would allow his brigade to move
on a southern axis of attack staged out of Bluff Cove while
Brigadier Thompson's 3 Commando Brigade attacked on a northern
axis from their present positions on the Mount Estancia-Kent-
Challenger line. The sticking point was the limit of availability
of helicopter lift to move 5 Brigade into position, since these
limited assets were already fully engaged in resupplying 3
Commando Brigade and in moving up artillery and ammunition for the
final assault.

While this campaign planning was underway, the Gurkhas had
made the "yomp" to Goose Green to relieve 2 Para, which then
reverted to 5 Brigade control. In the meantime the 2 Para
commander, with a clever use of civilian telephone lines,
discovered that the town of Fitzroy on the shore of Bluff Cove had
been evacuated by the Argentines. Brigadier Wilson, on his own
authority, commandeered a Chinook and airlifted a 2 Para rifle

company, followed shortly thereafter by yet another rifle company, onto the high ground above Bluff Cove. In putting 2 Para in this exposed position, Brigadier Wilson forced the decision in favor of a coordinated two-brigade attack on Port Stanley. The problem now became one of concentrating 5 Brigade into an attack position at Bluff Cove. The Welsh Guards began an overland approach march to move into position, but it soon became apparent that these mechanized infantry troops were not up to the task, and they had to be withdrawn back into the San Carlos Water perimeter.

It was particularly significant that in this modern age of troop movement by aircraft, helicopters, and sophisticated armored personnel carriers, the ability of infantry to move overland on foot became a strategic issue. As a result of the failure of the guard battalions to perform this most basic of infantry tasks (a task so basic, so old-fashioned, and so time-consuming that in the U.S. Army it is too often ignored, especially by mechanized infantry units who equate ability to move with vehicle maintenance), General Moore was forced into a difficult decision. The scarcity of helicopter support precluded movement of the entire 5 Brigade by air. The threat of Argentine air attack and severe weather made amphibious movement extremely hazardous. But because 5 Brigade was unable to march into battle, the risky amphibious operation became the only alternative.

At first the decision was to move them on the two available assault ships, Intrepid and Fearless. In particularly bad weather, the Scots Guards embarked on Intrepid on June 5th, and after seven hours at sea with winds gusting up to seventy knots, finally struggled ashore at Bluff Cove. After an attempt to move the Welsh Guards on the Fearless on June 6th failed because of bad weather, Northwood decided that hazarding their scarce assault ships was too risky. They would, however, reluctantly risk the smaller and more plentiful civilian-manned landing ships. On June 7th, elements of the Welsh Guards were loaded on the landing ship Sir Galahad, which dropped anchor in the exposed and relatively unprotected harbor at Bluff Cove on the morning of June 8th. Five hours later, through an evident lack of amphibious training compounded by what can only be assumed as a lack of a sense of danger of Argentine air attack, many of the Welsh guards were still on board Sir Galahad. At 1:10 p.m. the ship was attacked by four Argentine aircraft, resulting in thirty-three Welsh Guardsmen and eighteen other seamen and soldiers killed and forty-six others injured, the worst British losses of the entire campaign.

Tragic as they were, these losses had little tactical effect. Although two Welsh Guards rifle companies had been rendered combat ineffective by the attack on Sir Galahad, they were soon replaced by two companies from 40 Commando. The 5th Brigade was now in position for the final assault on Port Stanley.

THE FINAL ASSAULT

Even with his two brigades in position, General Moore faced a formidable task. Intelligence, including patrols from SAS, the SBS, and a cadre from the Royal Marine Mountain and Arctic Warfare School, had revealed that there were over eight thousand Argentine soldiers in the Port Stanley garrison. These troops were well provided with heavy guns and ammunition, including recoilless rifles, heavy machine guns, some thirty 105mm and four 155mm howitzers. The hill lines covering Port Stanley were covered by minefields and defended by Argentine soldiers whose equipment included excellent night-vision devices and who had had over six weeks to fortify their position.

Two courses of action were presented--to hold in the north and attack on the south, or to attack all along the front. General Moore selected the latter, and ordered 3 Commando Brigade, with 2 Para attached, to seize the next line of intermediate objectives-- the Mount Longdon-Two Sisters-Mount Harriet line. Once this line was secured, 2 Para, (the 3 Commando reserve), would make a supporting attack to seize the western edge of Wireless Ridge while 5 Brigade with the Scots Guards, Welsh Guards, and Gurkhas would pass through 3 Brigade to continue the attack. Leapfrogging the brigades, it was believed, was the best way to maintain momentum and keep the Argentines from regrouping.

On the night of June 11th, 3 Commando Brigade began the advance with three battalions abreast. The 3rd Paras were to attack Mount Longdon, 45 Commando to attack Two Sisters, and 42 Commando was to assault Mount Harriet. Although they lost some time because of the difficulty in night movement, both of the Commando battalions quickly seized their objectives. The 42 Commandos actually moved around the Argentine positions on Mount Harriet and overran them from the rear. But 3 Para had a tougher time of it. Tactical surprise was lost when one of their soldiers stepped on a mine and the Paras soon found that they were not facing a company as they had expected, but a battalion of the Argentine 7th Regiment. Under intense machine gun and recoilless rifle fire, the going was particularly tough. It was not until dawn that the tide of battle began to turn. Pressing their advantage with fixed bayonets, Mount Longdon was finally cleared on the morning of June 12th. For an attack on an entrenched position, British casualties were surprisingly light. The 3rd Paras lost twenty-three men killed and forty-seven wounded, while the two Commando battalions lost a total of five killed and twenty-one wounded.

The plan called for 5 Brigade to immediately pass through the Commandos on Harriet and Two Sisters and seize the next set of objectives on Tumbledown and Mount William. Their attack was scheduled for the night of June 12th, but a delay in helicopter movement and the need for 5 Brigade to reconnoiter their objectives forced a twenty-four hour delay. It was not until the night of the 13th that the Scots Guards jumped off to seize Mount Tumbledown.

As they approached the main heights of Tumbledown Mountain, the Scots Guards ran into heavy opposition. Instead of the hasty field fortifications that the British had faced earlier in the war, they came up against a strongly entrenched company of the Argentine 5th Marines supported by mortars and ten machine guns. A British artillery officer described these positions as "excep- tionally well-prepared. Many fire trenches had deep bunkers attached to them and these often burrowed under the natural over-

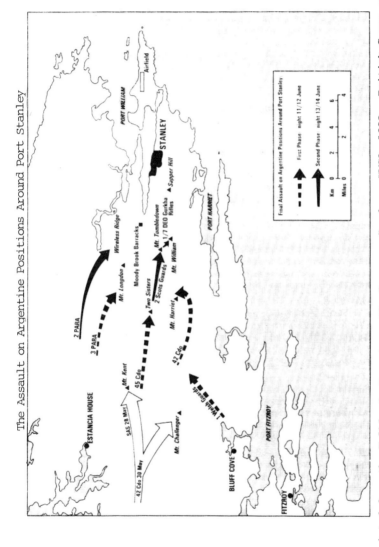

The Assault on Argentine Positions Around Port Stanley

Reprinted from the Falklands Campaign: The Lessons, London: HMSO, 1982. British Crown copyright; reproduced by permission of the Controller of Her Britannic Majesty's Stationery Office.

hang of rock." They were so well-established that "not one man in these well-prepared positions was wounded by British artillery. The detachments hid in their rock-roofed bunkers, often firing their guns on fixed lines remotely by string."[15]

The Guards may have had some difficulty in "yomping," but they proved that there was nothing wrong with their fighting ability. Using classic infantry fire and maneuver, the Scots Guards closed on the Argentine defenders and with rifles and grenades routed them out of their entrenchments. By noon on June 14th, the Scots Guards had completely eliminated all opposition on one of the most strongly defended Argentine positions of the war.

While the fight for Tumbledown Mountain was raging in the center of the line, 2 Para, to the north, jumped off to seize Wireless Ridge. Facing the Argentine 7th Regiment and elements of the Argentine 1st Parachute Regiment, the Paras leaned heavily on their fire support, which included two 105mm batteries, a Royal Navy frigate, and a troop of the Blues and Royals. Over six thousand rounds of artillery ammunition were fired in support of their attack. Although soldiers of the Argentine 1st Parachute Regiment launched an unexpected counterattack just as dawn was breaking, it was broken up by artillery fire and the Argentine defense collapsed into a rout, with soldiers fleeing in panic toward Port Stanley.

Meanwhile, to the south of the line, the Welsh Guards and Gurkhas advanced on Mount William and Sapper Hill, meeting little resistance. It is interesting to note that although the Gurkhas played a relatively small role in the final assault, their very presence had evidently sparked fear in the hearts of the Argentine defense. Although in actuality the Gurkhas fired few shots, took three prisoners, and suffered only a handful of casualties, the Argentines have enormously magnified the Gurkha role. In a recent article circulated widely in the Spanish-speaking world, Nobel Prize winner Gabriel Garcia Marquez quoted witnesses as saying how the Gurkhas beheaded Argentine soldiers "with their assassins' scimitars" and were so bloodthirsty that the English had to hand-cuff them to stop further killing after the Argentines had surrendered.[16]

With the collapse of Argentine forces on the Wireless Ridge-Tumbledown Mountain-Mount Williams-Sapper Hill line, the final assault was at an end. There was no need to attack Port Stanley, for white flags sprang up throughout the Argentine positions. At 9 p.m. on June 14th, the British land commander, Major General Jeremy Moore, accepted the surrender of Major General Mario Benjamin Menendez and the entire Argentine Malvinas force--almost ten thousand soldiers with their arms and equipment.

CONCLUSIONS

In 1973 when then US Army Chief of Staff General Creighton Abrams was briefed on the Yom Kippur War, he reacted with characteristic directness. "What this war proved," he said, "was that land forces have a vital role to play in national security." This simple statement had far-reaching implications. It led to the rejection of the notion that had plagued the US Army for almost two decades: that conventional war and conventional tactics were outmoded and irrelevant to the modern battlefield. It led to the publication by the Army's Training and Doctrine Command of a whole series of "How to Fight" manuals. Perhaps most importantly of all, it rescued military history and military art from a generation of neglect and spurred a "back-to-basics movement" within the Army that continues to this day. If General Abrams were alive today, he would see the British campaign in the Falkland Islands as a reaffirmation of his earlier conclusions.

There has been a tendency for many military analysts to discuss the Falkland Islands War as a historical curiosity, as an aberration with no lessons to offer. Such attitudes are remarkably similar to reactions to the Korean war a generation ago. Examining that war, Lieutenant Colonel John A. English of the Princess Patricia's Canadian Light Infantry observed that "Ironically, success in the first major war of the Atomic Age hinged not on high technology but on the performance of the old-fashioned soldier on foot, the ancient and unglamorous 'Cinderella' of the army."[17] The decisive role of infantry, far from being an aberration, is better seen as a constant, as the success of British Army and Royal Marine infantry in the most recent war in the Atomic Age has once again demonstrated.

The war in the Falklands has also validated the Army's current approach to military theory and military strategy. One of the consequences of the American failure in Vietnam was a rejection of the neo-Jominian approach to war exemplified by the mathematical models and cost-benefit analyses that masqueraded for strategy during the Vietnam war. Following the lead of the Air and Naval War Colleges, several years ago the Army War College began to stress the value of Clausewitzian theory to the conduct of war. Especially important was his rejection of quantified models and his stress on the importance of moral factors in the conduct of war.[18] The decisive battles in the Falkland Islands War were proof of the wisdom of that choice. By any mathematical model, the British should have had no chance of success against an Argentine land force, superior in both numbers and weaponry, fighting from prepared defensive positions. The critical difference was not material but moral. It is noteworthy in this respect that British analysts laid part of the blame for the Argentine defeat on their American training which "had taught them to rely too heavily on resources rather than human endeavor."[19]

Finally, the Falkland Islands War was a reaffirmation of basic Army doctrine which, while acknowledging that "control of seas and of air space is...vital to modern land warfare for without this extraterritorial security, land control is not likely to be achieved or sustained," emphasizes "the fundamental truth...that only ground forces possess the power to exercise direct, continuing, and comprehensive control over land, its resources, and its peoples and make permanent the otherwise transitory advantages achieved by air and naval forces."[20]

NOTES

1. Carl von Clausewitz, On War (edited and translated by Michael Howard and Peter Paret with introductory essays by Peter Paret, Michael Howard and Bernard Brodie and a commentary by Bernard Brodie) (Princeton: Princeton University Press, 1976), p. 143.

2. Thomas C. Leonard, Above the Battle: War-Making in America From Appomattox to Versailles, (New York: Oxford University Press, 1978), p. 79.

3. Ibid.

4. General Edward C. Meyer, Chief of Staff United States Army, "A Ready Land Force," Defense 83 (April 1983): 3.

5. Russell F. Weigley, Eisenhower's Lieutenants (Bloomington: Indiana University Press, 1981), pp. 108, 186-187.

6. Max Hastings and Simon Jenkins, Battle for the Falklands (London: Michael Joseph, 1983), pp. 179, 220; and also Rear Admiral E. F. Gueritz, "The Falklands: Joint Warfare Justified," RUSI Journal (September 1982): 48.

7. Hastings and Jenkins, pp. 230-231.

8. Principles of Strategy for an Independent Corps or Army in a Theater of Operations (Fort Leavenworth: Command and General Staff School Press, 1936), p. 20.

9. Hastings and Jenkins, p. 231.

10. Clausewitz, p. 606.

11. Hastings and Jenkins, pp. 239, 255-256. See discussion on how this leak occurred on pages 255-256.

12. Ibid., p. 252.

13. Clausewitz, pp. 89, 595-596.

14. For a detailed discussion on "yomping" (what the British Airborne evidently called "tabbing"), see the exchange of letters in the Correspondence Section of RUSI Journal (December 1982): 78, and (March 1983): 79-80.

15. Major J. G. A. Bailey, Royal Artillery, "Preplaced Hardened Field Defenses," British Army Review (August 1982).

16. Mark S. Smith, "Psychological Warfare Aided British," Washington Post (17 July 1982): A16; and Peter Osnos, "Myths of the Gurkhas," Washington Post (2 May 1983): A1.

17. Lieutenant Colonel John A. English, A Perspective on Infantry (New York: Praeger, 1981), p. 227.

18. Clausewitz, pp. 134-137.

19. Hastings and Jenkins, p. 324. See also Major General Moore's observations on Argentine discipline and morale in "The Falklands Experience," RUSI Journal (March 1983): 31.

20. Field Manual 100-1, The Army (Washington, DC: Department of the Army, 14 August 1981), p. 8.

7
Smart Weapons

William J. Ruhe

When the Argentine Exocet missile hit the British destroyer
Sheffield and destroyed it through the resulting fires, the world
media proclaimed that "smart" weapons had revolutionized naval
warfare. A single $200,000 weapon had sunk a $40 million ship!
It was expected that the further use of smart weapons in the
Falklands War would demonstrate the validity of this premise. In
fact, many more "smart" weapons were employed there--in naval
engagements as well as in air and ground actions. How revolutionary their effect was on today's wars is still a moot question,
but it is worth examining.

What a weapon's capabilities must be to make it "smart" is
arguable. Some of today's weapons have built-in electronic
features which allow the weapon by itself to carry out many functions. However, other weapons are "smart" in only one way. The
term "smart" weapon seems to be synonymous with the frequently
used term "precision-guided" weapon. That would mean that a
weapon's built-in capability can guide it to a precise hit on a
target. On the other hand, an operator might send signals to a
precision-guided weapon so that it intercepts a target. In any
case, today's weapons, which utilize electronic means for
achieving high hit probabilities, can be classified under the term
"smart" weapons.

At one end of the scale of smartness, a weapon can do only
one intelligent thing: it can be guided to a target by radio
signals which tell the weapon how to change its trajectory. Or
the weapon can just home on the illumination of a target by radar
or laser beams. In either case, the weapon is dependent upon an
operator far removed from the weapon while it is in flight. Since

such weapons are only marginally smart, they will be touched on briefly in this discussion. However, it will be pointed out how additional smartness in weapons provided significant payoffs in the Falklands War. At the other end of the scale are missiles which are totally divorced from the firing platform after launching--the so called fire-and-forget or "launch-and-leave" weapons. Such weapons may have programmed trajectories which: (1) avoid enemy defenses between the firing platform and the desired target; (2) prevent the location of the firing platform; (3) make the missile more difficult for enemy defense to cope with (flying at high altitudes to maximize speed to target, and descending to sea skimming in the terminal mode to reduce detectability, etc.); (4) pop up to an altitude to detect the target; (5) go into a programmed search pattern until a target is detected; (6) attack a target with a terminal maneuver while terminal-homing on a target; or (7) adjust the trajectory to maximize weapon damage to a target.

In addition, very smart missiles: (1) can distinguish between decoys and target; (2) through computerized logic may send back information on the target as observed by the missile; (3) can activate their homing devices at a programmed range; (4) may react to jamming of the missile's terminal-homing radar by shifting to a secondary means for homing or by shifting radar frequency; (5) may home on an emission with a specific identified frequency; (6) just possibly may identify their targets by scanning them with radar or infrared seeking devices; and (7) can shift terminal-homing mode (from active radar to passive infrared (IR), etc.).

Whether the use of smart weapons or the more commonly used "precision-guided" weapons in the Falklands War demonstrated a revolutionary effect on warfare needs further evaluation. In light of the impact of smart weapons on the fighting in the Arab-Israeli War of 1973, it would appear that much that happened in the Falklands War merely confirmed the results of a decade earlier. Moreover, for more than a decade, Soviet military writers have stressed that antiair missiles provided an umbrella of temporary air control over a battle area--despite the presence of manned aircraft for controlling the air in the traditional sense. This in itself implied a revolutionary effect on 20th century warfare and the Arab-Israeli War indicated that this premise has some validity.

At that time, the Israelis, with traditional control of the air over the battlefield, lost so many aircraft to ground-launched antiair missiles that they were forced to abandon the close support of troops by their attack aircraft--shifting to a longer range standoff delivery of their weapons. Additionally, in the ground fighting of that same war, the success of precision-guided antitank missiles against the armor of both sides led General Grechko, the then commander of the Armed Forces of the Soviet Union, to conclude that, rather than providing heavier armor for tanks and other mobile ground equipment, the answer lay in far greater mobility of units. This conclusion alone would indicate the revolutionizing effect of smart weapons.

Earlier, in 1967, the Egyptians had launched four Russian-made cruise missiles which sank the Israeli destroyer Eilat far at sea and a considerable distance from the small Arab patrol boats which conducted the attack. At that time many military observers speculated that smart missiles had revolutionized sea warfare.

In 1971, in the Indo-Pakistani War, the Indians employed more smart antiship Styx missiles with marked success. No counter-measures were used against these weapons, however. Later, in the 1973 Arab-Israeli War, when the Israelis used countermeasures, the previously successful Styx missiles failed to obtain a single hit --for some fifty-five such missiles employed by the Arab forces. On the other hand, the Israelis' smart antiship missile, the Gabriel, sank five of the Arab missile craft that were encountered, with the Arabs apparently not employing counter-measures. Interestingly, a decade later, when a similar smart antiship missile was employed--an Exocet cruise missile--and it destroyed a big warship, the event was treated as a new and important occurrence by the world news media.

Some perspective on the effect of such smart weapons on today's warfare can be gained from an initial examination of their impact in the naval operations of the Falklands War. First, the offensive use of smart antiship weapons is shown, followed by the use of smart defensive weapons. Later, the effect of smart weapons on the air and ground war will also be discussed.

The first use of a semi-smart antiship weapon occurred on April 25, 1982, when a British Lynx helicopter fired a six-kilo-meter-range AS-12 missile at the Argentine submarine Santa Fe as it entered port on the surface at South Georgia Island. The Santa Fe was hit and went aground to prevent it from sinking. This sub-sonic, rocket-propelled missile was tracked in flight by its tail-mounted flares. An operator in the helicopter, while optically sighting the target, used a control stick which generated radio commands to the missile to intercept the target. The transmitted radio signals were picked up by a wire trailed by the missile. The weapon then exploded on contact with the submarine. In sub-sequent actions, Lynx helicopters delivered more AS-12s against Argentine craft and damaged them.

Later, British helicopters launched similar but somewhat smarter Sea Skua missiles at Argentine patrol craft. The eight Sea Skuas which were fired at four small ships sank one and damaged two others. The Sea Skuas had about double the range of the AS-12s and used a different method for homing on their tar-gets. For the Sea Skua, an operator in the helicopter illuminated a target with a Sea Spray radar. The missile had a programmed altimeter that allowed it to skim across the sea at a minimum height above the waves consistent with the sea state; it then acquired its target passively by means of the reflected energy from the Sea Spray radar and flew in to strike the target. The Sea Skua also had a programmed terminal maneuver to make it more difficult to shoot down in its last moments of attack. Although this missile had a small thirty-kilogram warhead designed pri-marily for protection against missile-carrying boats (like those used in the Mideast War of 1973), it was useful in the Falklands War against other different types of small ships.

When the Argentine cruiser General Belgrano was torpedoed on May 2nd and sunk by two torpedoes--one in the bow and one in the stern--the news media reported that the British nuclear submarine Conqueror used the Tigerfish torpedo to accomplish the sinking. However, it became known that two old pre-World War II MK VIII straight-running British torpedoes, and not the smart Tigerfish torpedo, had done the damage. The MK VIIIs have no electronic features and even their fuses are activated mechanically. This illustrates that technological improvements in parts of a weapon system other than the weapon itself can significantly improve a weapon's hit probabilities. In this case, the high submerged mobility of the nuclear submarine ensured the simple, "dumb," straight-running torpedo a far better chance of hitting its target.

When on May 4th an Argentine Super Etendard aircraft launched the Exocet which hit and eventually destroyed the Sheffield, it seemed that smart weapons had reached a maturity which signalled a radical change in the character of sea warfare. The Exocet, a fire-and-forget weapon, was launched from a low-flying aircraft at a range of more than twenty miles from the Sheffield. The aircraft was apparently undetected by the Sheffield's radar, but had itself momentarily acquired the Sheffield with its own radar before descending to a lower altitude. The missile flew such a low trajectory that the Sheffield's crew were aware of the attack only a few seconds before it struck the starboard side of the destroyer, just aft of the bridge. Flying at high subsonic speed, about mach 0.93 or about 600 miles per hour, its terminal approach was only a few feet above the waves, too low and too quick for the Sheffield to react to this threat.

In fact, it was this very low sea-skimming capability that made the Exocet so attractive to many third power navies. The Exocet's trajectory is so low that any ship is unlikely to acquire it by radar until it is very close aboard. However, sophisticated target ships may be able to receive a few more seconds of warning by intercepting either the Exocet's own acquisition radar, or the radar of the Super Etendard or other launch platform, prior to the missile being detected visually or by the ship's air defense radar. But at 600 mph the missile is traveling at ten miles per minute, so a launch at a range of twenty miles provides the defenders with a maximum warning time of only 120 seconds. In this case, it appears that the Sheffield's electronic emission intercept system was not programmed for a missile produced by a nation of the West.

The Exocet, its altitude controlled by a radio altimeter, cruises at about fifteen meters with its programmed course maintained by inertial guidance. At a distance of twelve kilometers from the target, the missile's nose-acquisition radar activates and begins a wide lateral-sweeping terminal search for the target. Once acquiring the target, the missile homes automatically and descends to a pre-programmed wave-hugging altitude, which can be as low as two meters. By proportional navigation, which is part of the missile's computerized logic, it intercepts the moving target rather than flying toward it in a tail chase.

The 165-kilogram high-explosive warhead in the Exocet is fused to detonate inside the hull of a ship; hence the small hole punched in the side of the Sheffield, as indicated by early photographs, did not seem unusual. However, the heavy black smoke and great heat produced by a weapon whose rocket fuel should have been expended by the time it went into the Sheffield indicated that the explosive material in the warhead had not detonated but rather had burned up. The Sheffield's skipper, Commander Salt, reported that the intense heat and fires overwhelmed all damage control efforts. Eventually, it was fire which destroyed the Sheffield. Had the weapon detonated on impact, it is unlikely that the blast damage would have been sufficient to sink the ship.

Moreover, the Exocet, with its relatively light warhead, was designed primarily for smaller targets. Exocet's air-launched version, the AM39, is an all-weather weapon, weighs 654 kilograms, is 4.69 meters long, is thirty-five centimeters in diameter, and uses a dual-thrust rocket propulsion system with the booster burning for 2.1 seconds and the sustaining hard rocket fuel burning for 105 seconds. Thus the Exocet fired at the Sheffield from twenty-three miles should have burned out before reaching its target.

From then on, the British expected to see Exocets fired against their two aircraft carriers, the Hermes and Invincible, and took extraordinary measures to ensure that this smart weapon would not hit their ships. When the British believed that an air attack was imminent and that Exocets might be used, a continuous chaff barrage was laid at some distance from the major ships to decoy the missiles away from their intended targets. Chaff is, in effect, chopped up silver foil which reflects radar. Large clouds of bits of foil make the missile's radar see a larger target than the ship it should home in on; hopefully, the missile will lock on the chaff and fall harmlessly into the sea.

This is what happened on May 25th, when two Argentine Super Etendards attacked the British fleet. The Argentines launched two Exocet missiles from long range at what they believed was a British carrier. When the planes had popped up to 500 feet for a radar look at the area where their reconnaissance aircraft had reported the presence of British ships, the Argentine pilots detected a large radar blip surrounded by many smaller blips. The Exocets were then decoyed by the chaff clouds thrown up a mile or more away from the carrier's position. The artificial radar targets evidently fooled the Exocets, which passed on through the chaff clouds and locked on the container ship Atlantic Conveyor. The missiles then hit the container ship, which was about five kilometers away from the carrier. Like the Sheffield, the Atlantic Conveyor was destroyed by fire.

Neither the pilots nor the smart missiles could on radar tell the difference between an aircraft carrier and a big merchant ship, or between a chaff cloud and an actual ship. The Argentine flyers, moreover, were certain that they had struck the carrier at least once, and rejoiced when they returned to base.

On the last day of the war, an Exocet fired from an unidentified shore battery hit the British destroyer Glamorgan lying off shore. Its use was so unexpected that the Glamorgan is not known to have had time to launch chaff. Although thirteen men were killed, the Glamorgan was quickly back in action.

Significantly, no attempt was made to use the Exocet against British warships in the restricted waters off San Carlos, because the nearby land was likely to divert the missile away from its intended target.

There was one other smart weapon in use that has had virtually no publicity and tends to be overlooked, though it is an important part of naval warfare: the mine. Although the Argentines had smart bottom mines which could discriminate between light ships like minesweeping trawlers and heavier warships, they were used only in the approaches to Port Stanley and had no effect on the war's outcome. They were swept when the war was over. However, had these mines been laid in the inlet of San Carlos, they might have seriously delayed the British landings.

It is noteworthy that Argentine attack aircraft scored many hits with simple, unguided bombs--and getting bomb hits on maneuvering ships is a difficult problem. However, Argentine general purpose "conventional" bombs destroyed three major warships plus the landing ship Sir Galahad, and seriously damaged three more big warships. Much of this success can be credited to far better, modern air-delivery avionics. Like the old British MK VIII torpedoes, iron bombs have a greatly improved lethality without being "smart." However, it should be recognized that the Argentine flyers, in trying to avoid the British defensive missile systems, flew in to their targets at a very low altitude and frequently delivered their iron bombs at too low an altitude over their targets. The result was that the bomb fuses may not have had time to arm before the bombs hit. A half-dozen more ships would have been destroyed or damaged had all of these bombs exploded.

Harriers used laser-guided bombs in close support of British troops. The ten-foot accuracy and elimination of spurious targets was a great improvement on "dumb" bombs.

One other smart weapon, which was deployed, should be noted. Argentina's large air search radar, a TPS43 located on the highest hill overlooking Port Stanley, had to be destroyed since it was detecting the movements of British aircraft attacking Port Stanley's airfield. When British Vulcan bombers flying from Ascension Island failed to knock out this ground radar installation with conventional bombs, a Shrike antiradiation missile was mounted for the next attack. Shrike is a small air-to-surface, solid rocket-fueled, mach 2.0, ten mile-range missile which homes on a radar emission; its sixty-six-kilogram high-explosive fragmentation warhead then destroys the target radar. It can be countered by turning the radar off when Shrike is detected in its attack. Whether the British hit this radar is unclear, but a

Shrike did hit a fire control radar belonging to an antiaircraft artillery battery.

The attractiveness of these smart weapons which home on an enemy's electronic emissions is enhanced by providing the weapon with a trajectory logic so that when the enemy's emitter is turned off, the missile can still attack the spot from where the emanations came. This has been introduced into the latest antiradiation missiles.

The smart missiles used for British anti-air defense had an equally interesting employment in the Falklands War. The Argentines recognized that the long-range Sea Darts on the British Type-42 destroyers were effective against high-altitude aircraft. The Argentines also had the Sea Dart and had tested it extensively before the war. Sea Dart has a fifty-mile range and can kill aircraft with its proximity-fused warhead at high altitudes (up to 25,000 meters). When a ship's radar detects an enemy aircraft, a Sea Dart can be launched to semi-actively home on the reflected radar signal. K-band radar, of very high frequency and very short wave length, is used to illuminate enemy aircraft. This minimizes the effects of weather and reflections from the sea's surface. Flying at over mach-3 and capable of engaging crossing targets as well as closing ones, British Sea Darts scored eight kills against Argentine aircraft.

The Sea Darts on the Type-22 destroyers were obsolescent (1968 design), and less efficient than today's improved Sea Darts. However, they forced Argentine pilots to approach their targets at very low altitudes so that the British radars could not detect the attackers at long range. Realizing that the Sea Dart could not be employed at ranges under twenty-three miles, Argentine pilots flew back up to 500 feet when inside this boundary in order to better acquire their targets on radar.

A few British warships carried the Sea Slug, a long-range, high-altitude surface-to-air missile. This older supersonic weapon was not credited with any kills of Argentine aircraft, if it even saw use.

The British used the Sea Wolf and the older Sea Cat for close-in defense. The Sea Wolf, first operational in 1980, was aboard two British destroyers, Broadsword and Brilliant. This weapon was so successful that neither destroyer was seriously damaged while scoring six kills, one of which was reported to be an air-to-surface missile; the other five were Argentine aircraft.

The Sea Wolf is a short-range (5.6-kilometer) naval weapon. The solid-fuel rocket motor propels it to speeds over mach 2. It is an all-weather system, weighs eighty kilograms, and is 1.98 meters long. Installed in a six-barrel launcher on a destroyer, it is fired when the ship's tracking radar is locked on an aircraft. The fire control radar is a dual-band, pulse doppler radar which overcomes multi-path radar reflections, making the missile effective against low-flying targets. A radar tracks both the missile and the closing aircraft and through a command transmission to the missile corrects the Sea Wolf's flight path to intercept the target. Impact and proximity fuses in the Sea Wolf ensure a detonation on or near the target. In manual operation, a television sight is used and the operator generates commands to the missile through a control-stick. When this mode was used in the Falklands, the missile's exhaust blanked out the target to which it was heading. Thus it was fired with an offset and brought to the target only when close to the attacking aircraft.

Other British warships carried the Sea Cat short-range defense missile, which is similar to the Sea Wolf but smaller, subsonic, and less sophisticated. In its recent modification, it was provided with a limited low-altitude defense capability. The Sea Cats, which accounted for eight Argentine aircraft, are guided to the target by radio commands to the missile. These commands are sent by an operator who tracks the target and the missile either through binoculars, a TV optical system, or radar. The missile is detonated on contact or by proximity fuse. Although the Argentine Navy also had Sea Cat, it never used this missile in combat.

One other short-range (four-mile), surface-to-air missile figured in the naval engagements. At the San Carlos beachhead, Rapier land batteries were mounted on high ground overlooking the landing area. Although this frequently required a missile interception at the maximum range of six kilometers (resulting in some missiles not striking targets crossing in front of the battery), such missile attacks nevertheless disturbed the Argentine pilots as they delivered their bombs. Moreover, because of the extremely low levels at which the Argentine pilots approached the British ships, many of the kills made by Rapiers were ones where the missile was fired down at the attacking planes. Fortunately, the Rapier used a contact fuse in its warhead rather than a proximity fuse; this provided some measure of protection against hits by friendly forces. Additionally, when the Rapier's radar tracking system was saturated with land and sea returns when pointed down at the low-flying aircraft, it was possible to fire the Rapiers by using the secondary optical tracking system.

One problem which the Rapiers experienced was an interference between their system for identifying friend from foe (IFF) and their tracking radar. This was solved by shutting down the radar and using the optical tracking system.

The British-made Rapier weighs 43.6 kilograms, is 2.25 meters in length, 12.7 centimeters in diameter, and has a 2.7-kilogram high-explosive warhead. It is propelled by a two-stage solid-propellant rocket motor at better than mach 2 speed. This is the operational sequence: an enemy aircraft is picked up by a surveillance radar; it is then interrogated by IFF. If the target is unfriendly, the operator begins tracking the target by radar. A computer signals when the target is within range. The operator then fires, and the fire control radar, tracking the Rapier as well as the enemy aircraft, applies corrections to the Rapier's trajectory by means of a microwave-command transmission. The missile may also be directed to its target optically, with the operator keeping the target in his line of sight while a television unit tracks the missile's tail flares. The tracking unit then sends course correction signals to the missile.

British land surface-to-air missiles, the Rapier and Blowpipe, were well tested prior to this conflict. Both are light, portable, optically-guided air defense weapons which are simple to operate manually. They had great success, destroying twenty-three aircraft. The Rapiers destroyed fourteen of these aircraft with only forty-five missiles fired, whereas for each kill by a Blowpipe, about ten missiles were fired. On the other hand, Argentina's French-made Roland missiles--similar light-weight, optically-guided, short-range air defense missiles--failed to down any British aircraft, although at least seven Rolands exploded close to their targets (which included Vulcan bombers and Sea Harriers). The Vulcans used radar jamming against the Roland's radar, while the Sea Harriers, alerted by their tail-mounted warning system, dispensed chaff to divert the attacking missiles.

The truly low-cost missile used in the Falklands War was the Blowpipe, a shoulder-launched guided missile. Although this wea-pon barely qualifies as a smart weapon, later weapons of this type will be truly smart and will have a significant impact on both land and sea war. These weapons have been acquired by many armies of the world and the British have also adapted it to some of their submarines and suface ships. The original missile from which Blowpipe stems was the US Redeye, first seen in 1967. In the Arab-Israeli War of 1973, several thousand Russian SA-7 Grails were fired, causing the Israeli Air Force to radically curtail their close-air support of troops due to their unexpectedly high losses.

During the war about 100 Blowpipe missiles were fired at enemy aircraft, downing nine. A British Harrier was also downed by an Argentine Blowpipe. Given the number of Blowpipes fired, this is a reasonably good success rate. However, the Blowpipe had several shortcomings which caused this low performance. More modern weapons of this type have been modified to rectify these deficiencies.

The Blowpipe is a small (12.7-kilogram) missile in a fiberglass canister. An aiming unit is clipped to the cannister. The missile is 1.39 meters long, 19.6 centimeters in diameter when in its container, and 26.7 centimeters in diameter with its wings extended. The Blowpipe, with a range of 6.5 kilometers, is shoulder-fired by a single man at a low-flying aircraft. The air-craft may be identified by an IFF attachment on the firing can-nister. An explosive charge expels the missile from its container. The exploding debris is ejected from the rear end of the cannister and serves as a hazard to those near the blast. When the missile has left the tube and its sustainer motor has ignited, the operator, sighting on the missile's tail flares through a monocular sight, guides the missile with a thumb-operated flight controller. The missile follows the directions generated by means of radio signals broadcast to it from a small transmitter in the flight controller unit. The missile, with a proximity fuse, is designed to explode close to its target and its two-kilogram warhead does serious damage to the aircraft.

Since the Blowpipe missile homes on only an aircraft's exhaust, the thumb control of the missile proved to be a clumsy means of fire control. Heat flares dropped from aircraft, including helicopters, easily decoyed it. The very small warhead used in a proximity explosion mode frequently proved less than lethal to its aircraft target. Because of its mach 1.5 speed, it only proved adequate for firing at aircraft in the subsonic speed range. The target's movement across the operator's line of sight made manual guidance of the missile virtually impossible. Some of these shortcomings are being rectified by use of a television vidicom unit, which provides semi-automatic guidance for the weapon.

When Blowpipe is used on a submarine, it is configured in a battery of six missiles centered around a television vidicom system, which is mounted inside the bridge on the submarine's sail. For surface ships, a battery of two to ten launchers has been developed, also using the television vidicom system for guiding the missiles.

The most modern version of this family of weapons, the Stinger, is an all-aspect (can be fired at any aspect of its aircraft target) fire-and-forget, heat-seeking infra-red weapon, with a built-in logic for distinguishing between decoy heat flares and an aircraft heat source. The Stinger is fired to lead the target like duck shooting, and the supersonic weapon homes on the aircraft. Apparently, only a few Stingers were used in the war, but their kill ratio was probably far better than the Blowpipe's.

Both the British nuclear submarines and the Argentine German-built 209s had smart torpedoes, but they were not used successfully. The sinking of the Argentine cruiser General Belgrano is discussed elsewhere. Reportedly the British did not fire Tigerfish torpedoes, but used Mark VIII torpedoes instead. Tigerfish has a dual-wire system for giving the weapon command when it is en route to its target, and can passively home on a target's propeller noises or actively home (with its nose-mounted sonar) on the target's hull. It appears that the complexity of smart underseas weapons makes them more difficult to fire than the less sophisticated torpedoes of the past.

In the air war, the effect of smartness in weapons was most dramatically demonstrated. The British Harriers used the AIM-9L Sidewinder while the Argentines evidently used the French Matra R.530 missile. Both weapons were of about the same range (eleven miles) and speed (more than mach 2.5) and both have been sold to many countries. Both weapons are considered to be all-weather and all-aspect. In the case of the 530s, they semi-actively home on radar energy reflected by the target. The Sidewinders, however, home on the infra-red hot spots of an aircraft (the engine exhaust or aerodynamic hot spots). The warhead on the R530 is about one-third the size of the AIM-9L, although the AIM-9L is smaller. But the slightly better Sidewinder, a fire-and-forget weapon, killed twenty-four Argentine aircraft with only twenty-seven missiles fired by Harriers. On the other hand, there were no known Harrier losses to R530 firings. When the Argentines did launch their 530s from Mirage IIIs, it was reported that the Argentine pilots broke away from the engagements after launching their weapons, breaking their radar lock on the Harriers before the missiles had a chance to home on the reflected beam of radar energy from its target.

MILITARY LESSONS LEARNED

The use of high technology weaponry caused a marked advantage for the offensive over the defensive. While more than a billion dollars worth of equipment was expended by both sides, the casualty rates show the British losing only 255 men and the Argentines about three times as many.

The war demonstrated that:

1.   The antiship missiles used tended to hit well above the waterline of a ship and destroy it more by the resulting fires than by blast damage.

2.   Missiles were efficient in all-weather conditions and were usable around the clock. The heavy seas and low visibility conditions of the Falklands area seemed to have little effect on missile performance.

3.   Because of their relatively high cost, smart missiles were in short supply and were husbanded for use against selected high-value targets. However, in the press of conflict, they were expended against lesser targets.

4.   Antiship missiles were best used when they had a high element of tactical surprise. The Exocet hits were on targets which were virtually unaware of an impending missile attack. When antiship missiles were expected, the use of decoys proved to be effective in preventing them from hitting their targets.

5.   An antiship missile fired from a shore battery with its land background enjoyed a high element of surprise since the land clutter prevented detection of the firing units, and only when the missile was well clear of land was it detected.

6.   Amphibious landings which used the protection of a land background made it extremely difficult for a smart antiship missile to acquire its target. Therefore, such landings were done best in coves or up estuaries rather than on an ocean-fronted beach with a clear view out to sea.

7.   The sea-skimmers, whether missiles or aircraft, proved most difficult to combat. The lower the trajectory, the more difficult it was for fire control systems to weed out sea return and the confusing multipath radar returns which made tracking of the missile particularly difficult.

8.   Fire-and-forget missiles showed a marked tactical advantage over missiles which required the illumination of a target to home on. The attacking aircraft had to maintain a radar lock on the target until weapon impact. This not only greatly hazarded the aircraft but restricted the range of the weapon.

9.   The employment of low-cost Sea Skua missiles in inshore waters against low-value but militarily important targets indi-

cated the need for such a smart standoff weapon. Moreover, the range of the Sea Skuas allowed the delivery of the weapon outside the range of point defense systems, particularly those of low-cost simple operation, such as Blowpipes or Rapiers.

10. The need to program electronic emission interception and analyzing equipment (ESM) for emissions of smart missiles of western manufacture was evident as British equipment appeared to have been programmed for Soviet weapons rather than for the Exocet's terminal-homing radar emissions.

11. In the sea battles, the smart antiship weapons such as Exocet, Sea Skua, and AS-12 did not demonstrate a definitive superiority over plain iron bombs.

12. Naval air defense was layered to combat smart missiles like the Exocet. Long-range surface-to-air missiles forced air-craft weapon delivery below the targeted ship's air search radar horizon. And short-range point defense systems provided addi-tional protection against penetrators.

13. The level of control of the air achieved over both the sea and ground battlefields was achieved mainly by suface-to-air missiles. Neither the British nor Argentine-manned aircraft achieved control of the air in the traditional sense. Those British warships that were adequately armed with antiair missiles established a significant level of air control in the form of an umbrella over the individual ships.

14. The combination of long-range surface-to-air missiles and short-range point defense weapons forced the Argentine pilots into more hazardous types of attacks.

15. The failure to detect Argentine aircraft before they released long-range missiles indicated a need for an early warning aircraft. Much of the British ship damage, at least that part attributed to smart weapons, would have been prevented with better warning of Argentine aircraft attacks.

FUTURE IMPLICATIONS

The above lessons have the following logical implication for warfare in the future:

1. Antiship missiles like the Exocet, which are launchable from small craft as well as aircraft and shore batteries, give smaller navies a weapon power virtually unrelated to the size of the launching ship.

2. The simple shoulder-launched antiair missile tends to force attacking aircraft into a standoff weapon delivery mode, which limits the use of bombs, rockets, and guns and reduces their delivery accuracy.

3. If simple, shoulder-held antiair missiles are used on merchant, auxiliary and warships, then aircraft will be forced to use far more expensive, sophisticated weapons for attack. These weapons will necessarily be in short supply, and thus attrition of such simply-armed ships by aircraft attack is likely to be lower.

4. It is advantageous for a smart missile to be able to distinguish decoys such as chaff and flares from actual targets and to be resistant to countermeasures such as jamming, shut down of electronic emissions, and break-lock systems.

5. With the proliferation of a country's missiles to many other nations, it is desireable to program ESM equipment for one's own missiles as well as those of the enemy.

6. Due to the effectiveness of modern weapons, it has become highly desirable to intercept aircraft outside of their weapon delivery range.

7. Because of the premium placed on a long-range AEW capability to prevent the delivery of smart long-range weapons, there is a high likelihood that for the destruction of AEW aircraft smart antiradiation missiles will be developed and be employed by submarines or aircraft.

8. Surprise (technological or tactical) is increasingly necessary in firing a smart weapon because electronic countermeasures can neutralize its effectiveness.

Finally, the war seemed to show with respect to the revolutionizing effect of smart weapons--whether sophisticated Exocets or simpler laser-guided bombs--that they are likely to dominate a conflict only if there is a marked disparity between the technologies of the adversaries.

8
Intelligence and Warning Lessons

Gerald W. Hopple

Was the Falkland Islands War preventable? Was it foreseeable? Almost inevitably, these two questions arise when a war erupts. The focus here is political and strategic rather than tactical warning. What kinds of political preconceptions and strategic assumptions impinged on and shaped the decisions and actions of the two protagonists? The potential lessons are manifold, but we must guard against premature or misapplied lessons. The basic theme of this essay is that the conflict was essentially not foreseeable. Whether it was preventable is another and more difficult question. In the short term, it was probably not avoidable, but long term British defense policy and posture decisions as well as strategic assumptions on both sides led to what may have been an unnecessary war. In addition, the lessons of the war must be viewed in the context of the changing nature of the international system and in light of the prospects for crisis and conflict between allies and in the Third World in the 1980s. These central issues will be explored in some detail, and more general implications for intelligence and warning will also be considered.

THE CENTRAL ISSUES

Major wars often begin with sudden attacks.[1] In the aftermath of such an armed conflict, there is a common analytical syndrome: a postmortem is conducted and the conclusion is advanced that there has been an "intelligence failure." Any national intelligence bureaucracy includes one or more components tasked with tracking current affairs and trying to anticipate the threatening behavior of actual or potential adversaries. Therefore, if the other side attacks, the warning analyst has failed to warn.

This plausible generalization is intrinsically facile and quite frequently wrong. A powerful and pervasive fallacy--the hindsight bias ("I knew it would happen all along")--encourages us to assume that what we know after the fact could have been foreseen.[2] Nothing could be further from the truth. The hindsight bias--what Baruch Fischhoff calls the "silly certainty of hindsight"--is an insidious manifestation of a common failure in human thinking and perceiving. It is only one of many cognitive psychological obstacles to effective and error-free inference and analysis.[3]

There have been many case studies of warning or intelligence failure.[4] All of the cases, it should be emphasized, are potentially susceptible to the hindsight bias. They also tend to share other characteristics. For example, in retrospect we can see that many military attacks featured a variety of warning signals--embedded in a maze of both noise and deception. Furthermore, most occurred in the context of heightened tension that had been building for some time. Often, there had been several previous alerts which turned out to be false alarms. The Pearl Harbor case illustrates this recurring pattern vividly; after June 1940, there had been three distinct periods of very high tension and alerts in US-Japanese relations (including November 1941, the month prior to the attack).

Based on single and comparative case studies and some quantitative data, there has been some movement toward a "theory" of surprise and warning. Several explicitly comparative analyses have attempted to develop a portrait or theory-sketch of prewar warning and response. One focuses on deception and the other, Richard Betts' study, is more ambitious.[5]

The Falklands case seems to fit the reconstructed general pattern. Like Pearl Harbor, the German attack on the Soviet Union in 1941, the outbreak of the Korean War in June of 1950 and the Chinese intervention in November, and many other comparable attacks during World War II and since, the Argentine invasion was preceded by warning signals. The attack was the culmination of several weeks of tension. If we take the extended historical record as our frame of reference, the Anglo-Argentine conflict dates back in an active sense to 1965 (when the United Nations urged Britain and Argentina to negotiate) and ultimately to 1833 (when the British occupied the Falklands after a brief period of Argentine rule). There had been a number of previous invasion threats (particularly in 1977) and Argentina almost routinely indulged in sabre-rattling prior to yearly rounds of negotiation with the British.

In a more fundamental sense, the genesis of the war can be attributed to an intellectual syndrome in which one or both sides rely on certain reassuring but misleading political and/or strategic assumptions. The preconceptions typically refer to "facts" about one's own capabilities and the other's capabilities, intentions, and risk calculations.

Perhaps the most dramatic recent illustration of the disastrous impact of such strategic assumptions was the Israeli belief in 1973 that Egypt would not attack until it had attained air superiority.[6] This central premise, the master belief in the Israeli strategic calculus, was accompanied by a secondary belief: Syria would not attack unless Egypt did. These two assumptions formed the Israeli "conception." Together, the two core assumptions operated as a strategic conceptual straitjacket, suppressing, shaping, and biasing the interpretation of an incoming stream of contrary tactical indications.

To what extent did analogous political/strategic assumptions dominate the Argentine and British decision processes in the eight weeks preceding the invasion on April 2, 1982? This is the central analytical issue in the "postmortem" below. However, other considerations must also be introduced. These include additional potential causal forces, the lessons of the war from the perspective of the United States, and some crucial caveats and tentative lessons for the warning analyst who must constantly navigate through the misty and mystifying world. Despite the mist and the mystery, the warning analyst is expected to predict the unpredictable, "to extract certainty from uncertainty and to facilitate coherent decision in an incoherent environment."[7]

POSITIONS OF THE PROPONENTS

Most strategic warning analysts agree that we can never eliminate surprise, banish deception, or develop a foolproof or infallible system of indicators. Even if consensus crystallizes around a forecast that X will attack, whether someone will launch war is only the most general analytical question. We must also confront the multiple and vexing issues of when, where, and how.[8]

Roberta Wohlstetter's masterful retrospective analysis of the Pearl Harbor case starts out with the fundamental and quite illuminating point that a Japanese attack was fully expected.[9] Although the other side expected such a Japanese attack in late 1941, when, how, and even where it would occur were open questions. Siberia, Southeast Asia, and the Philippines were among the many potential Japanese targets.

Perhaps more than anyone else, Richard Betts has written about strategic warning cogently, systematically, and theoretically.[10] While work on intelligence and warning tends to be regrettably ad hoc and narrowly case-specific, Betts has pursued an explicitly comparative research approach. He has tried to extract relevant lessons and theoretical generalizations from past cases while remaining sensitive to the subtleties and ultimately unresolvable tradeoffs involved in strategic warning analysis. He has surveyed and assessed the nature and costs and benefits of alternative intellectual and organizational solutions, recognizing that few of them offer permanent panaceas, almost all of them reduce one vulnerability at the cost of increasing another, and some intelligence failure is inevitable. Furthermore, what we think of as an intelligence failure is often political failure. In searching for "culprits," Betts advises us to subpoena the decisionmaker as well as--and probably with more justification than--the intelligence analyst.[11]

In his book Surprise Attack, Betts puts forth three propositions which define the parameters of his theoretical argument. First, the key cause of surprise is political failure, not intelligence failure. Secondly, sudden attacks occur in situations of prolonged tension; there have been no significant cases of "bolts from the blue" in the twentieth century. Thirdly, the victim's strategic assumptions trigger the critical miscalculations which produce surprise.

These three propositions constitute a useful point of departure for analyzing the Falklands War from the vantage point of warning and intelligence. The first is the most crucial from the perspective of the discussion here. Betts demonstrates conclusively that military attacks which start wars are often "surprises," but the defender has nevertheless received significant warnings during both the political and strategic phases of warning.[12] Sometimes there are literally hundreds of incidents and other indicators as well as several major alert "false alarms."[13]

Is a surprise attack an intelligence failure or a political failure? To an extent, many failures of warning undoubtedly mix the two dimensions in an indissoluble blend. For most of the cases which he examines, Betts exaggerates the extent to which genuine warnings emanated from the intelligence bureaucracy. Typically, intelligence analysts reflect the political premises and biases of decision makers--either because they have no choice (dissent from official preconceptions would be ridiculed or punished), or they share central beliefs with the policy community.[14]

Rather than positing a sharp and unrealistic dichotomy between intelligence failure and political failure, we ought to think more in terms of "analysis failure." Analysis is different from the collection of information; it is the job of both the intelligence professional and the political decision maker to do analysis. One of the intelligence analyst's most important tasks is to create a context for the decision maker's judgment and offer a solid foundation for delineating options and selecting an alternative course of action.

The unfortunate connotations of the failure part of the analysis concept should be clearly recognized. Failure implies that there is a culprit who should be punished. Warning intelligence is extraordinarily difficult even under the best of circumstances. Its hit rate will inevitably be low (especially the perceived hit rate, since the many successes are easily forgotten when the occasional but salient failure occurs).

We should distinguish between political failure which is a direct outgrowth of a nation's defense posture (and other policy flaws) and pure analysis or technical warning failure. From the British viewpoint, fundamental policy errors seemed to contribute disproportionately to the outbreak of the war.[15] The Czech case in 1968, in contrast, seems to have been more of an analysis failure (from the Western perspective). Technical warning failure, when the relevant information is simply not collected or processed quickly enough, is relatively rare with respect to major military attacks, although processing and distribution snafus are far from irrelevant. Essentially, policy failure probably arises most blatantly when the deterrence-provocation dilemma is incorrectly diagnosed. Using Robert Jervis's deterrence (Munich) and spiral (World War I) models,[16] we can classify World War II as a "policy failure" and World War I as an "analysis failure."

Obviously, the typology of policy failure, analysis failure, and technical warning failure is simplistic and misleading. Very few real world cases would fall unambiguously into one of the three categories. Even with hindsight, people will disagree vehemently about particular cases. But the ideal types of pure policy failure and pure analysis failure at least alert us to the fact that "policy without intelligence" can be the real cause of what is labelled an "intelligence failure."[17] The distinction between analysis failure and technical warning failure, which is also simplistic, is nevertheless of undeniable value for the purpose of assessing intelligence performance. Warning is not just sensors and hardware; it is also analysis. More generally, intelligence is not simply "facts" in the form of data; it is also analysis and interpretation. Intelligence "failures" typically lead to injunctions about the need to collect more data. This is a myth; the problem is not generally the need for more data (analysts are often inundated with data), but the indispensable necessity for more and better analysis. Analysis is the human process which intervenes between data (the input) and the intelligence assessment/appraisal/warning (the output). Discussions about the "I" in C^3I (command, control, communications, and intelligence) often black box the "system" (the human analyst or decision maker) which intervenes between the input and the output. This happens equally pervasively and perversely in C^3 more generally.[18]

The popular definition of intelligence as evaluated information underlines this point. Although the work of Betts provides the basic context for the discussion in this section, it should be emphasized that he is in no way associated with the view that intelligence is simply data. In fact, he emphasizes that intelligence is not just a process of finding and presenting the facts; the facts never speak for themselves.[19] When the facts are indisputable or relatively clear, as is sometimes the situation in basic intelligence, then the product is a report or survey rather than an assessment or estimate.

Analysis failure occurs in part because of the well known dichotomy between intelligence and policy. While this is a necessary and useful rule for a number of reasons, it may warrant at least a little revision. Betts uses the example of including strategic net assessments in such intelligence community documents as National Intelligence Estimates.[20] While analysts should not be encouraged--or compelled--to become immersed in internal policy debates, the strict injunction against getting into this area inhibits analysis and reduces the value of intelligence outputs. For example, the explicit consideration of one's own alternative policy options as a basis for different analytical estimates and appraisals is at least worth considering.

We need to emphasize what analysis can contribute to minimizing warning failure. Consumers want answers; producers, however, can often contribute the most by posing questions.[21] In addition to asking the most relevant and difficult questions, warning intelligence should highlight the critical gaps in the knowledge of decision makers, illuminate the key uncertainties, clarify the ambiguities to the extent possible, and provoke debate whenever necessary.

The second proposition, that there have been no real "bolts from the blue" in the case of modern wars, is fundamentally valid and frequently ignored. As the next section will show, the Falklands case fits this pattern. The problem for the intelligence analyst, however, is twofold. One is the hindsight bias: can we ever distinguish between the X case when war does occur and the few or many earlier Xs when tension rose, indicators were fully consistent with a reading of "significant danger of hostilities," but peace prevailed?

The second is the challenge of attempting to analyze and forecast events of very low probability but very high consequences. On any given day there are many potential crises that could escalate into wars. There have been thirty long-term bilateral conflict situations in Latin America alone since 1945, many of which are still active.[22] Coupled with the hindsight bias, the methodological difficulties of trying to explain and forecast rare but catastrophic events makes the job of the warning analyst more than challenging.

The third proposition identified above is that surprise attack is linked intimately with the victim's strategic assumptions.[23] In one sense, this proposition is simultaneously unobjectionable and patently obvious. The attacker exploits the opponent's strategic premises; aside from instances in which the capability differential is extreme, if such assumptions did not exist, there would be nothing to exploit and no basis for launching a successful surprise attack.

But in a more basic sense, strategic assumptions often emerge as genuine causal forces in a nontrivial way. When strategic assumptions account for surprise attack, they do so as necessary (if not sufficient) determinants. The Israelis _assumed_ that Egypt would not attack unless it had achieved air superiority, which it did not have in 1973 and was not expected to have until 1975. Stalin _assumed_ in 1941 that Hitler would present an ultimatum before attacking. The West _assumed_ that a North Korean attack in 1950 would inevitably be an adjunct to a more general war.

Strategic assumptions are almost invariably plausible--at least before the fact. They are also often reinforced by the other side's active deception. Strategic assumptions may refer to capabilities or intentions (or both); they may concern basic defense postures and often reflect sensible but ultimately wrong recipes for preventing war. For example, Stalin tried to deter Hitler by avoiding provocation. In other cases, warning stimuli are simply rejected because they do not conform to the prevailing belief system.

People naturally become wedded to their basic beliefs and vigorously resist their elimination. This unwillingness to look at evidence in the light of alternative beliefs leads to warning disasters. The situation becomes even more problematic when, as is often the case, previous false alarms dull sensitivity and leave the strategic assumptions intact.

THE FALKLANDS WAR: THE WARNING CONTEXT

The Falklands conflict began on April 2, 1982.[24] Although the immediate precrisis period spanned only the preceding month, Argentina had consistently demonstrated the seriousness of its purpose and shown its willingness to consider a resort to force since 1945. The dispute itself, of course, dates back to the late

1700s.

In 1965 the United Nations General Assembly invited Britain and Argentina to negotiate for a peaceful solution to the dispute. There have been many rounds of negotiation since 1965, with the period since 1976 being characterized by a more determined effort, especially on the part of the British, to achieve a negotiated settlement.

The Falklands dispute has had many periods of relative quiet since the serious reassertion of Argentine sovereignty in the 1880s. Occasional crises, such as in 1927-1928, 1933, 1966, and 1976, have interrupted the sometimes long periods of quiesence.

There was a particularly serious invasion threat in late 1977.[25] Relations between Argentina and Britain were very strained, a British ship had been fired upon, and fuel supplies to the islands (which had been declared a province by Argentina several years earlier) had been cut off. Intelligence reports highlighted both Belize and the Falklands as potential flashpoints. The British secretly sent a submarine as a precaution. The ensuing negotiations progressed well enough that the threat of invasion subsided. This "false alarm" is particularly important in the light of the events and interpretations of March 1982 because the Foreign Office had "cried wolf" once and had thereby weakened its case the next time around.

Since 1976, frequent Anglo-Argentine talks have occurred in New York, Lima, and Geneva. Exploratory negotiations in New York in April 1980 provided the background for a British policy initiative in November 1980 and facilitated further talks during February 1981. The initiative constituted a significant breakthrough since the British publicly proclaimed their willingness to consider a solution which would involve Argentine sovereignty.

The February talks, scheduled for resumption in December 1981, were postponed by the fall of General Viola as head of the junta and his replacement by General Galtieri. The negotiations were held in February 1982 in New York. On February 26th, the two sides agreed to a compromise for a "negotiating commission" which would meet on a regular basis and the talks ended with a communique which referred to the "positive and cordial atmosphere." The war itself started a little over a month afterwards, with a successful Argentine invasion on April 2nd. Ten weeks later, Argentina surrendered to the British and conflict ended.

Strategic Warning: The Combatants

What went wrong? What happened between February 26th and April 2nd? Initially, the Argentine junta virtually repudiated its negotiator. War fever intensified in the press. The British representative to the New York talks, Richard Luce, conveyed his concern about the reaction in Buenos Aires to Lord Carrington. However, neither Luce nor Carrington felt that the situation warranted a formal request to send a tripwire or deterrent force. Previously, a decision had been made in June 1981 to scrap the ice-patrol ship HMS Endurance, the only regular British naval presence in the South Atlantic.[26]

Two factors probably accounted for the failure to request a deterrent force.[27] One was budgetary, a climate of "total obsession with money," with the defense ministry "under perpetual siege."[28] The second was the absence of intelligence data which would have supported such an action. Apparently, neither the relevant Foreign Office analysts nor the Joint Intelligence Committee, an institutionally separate group within the Cabinet, produced assessments which would have justified a deterrent force decision.

Intelligence sources have since asserted that their raw material was significantly more alarmist than the assessment of it which went to ministers. The assessments minimized the probability of an invasion, drawing on:

...the old-hat nature of the threats, General Galtieri's preoccupation with domestic issues, improved relations between his regime and Europe and America, the "cordiality" of the New York talks and their one-year deadline. This was used to explain even the statement issued in Buenos Aires on March 3rd that the regime was about to "seek other means" of regaining the Falklands. This statement itself suggests the junta had not yet made any decision to invade--or it would surely not have issued it.[29]

The Economist concludes that a recommendation for a precautionary expedition would have required considerably more than circumstantial evidence. This was not available until March 29th, the Monday before the invasion. By then, warning indicators had proliferated. The British reacted by sending a submarine plus support ships from the Mediterranean to the South Atlantic. By the time Prime Minister Thatcher called the first crisis meeting on Wednesday evening, deterrence with anything more than verbiage was out of the question.

In contrast to many wars, the active prewar crisis period was unusually abbreviated. Furthermore, the British and Americans have since concluded that the junta had not made a definite decision to invade even on Monday. It was still an active option, but no final decision had been reached.[30]

As in so many other crises of this nature, the victim was at least somewhat distracted by other issues. The Foreign Secretary's trip to Israel and another battle about the European Community's budget both diverted attention from the Falklands.[31] In October 1973, the Israelis had been similarly distracted by a PLO attack on Russian Jewish emigrants in Vienna. In November and December 1941, the war in Europe and other potential Japanese targets preoccupied US decision makers. In addition to false alarms, then, which reduce sensitivity through the false alarm effect, distraction militates against warning by diffusing attention.

Strategic assumptions played a role on both sides.[32] The British assumed that Argentina would not try to take by force what it could not achieve by negotiations. This assumption was reinforced by the length of the dispute, the earlier false alarms, and the consistently strident Argentine rhetoric. Verbally, Argentina had repeatedly threatened invasion; this rhetoric came to be perceived as meaningless diplomatic posturing (and also as a flourish for domestic consumption, a theme to which we shall return in the following section). If anything, General Galtieri, with his Anglophile foreign minister, less draconian human rights policy, total neglect of the Falklands issue in his initial speeches, and decision to combat inflation by cutting defense spending (with the navy sustaining the largest reduction) seemed to offer a respite rather than a threat.

Another analytical flaw in the British perception of the situation was the serious underestimation of the strength of Argentina's feelings about the Falklands.[33] The British pursued a policy in which they attempted to substitute bluff for a credible defense posture vis-a-vis Argentina. The reason for this (and the consistent roadblock to a mutually acceptable solution of the conflict all along) was the feelings of the islanders, who were avowedly British in attitude and psychological identification and equally adamant in their opposition to any form of Argentine rule. The Foreign Office was further restrained by Parliament, which backed the islanders without reservation. By early 1982, the British "could offer neither compromise to Argentina nor a credible long-term commitment to the Falkland Islands. The only negotiating posture left was prevarication."[34] Bluff and stalling were hardly ideal negotiating postures for preventing a blowup when the other side felt as intensely as Argentina did.

Intensity is a far from infallible but nevertheless very useful guide to intentions and their link with behavior. Prior to the invasion, Argentina clearly felt much more intensely than the British. Although the Argentines may have thought that the British lacked the capability to retake the islands militarily,[35] the sheer intensity of their grievance--as perceived from Buenos Aires and in comparison to Britain's commitment, which was reluctant, halfhearted, and ambivalent--undoubtedly played a role in the junta's final decision. The fact that the 150th anniversary of the British seizure would come in January 1983 must have added a powerful symbolic variable to the Argentine emotional equation.

Deterrence, defense, and escalation through miscalculation are three intertwined strategic concepts.[36] In her analysis of Israeli intelligence and decision making in the prewar environment in 1973, Stein explores the assumptions which governed the assessment and interpretation of information. As she notes, strategic arguments about deterrence, defense, and miscalculated escalation revolve around five distinct factors and their interrelationships: evaluation of the interests at stake; assessment of the challenge to be deterred; examination of the adversary's intentions and calculations of the options available; consideration of the credibility of the commitment to respond; and discussion of the appropriate response to the failure of deterrence.

In addition to not making credible judgments about deterrence, defense, and the danger of escalation through miscalculation (because of the assumption that Argentina would not resort to war), there is no public evidence that the British made realistic or even explicit assessments of the competing interests at stake or the challenge to be deterred. These are the two factors that are ordinarily attended to most assiduously in foreign policy decision making.

Based on the available evidence, it can be concluded that the quality of the British strategic concept was abysmal. As Stein points out, the basic problem is not the use of some kind of organizing concept; this is necessary for both analysis and decision making.[37] The real issue is the concept's logical coherence and completeness, its relationship to other concepts in the larger system of beliefs, and the way in which the concept is used. If, as Stein concludes, the Israeli concept in 1973 was incompletely articulated and this led to poor problem diagnosis and suboptimal consideration of options (as well as aggravating biased information processing), then the Argentine attack was perfectly understandable from this perspective, since, for all practical purposes, the British did not have a meaningful or workable strategic concept.

Why was this so? The easy answer is because the basic British assumption was that Argentina would not go to war. But this is the kind of crude and wishful thinking-derived assumption which suggests that it was decidedly epiphenomenal in character, that it constituted an apparent but illusory causal factor.

A higher order assumption--or set of assumptions--beyond the Anglo-Argentine strategic context may be discerned. This refers to the fundamental British defense strategy and posture with respect to the conflict and, even more primordially, to the shopworn but valid adage that a nation must be sure that its "political objectives can be achieved with the available military forces and strategy."[38]

The British refused to cede the Falklands or make a real defense commitment to them. The latter would have required a decision that would have been perceived to be politically damaging (if not suicidal) and economically unthinkable. But by early March it was too late; a decision to send a deterrent force at that time would not have sufficed.[39] What would have been necessary for the purpose of deterring an attack would have been an earlier and substantial military commitment in the South Atlantic and preferably on the islands:

> Perhaps the most important operational lesson of the Falklands war is the crucial value of having forces already on station in a crisis area in advance of potential hostilities. The deterrent value of forces on the spot is undeniable, and in retrospect it can be convincingly argued that the junta's refusal to believe that the British would fight for the Falklands was fatally encouraged by the absence of all but a token British force presence on the islands or in the South Atlantic prior to the Argentine invasion.[40]

From the British perspective, the Falklands War is an almost classic decision disaster or policy failure. There were also analytical failures lockstitched into the fabric of the fiasco, but they were the kind of flaws which fall almost exclusively in the province of policymakers (e.g., establishing and assessing one's own defense-deterrence strategy in a conflict arena).

Surprise attacks can be made least likely by overinsurance in force levels or very high levels of readiness; both are extremely expensive and neither is palatable.[41] However, British deterrence would have required neither overinsurance nor an unacceptably high readiness level. A credible deterrent force might have been sufficient and, if an extremely improbable attack did occur, would have greatly facilitated the defense of the islands.

Deterrence may be provocative in certain contexts. The deterrence-miscalculated escalation tradeoff is particularly relevant to the analysis of certain defense situations. However, the Falklands situation was probably analogous to the Korean arena, where the danger is insufficient deterrence of a North Korean attack, not provocation.[42]

The argument above assumes a rational opponent (rational in the sense of weighing comparative capabilities and trying to maximize one's expected utility). We have very little knowledge of the process which led to Argentina's decision to invade. Extensive evidence does indicate rather clearly, however, that strategic assumptions shaped the junta's decision as much as equally wrong assumptions accounted for the failure to anticipate war in Britain. If anything, the premise in Buenos Aires that the other side would not fight was held more strongly and perhaps with considerably more justification (based on signals and indications) than the equivalent assumption in London that Argentina simply would not go to war.

Argentina was reacting to the many British signals that the latter would neither make a long-term military commitment to the Falklands nor resolve the issue diplomatically. The decision to withdraw the Endurance from the area, which was postponed only because of the strange and semicomical South Georgia incident on March 19th, had conveyed a signficant message to Foreign Minister Costa Mendes. Other verbal and physical signals and indications emanated from London and were undoubtedly picked up in Buenos Aires.

The timing of the invasion shows a lack of concern for minimizing Britain's ability to react, underlining the plausibility of the argument that the junta assumed that Britain would not go to war (or would have satisfied itself with face-saving but essentially meaningless harassment).[43] Much of the British fleet at the time was back home for Easter when the Argentines invaded, a fact which later facilitated the very rapid assembly of a powerful British task force. If Argentina had waited for only two more months, the fleet would have been dispersed (with a group of warships in the Indian Ocean).

If Argentina had been willing to wait for eighteen months, they would have faced a Royal Navy stripped of any sea-based air power.[44] The aircraft carriers Hermes and Invincible, the backbone of the successful British attempt to retake the islands, were slated for retirement and sale to Australia; the government had cancelled plans and contracts for any new carrier construction. Furthermore, Argentina was in the process of acquiring new arms and would have been much better equipped a few months later. The latter fact and the concentration of the British fleet at home both point to a decision which rested on a firm--and logical--

conviction that the British would not react militarily or, at the most, would indulge in some posturing.

A second assumption, which was ancillary to the first, was that the United States would prevent the British from going to war. As was the case with Israel's two linked assumptions in 1973, these two premises were plausible, interrelated, and powerful enough to drive out any second thoughts that may have materialized. When war broke out, The Economist depicted the US as trying to play the role of "everybody's friend."[45]

Militarily, there was another key Argentine strategic error: the failure to move its air power from the mainland to the Falklands.[46] Because of this failure, the potential superiority of the Argentine Air Force was cancelled out since it was forced to operate from the mainland, 400 miles from the Falklands. The war could have turned out quite differently if the air force had been moved to the islands, adding further support to the hypothesis that Argentina simply assumed that Britain did not intend to go to war.

Argentina also probably reasoned that its gunboat diplomacy would succeed. This was a lesson of recent history that was well-grounded and, in fact, made the invasion decision seem like a prospect with a low cost, an extremely low probability of failure, and, given the intensity of Argentine feeling about the justice of its cause, a high payoff. During the 1970s, five islands, groups of islands, or parts of islands were seized successfully through an application of force that was "appropriate, limited, and naval."[47] Iran took several islands at the mouth of the Persian Gulf; China seized the Paracels; Vietnam occupied the Spratleys; Indonesia assumed control of East Timor; and Turkey took over a part of Cyprus. Protest greeted all of these operations and reversed none of them. Precedents therefore abounded for the logic and probability of success of such a venture.

For the British, then, warning signals existed but probably could not have been distinguished from previous invasion scares. For both sides, faulty assumptions were discernible (at least retrospectively). But we can ransack history's wars and ferret out fundamental but wrong assumptions as the precursors to almost every dyadic case which evolved into armed hostilities.

We know that the Falklands conflict occurred and that inevitably colors our reactions and interpretations. But if we look at the case from the vantage point of a British or even an Argentine analyst in January 1982, what would the analytical landscape have looked like? We would see the following general picture.

The Falklands is a permanent crisis arena, one of about thirty bilateral conflicts in Latin America since 1945. The majority of these are still active at some level; few have been resolved; some have tottered on the brink of war (such as Cuba-US in 1962, and Guatemala-Belize several years ago); and a few have escalated into warfare (e.g., El Salvador and Honduras in 1969). Since 1832, in fact, there have been ten wars in the general area (five in the 1800s, three before 1945, and two since).[48]

In the period between 1965 and 1981, there has been more overt conflict, a fact which is unarguably related to the perceptible decline of US hegemony in the region and the passing of the dominance of Cold War issues (compared to the 1948-1965 period). A new type of military regime has appeared in South America, one which actively promotes modernization. The former emphasis on internal security has been replaced by the achievement of an irreducible core of internal control and the advent of sharper interstate competition, heralding the transition from the "doctrine of national security" to the "diplomacy of national security."

Territorial claims and resource competition fuel many of the conflicts. Ideological and hegemonic conflicts have been decreasing.[49] Conflicts oriented around migration can be expected to increase in number and intensity. Many conflict constellations are a mix of the five types. The Anglo-Argentine conflict is hegemonic, territorial, and resource-oriented in character.

We can portray the general contours of the Latin American conflict environment in early 1982 fairly well. But this is a considerable distance from being able to estimate the probability that any specific conflict will escalate into a war. If we descend to the level of the specific dyad with which we are concerned, we soon discover that we can profile the relationship accurately, but the descriptive analysis does not provide any real basis for reliable, valid prediction.

In a scholarly essay on the Anglo-Argentine conflict which appeared in print several months prior to the war and covered the period from 1968 through 1981, the dispute is characterized as one of "cooperative confrontation."[50] The overall assessment was that there were "...clear signs that both disputants are imbued with a willingness to settle in order to provide a foundation both for improved Anglo-Argentine relations and for the cooperative development of the islands' offshore economic potential. In practice, however, certain factors militate against a settlement..."[51] At the same time, it was emphasized that "...there is still the matter of whether Argentina, which has proved more inflexible throughout the dispute, interprets Britain's search for a detente as a genuine gesture of conciliation rather than a sign of weakness to be exploited."[52]

It is highly unlikely that a current intelligence assessment in January 1982 would have been fundamentally different from the above academic account. Nor would the February negotiations have necessarily changed the outlook. Whether attack warning indicators--immediate precrisis signals--could have penetrated the fog of wishful thinking on both sides is debatable. We do not have access to the relevant evidence on either side, although, as noted, The Economist reported that the raw data were more alarmist than the finished intelligence assessments. In any case, trying to put oneself in the seat of the analyst with foresight responsibilities rather than hindsight knowledge invests "intelligence failures," the term that so many use so loosely, with a completely different aura.

Improvement must concentrate on doing whatever helps to make analysis better at the margin. One idea that is directly relevant to this case and has much more general applicability concerns strategic assumptions and arguments. Stein assesses the quality of strategic analysis in Israel in 1973, focusing on the logic of the prevailing strategic argument.[53]

The discussion above, which is admittedly quite tentative and ad hoc in nature, does suggest that strategic assumptions played a significant role in the prewar analysis and decision processes. As Stein points out, flaws in the Israeli strategic logic were not attributable to the need to rapidly develop or flesh out the structure of the argument in a threat-saturated crisis context. The process of conceptualization was able to unfold at a leisurely pace.

With respect to the British, the same is true. In fact, political and military leaders had an appreciably longer period of time to develop, analyze, assess, and modify as necessary their strategic conceptual tools and the accompanying logic. The almost ritualistic quality of the assumption that Argentina would not resort to war and the lack of evidence that other assumptions and conceptual structures were considered worthy of sustained and careful (and comparative) analysis cannot be blamed on time pressures. However we might wish to characterize the origins, the conflict dates back a long time (to 1965, 1945, the 1880s, 1833, or the 1770s, depending on one's perspective). Stein's conclusion is clearly generalizable to this case: "Strategic arguments developed over time can be remedied over time and, if they can be, error may be at least partly avoidable."[54]

Although the explanatory power of strategic concepts seems to be impressive, Stein readily acknowledges that the relative impact of poor logic compared to other determinants of failures in estimation and analysis has yet to be ascertained for the prewar 1973 Israeli case. This caveat applies with even more force to this preliminary discussion of the Falklands case.

Strategic Warning: The United States

For the United States, the Falklands conflict was a secondary rather than a primary crisis. However, there is no doubt that the war put the US in an awkward position since it has ties of friendship and alliances with both of the combatants. The "honest broker" role soon gave way to a tilt toward Britain, but it would clearly have been preferable from the US vantage point if war had been averted and the need to choose had never arisen.

It has been charged that the US had ample indications of the impending conflict, but ignored them.[55] Strategic warning of secondary crises is of importance for a variety of reasons, especially to a power with global interests and relationships. Secondary crises may become second-order crises, to use Thomas Belden's term, when a conflict between A and B spills over into a conflict between C and D.[56] The 1973 Middle East war exemplifies this syndrome; the Arab-Israeli conflict set off the US-Soviet alert crisis.

Even if the second-order crisis danger does not materialize, secondary crises can and do pose threats to primary US interests. This is particularly true when the crisis involves two allies or friendly powers, but a secondary crisis between two adversaries or non-allies (e.g., China-Vietnam, Soviet Union-Poland) is far from

totally irrelevant to US concerns and interests.
We live in a complex and interdependent global system, and the system shows every sign of becoming both more complex and interdependent. Therefore, analysis and strategic warning of secondary crises and conflicts will become even more vital in the future. What the US should do about a particular secondary (or any other) crisis is a policy matter, but what the situation is, what its roots are, and what is likely to unfold between the antagonists are all questions for which the intelligence community is properly responsible.

IMPLICATIONS, CAVEATS, AND LESSONS

The Falklands War has made a solution of the dispute which led to it less likely than ever. Attitudes on both sides have hardened and the islanders, never supportive of any kind of a settlement which introduced Argentine sovereignty, are even more negatively disposed toward Buenos Aires than before the conflict. The British had tried to substitute bluffing for a credible commitment and ended up with the very commitment they had consistently avoided. Argentina attempted to seize what they saw as rightfully theirs and are now much further from the goal than before. If the war was launched to prop up General Galtieri's regime, as some have speculated, the outcome and its aftermath were about as inconsistent with that goal as could be imagined.
Warning intelligence functions to provide foresight and thereby prevent war (if possible). It succeeded in accomplishing neither objective in this instance, although intelligence per se may not be the primary or real culprit. Although the analysis here has focused on attack warning and has ignored wartime intelligence and only touched on planning,[57] the recent Israeli-PLO War, the Falklands, and the ongoing Iran-Iraq conflict all reaffirm the importance of intelligence both prior to and during a conflict.[58]
Iraqi President Hussein's miscalculations included the capability of Iran's forces as well as his own and the expected impact of his attack on Iran's domestic situation. Israeli electronic intelligence was vital in determining how to destroy Syria's missiles in the Bekaa valley. The British skillfully meshed analysis of photo reconnaissance pictures and reports from small units as the basis for their decision about the best possible landing site.
Defense planning, including the realistic assessment of one's own capabilities and the capabilities and intentions of the opposition, turned out to be crucial in these recent wars. Careful and honest net assessments and attention to strategy (both in the political and military senses of the concept) are both indispensable. Neither Iraq nor Argentina devoted enough thought to these issues.
The lessons and implications of the Falklands War have relevance beyond the direct participants. All of the evidence we have about international crises and wars since 1945 points to the conclusion that there was nothing so unique about this case. Images of the international crisis that draw on the Cuban Missile Crisis of 1962 or associate crises with the superpowers or the

East-West conflict axis are not representative of the range or variety of crises in the contemporary international arena. Crises have occurred throughout the world and have involved confrontations between nations of all types. Especially within the Third World, endemic conflicts have often erupted into crises and some have led to actual warfare.

Table 1 presents forty-eight crisis dyads from 1966 through 1978. These pairs of international crisis actors constituted the empirical data base for a computerized crisis warning and monitoring system which was developed and tested by the US Defense Advanced Research Projects Agency.[59] This list reflects a Western bias; crisis chronologies of Soviet, Chinese, and other actors would differ appreciably.[60] Furthermore, the data base is not designed to be exhaustive in coverage; only the most salient international crises during the time frame are featured.

TABLE 1

CRISIS LISTS: 48 CRISIS DYADS, 1966-1978

DYAD	START DATE	COMMENT
1. Syria - Jordan	1 Dec 1966	
PLO - Jordan		
2. USSR - China	11 Jan 1967	
3. Israel - Syria	5 Jun 1967	
Israel - Egypt		
Israel - Jordan		
4. UNK - China	27 Jun 1967	Hong Kong dispute
5. Greece - Turkey	15 Nov 1967	
Greece - Cyprus (Turkey)		
Turkey - Cyprus		
6. Israel - Jordan	2 Jan 1968	
7. USA - North Korea	23 Jan 1968	Pueblo
8. USSR - Czechoslovakia	20 Aug 1968	
9. Israel - Egypt	24 Feb 1969	
Israel - Syria		
10. USSR - China	2 Mar 1969	
11. Honduras - El Salvador	30 Jun 1969	
12. North Vietnam - USA	18 Mar 1970	
North Vietnam - Cambodia		
North Vietnam - South Vietnam		
13. Uganda - Tanzania	9 Jul 1970	
14. Jordan - Syria	1 Sep 1970	
Jordan - PLO		
Jordan - Iraq		
USA - Syria		
USA - USSR		
Israel - Syria		
15. India - Pakistan	21 Nov 1971	
16. Uganda - Tanzania	17 Sep 1972	
17. Rhodesia - Zambia	9 Jan 1973	

18. Israel - Egypt	6 Oct 1973	
Israel - Syria		
19. USA - USSR	24 Oct 1973	Global alert
20. Greece - Turkey	15 Jul 1974	
Cyprus - Cyprus (Turkey)		
21. USA - Cambodia	12 May 1975	Mayaguez
22. Morocco - Spain	27 May 1975	
23. Morocco - Algeria	9 Dec 1975	
24. Syria - Lebanon	1 Jun 1976	
Syria - PLO		
Syria - Israel		
25. Angola - Zaire	10 Mar 1977	
26. Egypt - Libya	19 Jul 1977	
27. Somalia - Ethiopia	8 Aug 1977	
28. Israel - Syria	19 Sep 1977	
Israel - PLO		
29. Uganda - Tanzania	31 Oct 1978	
30. Cambodia - Vietnam	28 Dec 1978	

Despite these qualifications, it is clear that the list in Table 1 depicts the volume and variety of crises in the global arena. The Middle East (defined as crisis contexts involving Israel and one or more Arab opponents as well as related conflict episodes, such as the Syria-Jordan and PLO-Jordan pairs in 1970) dominates the empirical universe of world crises in the 1966 to 1978 period. The next most frequent type of crisis occurred between nonaligned Third World opponents (a total of fourteen, including five Middle East cases). Included are the Honduras-El Salvador War (1969), several significant crises between Uganda and Tanzania, several additional crises involving African nations, and India-Pakistan.

In contrast, other crises types are relatively rare. Only four superpower crises cases appear on the list (two between the US and the Soviets and two between the Soviets and China). There are eight East-West crises and four involving internecine disputes within the Communist world. All five Western crises are accounted for by dyads in the Greece-Turkey-Cyprus arena. Finally, two West-South crises (US-Syria in 1973 and Morocco-Spain in 1975) occurred during the period. There were no East-South crises.

What all of this reflects is an international system in which power has become significantly more dispersed. The tight and loose bipolar systems of the 1945 to 1960 period enabled the superpowers to orchestrate international political trends to a much greater extent and forced a considerable amount of international crisis and conflict into the Cold War channel. As bipolarity eroded, conflicts within the West and East surfaced and intensified. The international system became multipolar in the 1960s and this polycentric pattern accelerated in the 1970s, increasing the probability and incidence of crises within the West, East, and South (as well as between the West and East). The diffusion of power process is continuing and the world is becoming increasingly complex; almost invariably, this pattern will dominate the 1980s. Our expectations about conflict and crisis must flow initially from this fundamental structural configuration. The Falklands War, then, was neither deviant nor unprecedented. In terms of the larger implications, there are two that warrant mention. First, US policymakers and analysts can expect to continue to confront secondary crises, including ones between friendly powers or allies. High priority will have to be given to analyzing and anticipating such possibilities. The goal should not be to achieve an impossible degree of perfect warning, but to enhance the ability to react rapidly and decisively. One way to do this is by more explicitly and systematically monitoring and analyzing potential and actual conflict and crisis arenas, thereby providing for more rational and effective contingency planning.

Wars between allies can be projected for the future. In fact, this is one of the predictable consequences of a transition from a bipolar to a polycentric world political system. Not surprisingly in the light of trends in the international system, the Sino-Soviet and French-American conflicts both became overt and then escalated in the 1960s. The Western European reaction to pressure from the US on the Soviet pipeline deal, probes to the West for arms or economic aid and investment from Angola, Mozambique, and Iraq, daily pronouncements in Rumania and Israel, and a multitude of other subtle and blatant messages and events constantly remind decision makers in the Kremlin and Washington that allies can be a decidedly mixed blessing. In addition, if people are close friends, their relationship has nowhere to go but down.

The logic of the latter statement provides the basis for Bruce Bueno de Mesquita's initial argument that war between allies should not be shocking.[61] He analyzes seventy-six interstate war initiations from 1816 to 1974, discovering that in twenty-three cases, each belligerent had at least one ally. Of these twenty-three cases, fifteen involved a formal military agreement between the states at war. The fifteen instances of formal allies going to war represent twenty percent of the seventy-six wars. Even more revealing, allied dyads constituted only about seven percent of all annual regional dyads in the international system from 1816 to 1974. Thus, wars between allies are about three times more likely than would be expected on the basis of the distribution of bilateral military agreements.

The second implication concerns the Third World. A central arena for conflict, crisis, and war in the 1970s, the Third World will undoubtedly be a more dangerous environment in the 1980s.[62] For many reasons, domestic stresses and strains on Third World societies will probably experience a significant growth. To mention just one cluster of potent causal factors, the debt structure and other international economic aspects of the domestic reality which most countries of the South confront are currently deteriorating and are quite ominous in their implications for the future.

We can expect an upsurge of both internal and external crises and violence. Much of the growth of world military spending since 1968 can be attributed to developing states.[63] Every conceivable index--military expenditures (total and per capita), armed forces (total and per 1,000 of population), number of developing countries with advanced military systems (supersonic aircraft, missiles, armored fighting vehicles, modern warships), arms imports, and domestic defense production--dramatically highlights the increasing role and prominence of the Third World in international security affairs. Given the runaway military trends and the expanding array and heightened lethality of weapons and armaments obtained by developing societies (and increasingly produced indigenously as well), conflict will probably not only be a lot more frequent--it will probably be much more destructive.[64]

No part of the Third World is free from endemic internal and external conflict. This impacts directly on US concerns, both because it is a superpower with global interests and the developing world has been and will continue to be the primary surrogate arena of competition between the US and the Soviet Union.[65] The victory since 1975 of seven pro-Soviet communist parties in Asia and Africa only exacerbates the dangers and the potential for serious conflict and upheaval in strategically vital areas of the Third World.

Until recently, the US intelligence analytical bureaucracy lacked the resources necessary for studying developing societies in any real detail and with genuine sensitivity for the realities, complexities, and nuances of social, economic, political, and military trends and their interrelationships. In fact, it would not be unfair to charge that US analysis was sometimes so deficient that there was a lack of basic knowledge about exactly what was going on.

Donald Zagoria points out, for example, that, after the 1978 communist coup in South Yemen, the US State Department concluded that the country did not pose a genuine threat and was not worthy of much attention because it is small and had only 1.5 million people.[66] When this statement was made in August 1978, the fifteen Arab League states were in the process of organizing an across-the-board boycott directed against South Yemen. South Yemen has since been an expansionist state, threatening its neighbors and provoking serious concern in Saudi Arabia.

Zagoria sums up his position as follows:

> The challenge of dealing with communism in the Third World is as much a challenge to our understanding as it is to our policy. We need a much more sophisticated national understanding of radical movements and states than we presently have. Compared to the huge amounts of money and effort the government spends on collecting and evaluating military intelligence and "hardware," the amounts which it spends on political analysis are trivial. The problem is not merely a failure of gathering information or even a failure of proper evaluation. Even more serious, it is a failure to ask the right questions.[67]

Somewhat more analytical attention is currently being devoted to the South. However, it would be desirable and sensible to allocate even more effort. More information is needed, but data alone will not produce realistic assessments or accurate projections. In fact, flooding analysts with too much data will probably lead to the usual outcome of eliciting the common human tendency to be more confident about one's conclusions without being any more accurate. What is crucial is more and better analysis.

The Falklands War provides an excellent example. Did internal political conditions lead to the attack on the Falklands? What is the nature of the nexus between domestic politics and foreign affairs? Do internal crises produce foreign wars? We can never completely penetrate or open the black box of a foreign society, especially with respect to the decision making processes of elites. But the challenge nevertheless remains to attempt to use available indicators and other evidence to reduce uncertainty as much as possible, to unravel and clarify causal processes, and to illuminate the contours and dynamics of elite assessment, inference, and choice processes.[68]

The invasion, as The Economist noted soon after the war started, was "launched just as the popularity of Argentina's military rulers had tumbled to its lowest point since the coup of 1976."[69] Just three days before the attack was initiated, on March 30, 1982, disorders had erupted in Buenos Aires and other cities. The demonstration in the capital was the biggest since 1976.

The upsurge of Peronist agitation occurred against the backdrop of a desperate economic situation. The modest economic advances of the earlier years of military rule were evaporating as General Galtieri came to power. The inflation rate had reached 130 percent, the gross national product had declined by more than six percent, and unemployment was high.

The invasion brought about an immediate and dramatic increase in the regime's popularity, illustrating again one of the few iron laws of politics--that foreign crises and wars produce at least temporary rallies in a regime's popularity. However, unthinking acceptance of the plausible hypothesis that external conflict was welcomed as a means of solving a domestic problem would not be warranted. Lawrence Freedman presents evidence that unusually propitious international conditions also determined the timing.[70]

Argentine relations with both superpowers were positive. The US viewed the Galtieri regime as acceptable authoritarianism and the Soviets were grateful for Argentine wheat during the American grain embargo. Third World countries had consistently tended to side with Argentina in the United Nations on what looked on the surface like a classical anticolonial issue (although many subsequently refrained from supporting the attempt to impose a military solution).[71] Given the previously discussed British strategy of refusing to give in but signaling that it would not go to war, the international situation emerges as a complementary (if not competing) determinant of the decision to invade.

Warning analysts are concerned with the danger of war. But the Falklands crisis demonstrates vividly that internal politics cannot be neglected in the strategic warning analytical process. Theories of bureaucratic politics within a government also often enter into the equation.[72] Interservice rivalry in Argentina is almost a caricature of the bureaucratic politics model, but all governments tend to become institutionalized and, as a result, interservice, military-civilian, and other bureaucratic rivalries and differences of perspective affect the decision process in most nations. (This is becoming increasingly the case for most Third World states, many of which are well over twenty years old now.) The special role of Admiral Anaya as the architect of the invasion reaffirms the importance of probing bureaucratic politics and treating nations as something more than oversimplified unified, rational actors.

Thus, another lesson of the Falklands crisis and war is the need to conduct analysis in an integrated fashion. The intelligence analytical bureaucracy is functionally separated into economic, political, military, and other distinct components. William Colby decries the "almost uniformly bad" effect of chopping up analysis this way.[73] The real world simply does not operate in this fashion. Military intelligence needs to incorporate political, economic, and even cultural and sociological information and assessments into its analytical process. Strategic warning cannot be effective if it neglects or downgrades other areas of intelligence.

Several caveats about the conclusions advanced here should be explicitly highlighted. Both concern cognitive psychology and its impact on our thinking. The hindsight bias cautions us against indulging in the fantasy that we would have predicted something which others failed to foresee. We can always unearth warning indicators after the fact. We should always be humble about accusing others of being responsible for an "intelligence failure."

Secondly, another common bias is responsible for assigning too much significance to unrepresentative cases. Called the availability bias, it is based on the fact that we tend to emphasize cases that are available, not necessarily ones that are representative. The availability bias is especially likely if the case is dramatic or otherwise salient. Many statesmen in the 1940s and 1950s looked at every case through the filter of the Munich case; analogously, their successors in the 1970s used Vietnam as the exemplar for interpreting subsequent events and situations. In both instances, they were overgeneralizing a particularly salient crisis and consequently misapplying the alleged "lessons of history."

People rush into print about very recent cases. We should guard against the natural tendency to overemphasize the recent just because it is vivid in our memories. The Falklands may not be a representative case and may have little to tell us about crisis and conflict in the 1980s. This note of caution about overgeneralizing also applies, of course, to the many military "lessons" which have already been extracted from the experiences of Britain and Argentina in the Falklands battles.

With the caveats about the hindsight and availability biases out of the way, we can return to drawing inferences for the future from the Falklands conflict. Two final lessons will be catalogued. The first concerns what warning is and what it should attempt to accomplish. Was the Falklands War foreseeable and preventable? To what extent is any war predictable? The concept of analysis failure suggests that better analysis could have averted the outbreak of hostilities. Of course, we can never know this in a definitive sense. But the evidence of flawed analysis on both sides, the critical miscalculations that both governments made, and the wrong but reassuring assumptions that governed the two decision making processes all point to a failure of analysis.

Stein's juxtaposition of the intelligence and stupidity explanations for intelligence failure relates to this point.[74] The intelligence explanation emphasizes the intrinsically and inescapably complex, uncertain, and ambiguous nature of the task of intelligence and estimation. Error is inevitable and results from an unresolvable paradox. In contrast, interpretations that attribute failure to the "stupidity" of analysts or leaders stress endemic information processing biases or the suboptimal performance of leaders in a particular situation. The second version of the "stupidity" argument relies on evidence of cognitive rigidity, excessive commitment to only one interpretation, or the inappropriate utilization of a single concept or indicator.

The "intelligence" argument exonerates analysts and/or leaders, while the "stupidity" argument drastically underestimates the difficulty of the job of the warning analyst. Furthermore, a valid explanation would rank and interrelate the many potential causes of failure, factors that range from environmental constraints and stress to psychological, bureaucratic, political structural, and other routines, procedures, and processes.

The emphasis here has been on suboptimal analytical performance. This is the one area where we have some room (if only a little) for improvement. We cannot wish or define ambiguity and uncertainty out of existence. Nor, apparently, can we fundamentally affect or reform cognitive psychological processes; the extensive experimental evidence from cognitive and social psychology demonstrates that people continue to rely on biased heuristics and other suboptimal information processing routines even if they are informed and warned about them. But we can encourage better analysis when there is evidence of poor logic and other remediable shortcomings. People can be urged to think in terms of multiple and competing hypotheses, especially in the area of strategic assumptions and concepts, which usually emerge in a long-term and relatively stress-free environment.

Suppose the British had acted on the basis of an unequivocal warning. Would that have prevented war? It was probably too late; active deterrence at that point would have been provocative rather than simply defensive. As Betts argues, warning analysts must guard against the facile solution of always assuming the worst and issuing alerts on that basis.[75] To act on the basis of every threat from Buenos Aires would have been expensive and, because of the false alarm effect or cry-wolf syndrome, would have become routinized and therefore discredited. Always assuming the worst also risks preemption; precautionary escalation can become a self-fulfilling prophecy. Warning is not a process of issuing an alarm every time a set of indicators crosses a preestablished threshold; if it were, analysts could be computers.

The second general lesson concerns the issue of information versus analysis or technology versus thinking. We continue to indulge in the myth that technology and computers represent intelligence analysis. What is done with the information which is collected is the essence of good intelligence. Technical intelligence collection, computer-based aids, and electronic data storage, retrieval, and processing are irreplaceable adjuncts to analysis. But they are not substitutes for the evaluation of information, analysis, synthesis, interpretation, and drawing inferences, conclusions, and recommendations. That is the essence of warning and all other forms of strategic intelligence.

NOTES

1. Richard K. Betts, Surprise Attack: Lessons for Defense Planning (Washington, D.C.: Brookings Institution, 1982).

2. Baruch Fischhoff, "Hindsight ≠ Foresight: The Effect of Outcome Knowledge on Judgment Under Certainty," Journal of Experimental Psychology: Human Perception and Performance, 1 (1975): 288-299; Fischhoff, "The Silly Certainty of Hindsight," Psychology Today, 8 (April 1975): 70-76; Fischhoff and Ruth Beyth, "'I Knew It Would Happen': Remembered Probabilities of Once-Future Things," Organizational Behavior and Human Performance, 13 (1975): 1-16.

3. See especially: Albert Clarkson, Toward Effective Strategic Analysis: New Applications of Information Technology (Boulder, CO: Westview, 1981); Richard Nisbett and Lee Ross, Human Inference: Strategies and Shortcomings of Social Judgment (Englewood Cliffs, NJ: Prentice Hall, 1980).

4. Among the major case studies are: Abraham Ben-Zvi, "Hindsight and Foresight: A Conceptual Framework for the Analysis of Surprise Attack," World Politics, 28 (1976): 381-95; H. A. DeWeerd, "Strategic Surprise in the Korean War," Orbis, 6 (1962): 435-52; Michael I. Handel, "The Yom Kippur War and the Inevitability of Surprise," International Studies Quarterly, 21 (1977): 461-502; Klaus Knorr, "Failures in National Intelligence Estimates: The Case of the Cuban Missiles," World Politics, 28 (1976): 348-80; Barton Whaley, Codeword Barbarossa (Cambridge, MA: MIT Press, 1973); Roberta Wohlstetter, "Cuba and Pearl Harbor: Hindsight and Foresight," Foreign Affairs, 43 (1965): 691-707; Wohlstetter, Pearl Harbor: Warning and Decision (Stanford, CA: Stanford University Press, 1962).

5. See, respectively, Betts, Surprise Attack; Barton Whaley, "Strategem: Deception and Surprise in War" (Cambridge, MA: MIT, unpublished, 1969). Wohlstetter, "Cuba and Pearl Harbor," is a useful comparative case study. On surprise and diplomacy (as well a discussion of military versus diplomatic surprise), Michael I. Handel, The Diplomacy of Suprise: Hilter, Nixon, Sadat. Harvard Studies in International Affairs, Number 44 (Cambridge, MA: Center for International Affairs, Harvard University, 1981).

6. Janice Gross Stein, "'Intelligence' and 'Stupidity' Reconsidered: Estimation and Decision in Israel, 1973," Journal of Strategic Studies, 3 (September 1980): 155.

7. Richard K. Betts, "Analysis, War, and Decision: Why Intelligence Failures are Inevitable," World Politics, 31 (October 1978): 69.

8. Betts, Surprise Attack, p. 4.

9. Wohlstetter, Pearl Harbor.

10. See especially Betts, "Analysis, War, and Decision," and Surprise Attack.

11. This issue, which will be discussed in some detail below, surfaced in a direct and rather stark fashion in the Falklands "inquest" debate. As The Economist reported in June 1982 (283 (June 19-25): 35):

> Many members of parliament and members of the cabinet have been keen to see the inquiry (into the origins of the war) confine its investigations to the performance of the diplomatic and intelligence services immediately prior to the invasion. The diplomats' view, put by one of the fallen ministers, Mr. Richard K. Luce, is that it should cover "all departments concerned...and be free to examine the problem in the perspective of the last 15 or 20 years."

Editorially, The Economist said in the same issue, "The Inquest Into How It Began," p. 12:

> Although at first the inquiry was seen as "naming the guilty men," already it is clear that the blame is more diffused and more political than that...the root cause of Argentina's attack was a persistent weakness in the British defence of islands which its politicians were nevertheless not willing to give up...The inquiry will need to investigate not just intelligence raw material and Whitehall assessments, but the political and economic climate in which defence and foreign affairs judgments are made.

12. As opposed to the tactical phase of warning, which consists of "the initial movements of the attack itself, before combat is joined"(Betts, Surprise Attack, p. 5). The primary concern in Surprise Attack is political and especially strategic warning.

13. For example, there was a major invasion alert in South Korea on May 7, 1950, prior to the real North Korean attack in late June. During 1949, there had been 874 border violations in the Korean arena (Betts, Surprise Attack, pp. 53-54).

14. Policy and belief system pluralism may be desirable in intelligence analysis, but many realities and constraints minimize it. One of the most deeply rooted is the fact that the very nature of intelligence work places a high premium on recruiting people who share the regime value and belief systems (Chan, "The

Intelligence of Stupidity," p. 177).

15. For example, see the article "The Inquest," in The Economist, p. 12.

16. Robert Jervis, Perception and Misperception in International Politics (Princeton, NJ: Princeton University Press, 1976).

17. The most extreme example is policymaking without regular and meaningful inputs from intelligence. A much less extreme example of policy failure occurs when intelligence is "good" but policy turns out to be "bad." For example, intelligence may generate estimates which are fairly accurate and offer relatively valid warnings, but the decision maker may--for perfectly justifiable policy reasons--feel obligated to take action inconsistent with the inputs. Then, the disaster is a policy failure, not an intelligence failure. See Richard K. Betts, "Intelligence for Policymaking," in Gerald W. Hopple, Stephen J. Andriole, and Amos Freedy (eds.): National Security Crisis Forecasting and Management (Boulder, CO: Westview, 1983).

18. Stephen J. Andriole and Gerald W. Hopple, "They're Only Human: Decision Makers in Command and Control," Signal, 36 (March 1982): 45-49.

19. Richard K. Betts, "Strategic Intelligence Estimates: Let's Make Them Useful," Parameters, 10 (December 1980): 21. In general, see also Betts, "Intelligence For Policymaking."

20. Betts, "Strategic Intelligence Estimates," p. 22.

21. Betts, "Analysis, War, and Decision," p. 88.

22. Wolf Grabendorff, "Interstate Conflict Behavior and Regional Potential for Conflict in Latin America," Journal of Interamerican Studies and World Affairs, 24 (August 1982): 267-94.

23. Stein, "'Intelligence' and 'Stupidity.'"

24. The historical background is provided in: Peter J. Beck, "Cooperative Confrontation in the Falkland Islands Dispute: The Anglo-Argentine Search for a Way Forward, 1968-1981," Journal of Interamerican Studies and World Affairs, 24 (February 1982): 37-58; Peter Calvert, The Falklands Crisis: The Rights and the Wrongs (New York: St. Martin's Press, 1982); Lawrence Freedman, "The War of the Falkland Islands, 1982," Foreign Affairs, 61 (Fall 1982): 196-210; Jean Houbert, "The Falklands: A Hiccup of Decolonisation," Current Research on Peace and Violence, 5 (1/1982): 1-25. Also useful are The Economist issues of April 10-16 and June 19-25, 1982. See also the Rt Hon the Lord Franks, Falkland Islands Review: Report of a Committee of Privy

Counsellors (London: Her Majesty's Stationery Office, January 1983).

25. The Economist, 283 (June 19-25, 1982): 36.

26. At the time, the Foreign Office warned that this "could well be misread in Buenos Aires. This left a garrison of some seventy Royal Marines to deter Argentina from attempting to retake the Falkland Islands by force (Freedman, "The War," p. 198)." See also Calvert, The Falklands Crisis, p. 66.

27. The Economist, 283 (June 19-25, 1982): 36.

28. Ibid., p. 38.

29. Ibid.

30. Admiral Jorge Anaya, the chief of the Argentine Navy and the architect of the invasion, was actively lobbying for such an option. The invasion may have been triggered by the incident on March 19th, when some Argentine scrap metal merchants raised the Argentine flag on the dependency of South Georgia. The Endurance, which was already scheduled to be withdrawn from the area, was sent with a detachment of twenty-one Marines from Port Stanley to South Georgia. There has been speculation that this incident occurred with the knowledge and possible involvement of Anaya (Ibid., p. 43; Freedman, "The War," p. 199). Galtieri had pledged privately to take control of the Falklands by the time of the highly symbolic 150th anniversary of Britain's occupation (that is, by January 3, 1983) and the junta had made plans to prepare for an effective occupation before the February talks with the British (Calvert, The Falklands Crisis, p. 56). See also The Franks Report, Falkland Islands Review.

31. Freedman, "The War," p. 200. Well into 1981, Britain had been preoccupied with another potential flashpoint in Latin America: the Guatemala-Belize crisis (Calvert, The Falklands Crisis, pp. 68-9).

32. "Falkland Islands: The Origins of a War," The Economist, p. 35.

33. Ibid., p. 35; Jeffrey Record, "The Falklands War," Washington Quarterly, 5 (Autumn 1982): 45.

34. Freedman, "The War," p. 198.

35. Ibid., p. 199.

36. Stein, "'Intelligence' and 'Stupidity,'" p. 152.

37. Ibid., p. 152.

38. Michael Moodie, "Six Months of Conflict," Washington

Quarterly, 5 (Autumn 1982): 32. See also: Freedman, "The War," p. 198; Sir James Cable, "The Falklands Conflict," U.S. Naval Institute Proceedings, 108 (September 1982): 72; Admiral Thomas H. Moorer and Alvin J. Cottrell, "In the Wake of the Falklands Battle," Strategic Review (Summer 1982): 27; James D. Hessman, "The Lessons of the Falklands," Sea Power, 25 (July 1982): 16.

39. In fact, at that point, a deterrent force would have ignited a preemptive Argentine attack (forcing them to advance their timetable slightly). If it had been too small to be noticed or had been sent secretly (as occurred in response to the 1977 invasion scare), it would not have prevented the desperate junta from invading. See "Falkland Islands: The Origins of a War," The Economist, p. 43.

40. Record, "The Falklands War," p. 48.

41. Betts, Surprise Attack, pp. 309-10.

42. Ibid., p. 273.

43. Freedman, "The War," p. 199.

44. Record, "The Falklands War," p. 44.

45. "Falkland Islands: Will Two Weeks' Steaming Let Off the Pressure?," The Economist, 283 (April 10, 1982): 22. Former President Leopoldo Galtieri, the leader of the military junta during the war, maintained that Argentina would not have invaded if the junta had known the US would support Britain ("Argentine Military Arrests Chief During Falklands War," Washington Post, (April 13, 1983): A27.

46. Record, "The Falklands War," pp. 44-45.

47. Cable, "The Falklands Conflict," p. 73.

48. Grabendorff, "Interstate Conflict."

49. Ideological conflicts include disputes between dictatorships and democracies, civilian and military regimes, and capitalist and socialist alternatives. Big power claims to supremacy or hegemonic conflicts include as special cases the hegemony of a colonial power (Britain) and the hegemony of a regional power (Brazil).

50. Beck, "Cooperative Confrontation."

51. Ibid., p. 40.

52. Ibid., p. 54.

53. Stein, "'Intelligence' and 'Stupidity,'" p. 168.

54. Ibid.

55. "The Falklands: Warning, Intelligence, and Diplomacy," Armed Forces Journal International (September 1982): 30-31.

56. Thomas Belden, "Indications, Warning, and Crisis Operations," International Studies Quarterly, 21 (March 1977): 188-89.

57. Betts makes this tripartite breakdown in "Analysis, War, and Decision," pp. 63-65.

58. Moodie, "Six Months of Conflict," pp. 31-2.

59. Gerald W. Hopple, "Internal and External Crisis Early Warning and Monitoring," Technical Report (McLean, VA: International Public Policy Research Corporation, 1980).

60. DARPA sponsored research on international crises as perceived by both the Chinese and the Soviets (in addition to crises as defined from the US perspective); see Robert B. Mahoney, Jr., "Crisis Management: A Survey of Findings and Unresolved Problems," in Hopple, et al., National Security Crisis Forecasting and Management.

61. Bruce Bueno de Mesquita, The War Trap (New Haven and London: Yale University Press, 1981), p. 160.

62. Theodore H. Moran, "North-South Relations in the 1980s," Naval War College Review, 35 (September-October 1982): 29-30.

63. Edward A. Kolodziej and Robert Harkavy, "Developing States and the International Security System," pp. 19-47 in John J. Stremlau (ed.), The Foreign Policy Priorities of Third World States (Boulder, CO: Westview, 1982).

64. Moodie ("Six Months of Conflict," p. 29) amends this proposition slightly by arguing that arms inventories of LDCs are likely to feature a combination of simple and sophisticated weaponry.

65. For a particularly lucid and sophisticated analysis of recent Soviet activity in the Third World, see Donald S. Zagoria, "Into the Breach: New Soviet Alliances in the Third World," pp. 495-514 in Erik P. Hoffman and Frederic J. Fleron (eds.), The Conduct of Soviet Foreign Policy (New York: Aldine, 1980). On Soviet-US competition in Africa, see Kenneth Maxwell, "A New Scramble for Africa?," pp. 515-34 in ibid.

66. Zagoria, "Into the Breach," p. 511.

67. Ibid., p. 510.

68. A good example is the correlation recently unearthed

between the rhetoric which the Soviet finance minister uses in the annual budget message to describe future Soviet military spending and to discuss the nature of the US threat and annual changes in Soviet defense spending (as estimated in rubles by the US Central Intelligence Agency). This correlation, which has held up for twenty-five years, is alluded to in William Zimmerman, "What Do Scholars Know About Soviet Foreign Policy?," International Journal, 37 (Spring 1982): 218.

69. "Falkland Islands: Will Two Weeks' Steaming Let Off the Pressure?," The Economist, p. 21. In late 1974, Argentina was facing extreme threats from leftist and rightist terrorism and violence and a state of siege was proclaimed in November. The next month, newspapers urged an invasion of the Falklands to provide a diversion (Calvert, The Falklands Crisis, p. 44).

70. Freedman, "The War," p. 199. In addition, this was the ideal time of the year for an attack given the weather conditions. With the onset of winter, landing troops to retake the islands could be expected to be very difficult (Calvert, The Falklands Crisis, p. 86).

71. Reasons for Third World ambivalence toward Argentina prior to the war are discussed in Houbert, "The Falklands," p. 14. On Latin America's mixed reaction, see ibid., p. 22, and Calvert, The Falklands Crisis, pp. 103-104, 134-35, 160.

72. On bureaucratic politics, see Graham Allison, Essence of Decision (Boston, MA: Little, Brown, 1971). On interservice rivalry in Argentina, see Calvert, The Falklands Crisis, p. 50.

73. William E. Colby, "Decision and Surprise: Problems of Analysts and Analysis," pp. 91-97 in Robert L. Pfaltzgraff, Jr., Uri Ra'anan, and W. H. Milberg (eds.), Intelligence Policy and National Security (Archon Books, 1981), p. 95.

74. Stein, "'Intelligence' and 'Stupidity,'" p. 151.

75. Betts, "Analysis, War, and Decision," pp. 73-74.

9
Lessons Learned and Unlearned

Peter M. Dunn

In the United States, a great deal of time and money has been spent on studying the lessons of the Falklands campaign. However, as the preceding analyses suggest, senior military and political officials have discovered--if they did not already know it--that there were no new lessons to be learned from the Falklands conflict. This in itself is a lesser lesson of this campaign.

It is not surprising that such acute interest in the Falklands conflict was evinced by so many high-level Washington officials. For the senior military officers, here at last was a kind of war they recognized, and they felt comfortable in reading and discussing it. It was a clean, traditional war, with a proper battlefield, recognizable opponents in recognizable uniforms and positions, and no messy, scattered civil populations or guerrilla groups to complicate the situation. Here, then, was a conflict which could be chewed and digested with relish. It could be discussed intelligently by the various bureaucratic hierarchies, and so it was studied with zeal. The refreshing thing about it was that it did not end in a draw.

It is thus not so curious that someone else's little, relatively insignificant skirmish was studied so eagerly while the lessons of one's own vastly more important and disastrous war have been virtually assigned to the dustbin of history.

Having said that, it is still necessary to put the Falklands campaign into the context of modern politics and warfare. It has variously been said that this was the first Missile Age campaign; that large carrier battle groups would have flicked away the defending and attacking Argentines; that it was, in a sense, a revolutionary war (the revolution being in technology), and more.

First, apart from the inexorable advances in technology, there is nothing new under the sun (which itself has been setting off atomic explosions eons before the first humanoids appeared on earth). Contrary to the cacophony of discussion following the destruction of the HMS Sheffield by an Exocet antiship missile, that door was opened fifteen years earlier when another destroyer, the Israeli ship Eilat, was sunk by a cheap, small missile boat firing Soviet-made Styx missiles. But for years preceding even that earlier milestone, it was known that the Soviets had been perfecting and deploying these missiles.

Even the Exocet itself did not suddenly spring into view over the waters surrounding the Falklands. It, and others, had been destroying targets for years preceding this conflict, as it was developed, tested, and deployed in the West. In the eternal dialectic between the attack and the defense, the Theodosian walls surrounding Constantinople remain unique in their span of supremacy. Thus even as the Exocet appeared it could be, and was, defeated; as noted by William Ruhe, it can be confused or killed by electronic countermeasures (chaff and jamming), quick-firing guns, and missiles.

A great deal has been written to the effect that had the Royal Navy possessed large carrier battle groups it would have suffered less severely, if at all. This may or may not be true-- the author's own experience in attacking or in supporting attacks on defended targets (including warships at sea) in peacetime exercises and in combat suggests that at least some of any reasonably determined, sized, and trained attacking force will often get to the target, regardless of the defense employed. These "leakers" pose a more serious threat than bureaucracies with vested interests will admit; one leaker with a nuclear weapon will destroy the heart of a fleet. But the whole argument is vacuous in that only one or two nations have the money to spend on these larger systems.

There is no debate over the fundamental role of the giant carrier battle groups in Western maritime strategy; there is a growing appreciation of what smaller carrier groups can do, given smaller tasks. In today's turbulent world, for example, the small Harrier carrier would be well suited to evacuate citizens from a Third World country in revolutionary chaos.

Senior US Navy officials insist that the campaign has proved the need to build big carrier battle groups. In fact, it has tended to reinforce the opposite argument since victory was achieved without big carriers, while the possession of these ships has been almost immaterial in the military actions in Korea and Vietnam, neither of which resulted in clear-cut American victories. Neither China nor North Vietnam possessed any carriers; in fact, the latter had no navy at all, to speak of. But no one has argued that these dinosaurs are not needed, only that the smaller terriers also have a useful role to play in naval strategy. While in history dinosaurs were gloriously impressive and sometimes destructive creatures, they were expensive to maintain and eventually died out, and underfoot the tiny, lowly shrew and its descendants--including the reader--survived to inherit the earth.

If anything, the Falklands campaign has shown that the US Navy may have focused on the wrong problem. The major concern is the submarine threat. The Royal Navy, as skilled, sophisticated and experienced as the US Navy, was for weeks unable to destroy a single German-built Argentine conventional submarine which was stalking the British task force. It takes little imagination to realize the potential effect of an attack by, say, twenty nuclear-powered Soviet submarines on a task force.

The US Navy should, in addition, concern itself more with the state of the US merchant fleet. One has to wonder if in fact we could have mustered a hundred merchant ships at such short notice, ships which would be needed to sustain major land operations in Europe, the Persian Gulf and elsewhere. The Falklands again confirmed the need for heavy naval gunfire support of ground troops; this has been neglected over the years in the United States, and has been of great concern to the US Marine Corps. During the "Rolling Thunder" air campaign of America's Vietnam War, hundreds of sorties, including two strike support missions flown by the author, were launched against the Thanh Hoa Bridge in North Vietnam. Perhaps dozens of US Air Force and US Navy planes were lost, and scores of American crews killed or captured. The bridge was not destroyed in four years of repeated attacks, and still stood when Rolling Thunder ended on November 1, 1968. The battleship New Jersey could have fired its awesome salvos at the bridge, delivering the equivalent of a one-ton bomb from each barrel perhaps as accurately as a bomb dropped from an aircraft in those conditions--and perhaps 80 million dollars in lost aircraft, not to mention the lives of the lost air crews, may well have been saved. (Later, the measured and skillful use of technology, in the form of the laser-guided bomb, finally destroyed the Thanh Hoa bridge.)

In the Falklands, the Harriers of Strike Command and the Royal Navy--as did the short-range, single purpose Spitfires and Hurricanes of Fighter Command at Dunkirk--achieved air superiority not universally, but when and where it mattered, as stated by the Argentine garrison commander, General Menendez.[1]

The Harrier again proved to be a most magnificent flying machine in the hands of skilled and highly trained pilots. Its versatility is unlimited--it bombed, strafed, performed reconnaissance missions, flew from cargo ships, carriers, and sod strips, and killed Argentine aircraft with gun and missile. Its unique maneuvering characteristics make it a nasty opponent in the air, and despite its relatively low cost, in earlier trials it reportedly achieved a kill ratio of one to one in practice air combat against the US Air Force's vaunted (and horribly expensive) frontline fighters, the F-15 and F-16. Against the F-5 it was no contest, the Harrier being so vastly superior. So one lesson is that an airplane does not have to cost thirty or a hundred million dollars to be a winner.

The scrapping by Britain of the Gannet early warning aircraft may have been premature; that system would have complemented the SAS early warning effort. That grievous and potentially fatal omission was inevitable when the carrier Ark Royal, Britain's last big deck for the Fleet Air Arm, was retired. As has been stated, had the Argentines been less anxious for their circus the British would have scrapped the Vulcan bombers and delivered the carrier Invincible to the Australians. The thought of all this should make any Briton shudder.

At any rate, it is virtually impossible to establish an air-tight screen around any target area around the clock, and American critics of the air operation overlook the fact that the United States cannot seal its own border against the likes of airborne drug traffickers flying slow, propeller-driven aircraft, and a few years ago a MiG fighter from Cuba actually landed at the big US

Air Force base at Homestead, Florida, before anyone had known that it was even in the area.

A word should be said about the failure of diplomacy and the peculiar habit that politicians have of "sending signals," since there seemed to be a lot of mixed signals in this affair. During America's Vietnam War the author and his colleagues, flying missions over North Vietnam, often discussed what seemed to many in the field to be a waste of time--the sending of "signals." Diplomats often take the most expensive and most painful way of sending a message to the enemy. Certain types of military operations--perhaps a particular target, hitherto off limits--are often supposed to mean something to the other side. These signals are so often ignored or misunderstood that one wonders why, if a side wants to deliver a message, the sender does not save equipment and lives by writing it in plain language and sending it by mail to the enemy. But diplomacy seems to thrive on coyness and cute signals, and disaster often follows when these signals are so sophisticated that they are confusing and misunderstood.

As Gerald Hopple has noted, General Galtieri has since stated that had he known that the United States would oppose the Argentine invasion and back Britain, he would not have authorized the action.[2] Thus it seems that had the US Ambassador told Galtieri that the United States would oppose the Argentine aggression, the war would have been avoided. There was time to do this before the Argentine troops landed in the Falklands. Here some wires were crossed or signals lost.

The British, once more, experienced (one cannot, after so many examples of shortsightedness, say they have learned it) the unpleasant truth that all the praiseworthy social welfare programs in the world cannot provide for the security of the state. Securing the state and its interests is the fundamental responsibility of government.

Whatever the merits of the Falklands victory, no self-respecting professional military officer should confess to having learned anything from it. To admit that one discovered that superb fitness, high morale, superior fieldcraft, capable and courageous political and military leadership, a sound logistics system, intelligence, a sensible control of the news media, air and naval support, a sound strategy, skilled improvisation, and an intelligent use of technology (as opposed to a reliance on it) were necessary for victory is to admit that one is in the wrong business.

But while these neat, clean, traditional conflicts are the exercises of today and while they are relatively simple to plan and to fight, American generals will not fight such conflicts in their lifetimes. These are the big wars of yesterday. The wars of today are messier, and require a great deal of study, to say nothing of greater expertise and knowledge.

For the US officer corps, one lesson is that, as with American education, a return to basics should be accelerated. American officers spend hundreds of thousands of hours annually in studying for esoteric advanced academic degrees of questionable quality and usefulness in fields such as Management, Administration, Business, Counselling, Psychology, and the like. Hundreds of officers go off to study at such places as The Harvard Business School, Oxford, Princeton, and scores of other such institutions, studying just about everything except how to win a war, or how Mao, Giap and Timoshenko won theirs. Military sociologists have in the past bemoaned the fact that the emphasis on the serious study of war has all but vanished in the services.

A return to the study of the great captains, their campaigns, and the disastrous strategies and philosophies of the past, coupled with a renewed and desperately needed emphasis on integrity and team play, will go some distance to restoring what many have seen as the fading reputation of the American officer corps.

Many doubt that the Pentagon's inter-service squabbling which seems to accompany virtually every joint endeavor would have been resolved in the time that it took to get the British task force to sea. As others have noted, this lesson means that the present Joint Chiefs of Staff system should be restructured to allow the senior general or admiral to get the Chiefs all pulling in the same direction, as was done in the British Defence Staff.

Life is an unending succession of mixed blessings. The birth of a child brings happiness coupled with awesome responsibility; an inheritance is accompanied by a tax. And so it is with the reliance on computers and technology. To many, the microchip now becomes the deciding factor in war.

As Ibn Saud said of Lawrence of Arabia, technology is a double-edged sword. The reliance on technology brings the edge of triumph or disaster much closer. Victory can be swifter and cleaner, but as Norman Friedman noted, command and control systems can be countered and overloaded to invite equally swift disaster. An over-reliance on technology can invite disaster. In late 1972 when "The Computer" at Headquarters, 7th Air Force, Saigon, broke down for a few days, the air war over North Vietnam came to a halt. So dependent was the Air Force on its big computer that--in answer to the author's question at the time--the human brain and verbally transmitted orders to strike were deemed inadequate. The loss of the computer had paralyzed the headquarters. That is the problem with any infatuation--the heartbreak is so much the greater.

The Falklands, then, sustained the eternal supremacy of the human factor in war and reemphasized--if it needed reemphasizing-- the universality, and immortality, of both Clausewitz and Sun Tzu; it was the latter who observed that a long war was to no one's advantage.

If none of the preceding describes the fundamental lessons learned from the Falklands campaign, what then was the lesson learned? The answer is this: the winning side had itself learned a lesson.

By way of illustration, let us examine two cases, one involving a lesson learned, and one a lesson unlearned.

In the first case a military officer turned head of government of a developing nation seized the property of Power "A." The offended power assembled a task force and sailed to the area of dispute, but political timidity and vacillation produced a hesitant, half-hearted military campaign, and although A's military forces were undefeated by the enemy, humiliation and political defeat were the results.

A quarter of a century later, a military leader turned head of government of another developing nation again seized territory belonging to Power A. This time, with lightning speed, A assembled a task force, mounted a more difficult campaign with more slender resources, attacked superior numbers of defending troops, and achieved a smashing success.

A lesson had been learned.

For the reverse situation, let us follow Power "B." B mounted a costly expedition against a vastly weaker opponent, and despite having almost incomprehensible advantages in military and economic power, failed completely in all its military and political objectives, suffered humiliation and political defeat, and was forced to withdraw although its military forces were technically undefeated by the enemy. Political timidity, overlapping authority, and faulty strategy were the epitaph of that effort.

A decade later, an authoritarian head of state in another developing nation gravely offended Power B. B mounted another, if smaller, expedition to redress the grievance; land, sea, and air forces were again jointly employed. Once again, political timidity, overlapping authority, and faulty strategy were the epitaph of this humiliating failure.

A lesson had not been learned.

The first case, of course, involved Colonel Nasser's seizure of the Suez Canal in 1956 from Britain and France. The United States was not consulted by the offended powers, and the Anglo-French task force (under British command) assembled to retake the canal and bring down Nasser was crippled by indecision and doubt in the Cabinet in London. This hesitation was brought on in part by draconian American threats to weaken and perhaps destroy the monetary systems of Britain and France, threats which were reinforced by Soviet warnings. This half-hearted assault resulted in a stalemate. A humiliating withdrawal followed, and the Prime Minister fell from power.

Twenty-six years later, upon General Galtieri's seizure of the Falklands, the British took care to consult the United States before resorting to military force to retake the islands. Once the decision had been made in London to exercise the military option, corrosive bureaucratic and interservice rivalries were submerged, a supreme task force commander was appointed and endowed with authority, and the rest is history. The government at home was strengthened.

In the second case, rivers of words have flowed on what is now being called the "American way of war" in Vietnam. Political interference and timidity at the top, spotty quality and shallow training of the military officers, corrosive bureaucratic rivalries, overlapping authorities, faulty strategy, and more, brought on the humiliating American withdrawal from Vietnam and the mainland of Asia and the earlier collapse of an administration at home.

Within a decade the United States launched another expedition, this time to rescue its citizens held captive by the medieval despot, Khomeini. Political timidity, overlapping responsibility, bureaucratic rivalry, and faulty strategy were again influential in the humiliating American failure. A lesson had not been learned. When all is said and done, the lesson of the Falklands is that lessons from history must be learned--not briefed, heard, read or debated, nor optimized, bulletized, sanitized, or summarized--but learned. As Santayana wrote--and has been quoted to the point of exhaustion (yet in vain, it seems), bad history repeats itself when lessons are not learned.

NOTES

1. The Times (London), 28 March 1983.

2. Ibid. Also, The Washington Post (13 April 1983): A27.

Appendix: A Diary of the Falklands Conflict

Lawrence S. Germain

Approximately thirty Argentinian scrap-metal workers were landed at Leith Harbour on the north side of South Georgia Island from the Argentine Navy transport <u>Bahia Buen Suceso</u>. South Georgia Island is about 800 miles ESE of the Falkland Islands and at about the same latitude as Cape Horn. The island is about 105 miles long and eighteen miles across at the widest point with the long axis running ESE-WNW. Administratively, South Georgia is not a part of the Falkland Islands, but is a direct dependency of the United Kingdom.

The <u>Bahia Buen Suceso</u> is an unarmed transport of 3,100 tons standard displacement built by Canadian Vickers in Halifax in 1950. It has a standard complement of 100.

The scrap-metal workers were in the employ of Constantino Sergio Davidoff, who had a contract with the Christian Salvesen shipping firm of Edinburgh to remove the scrap metal left from four abandoned whaling stations. For a consideration of $200,000, Davidoff had the right to remove about 35,000 tons of scrap metal.

Thirty-five scientists of the British Antarctic Survey were also present on South Georgia at Grytviken, about twenty miles east of Leith Harbour. By sheer coincidence, four of the scientists discovered the presence of the scrap-metal workers and that they had raised the Argentine flag. The Argentines were told they did not have proper prior authority for the landing. The head of the British Antarctic Survey team reported the incident to Rex Hunt, the Governor of the Falkland Islands and a former Spitfire pilot.

March 20

The <u>Bahia Buen Suceso</u> departed South Georgia, leaving some of the scrap-metal workers at Leith Harbour.

The HMS <u>Endurance</u> was dispatched from Port Stanley with twenty-two Royal Marines aboard under the command of Lt. Keith Mills with instructions to arrange for the departure of the Argentines. The HMS <u>Endurance</u> was an ice patrol ship rather than a warship. It carried two Wasp helicopters and had two 20-mm guns.

The 3,600-ton ship had a complement of 119, including a detachment of thirteen Royal Marines, and had twelve spare berths for scientists. As a result of the 1981 Defence Review, HMS Endurance was slated to be scrapped.

March 22

Jeane Kirkpatrick, the US Ambassador to the UN, lunched with the Argentine Ambassador to the US in Washington. She was told that the Argentines viewed the Malvinas seriously and would not hesitate to take steps to retrieve them.

The British Foreign Office protested to the Argentine government that the Davidoff workers had illegally landed.

March 23

The HMS Endurance, only four hours out of Leith Harbour, was ordered by London to put into Grytviken and await further orders.

March 26

Over 100 Argentine troops under the command of Captain Alfredo Astiz were landed at Leith Harbour from the Bahia Paraiso, a 9,600-ton polar transport ship that carries two helicopters and a complement of 124 ship's company and eighty-two passengers. The landing was witnessed by three Frenchmen who had taken refuge in Leith Harbour because of severe storm damage to their forty-foot yacht. The landing was also witnessed by Lt. Mills, who covertly observed Leith Harbour. Consequently, London was informed almost immediately of this military invasion of British territory.

The Argentine frigates Drummond and Granville set sail from Puerto Belgrano. These two, along with the Guerrico, were the three French Type A 69 frigates in the Argentine Navy. Originally intended for South Africa, they were all built in France and commissioned between 1978 and 1981. The ships had a standard displacement of 950 tons and carried a company of ninety-three men. Several other ships of the Argentine Navy may have sailed at the same time.

March 27

The Bahia Paraiso sailed from Leith Harbour, leaving the Argentine troops ashore. The HMS Endurance was ordered to patrol the coast and assure that the Bahia Paraiso did not return to Leith Harbour. The Endurance discovered that the Bahia Paraiso had only gone the three-mile limit and was sailing parallel to the coast. Orders from London were to do nothing.

March 28

The British scientific survey vessel John Briscoe was en route from Montevideo, Uruguay, to Port Stanley with forty-three Royal Marines aboard, a relief detachment for the Falklands garrison that was about to complete its twelve months duty.

March 29

Five ships of the Argentine Navy were at sea ostensibly for naval exercises with Uruguay. An Argentine submarine was reported to be on its way to the Falklands.

Forty-three Royal Marines from the John Briscoe were landed at Port Stanley, reinforcing the remaining twenty-five of the resident detachment.

Foreign Secretary Lord Carrington indicated that the British government was reserving its military options should a diplomatic solution not be forthcoming. The Argentine Foreign Minister, Nicanor Costa Mendez, was reported to have said that his country-men in South Georgia were on national territory and could look to Argentina for protection. Costa Mendez also met with US Ambassador Harry Schlaudemann, answering the US offer to mediate the South Georgia issue to the effect that if the US wanted to help, they should not deal with the issue of South Georgia but of the Malvinas as a whole.

Admiral Sir John Fieldhouse ordered the nuclear submarine HMS Spartan to embark stores and weapons at Gilbraltar and deploy to the South Atlantic.

March 30

More ships of the Argentine Navy, including its only aircraft carrier the Veinticinco de Mayo (the former HMS Venerable) and two destroyers, put to sea. An Argentine C-130 Hercules aircraft overflew the Falklands. HMS Endurance was ordered to sail for the Falklands, leaving the Royal Marine detachment on South Georgia Island. Reports, which subsequently proved false, stated that submarine HMS Superb was headed for the South Atlantic. However, the nuclear submarine Splendid was ordered to deploy from Faslane to the South Atlantic.

March 31

Britain requested direct mediation by the US and proposed to Argentina that a special British emissary be sent to Buenos Aires.

Foreign Minister Lord Carrington departed for Israel.

An Argentine submarine was in the vicinity of the Falklands.

President Reagan telephoned Argentine President Leopoldo For-tunato Galtieri with inconclusive results. Argentine Foreign Minister Costa Mendez said that the diplomatic channel as a means of solving the dispute was closed. Britain requested an immediate meeting of the United Nations Security Council to discuss the Falklands crisis. After debate, the Security Council issued an appeal to Britain and Argentina to refrain from the use of or threat of force and to seek a diplomatic solution.

Seven Hercules transport planes left their base at Lyneham, Wiltshire, for Gibraltar. Some unloaded supplies for the naval ships including the frigates HMS Broadsword and HMS Yarmouth, then in Gibraltar. The other planes proceeded to Ascension Island. Instructions were given to secretly prepare a task force for South Atlantic operations.

April 1

The nuclear-powered hunter-killer submarine HMS Spartan departed Gibraltar. It is said that the Fort Austin, conveying SAS and SBS forces, departed for the South Atlantic.

April 2

About 120 Argentine commandos of the Buza Tactica were landed by helicopter at Mullett Creek about five miles southwest of Port Stanley before light. They had two objectives: the Marine Barracks at Moody Brook (about two miles west of Port Stanley) and the Government House in Port Stanley. One group arrived at the Marine Barracks at 6 a.m. (about first light) and found them deserted. Nonetheless they mounted a "house clearance," systematically kicking down every door, throwing in a grenade, and following that with a burst of gunfire. At about the same time, the second group found Government House defended by thirty-three Royal Marines and placed the building under attack. Sixteen Royal Marines who had been at various locations combined and attempted to relieve Government House but without success.

If the Argentine plan had been to capture both the Moody Brook Barracks and Government House with the commandos, that plan had been thwarted. Reinforcements were put ashore at a location about two miles northeast of Port Stanley and just north of the airstrip from the only tank landing ship (LST) in the Argentine Navy, the Cabo San Antonio. This Argentine-built ship was commissioned in 1978, had a displacement of 8,000 tons, and carried a complement of 124. Also present at Port Stanley but standing outside of York Bay were the frigates Drummond and Granville (over from South Georgia), the destroyers Santisima Trinidad and Hercules (British Type 42 ships), and the Antarctic support ship Almirante Irizar. This Finnish-built ship was commissioned in 1978, had a displacement of 11,811 tons, and carried a ship's company of 133 plus 100 passengers. It had been fitted to carry helicopters and landing craft and may have served as a troop ship. About 600 Argentine marines, 280 Army and Air Force personnel, and eighteen armored personnel carriers were finally landed. The British destroyed one armored personnel carrier with a round from a Swedish-built 84-mm Carl Gustav shoulder-fired antitank weapon.

Governor Rex Hunt was soon obliged to surrender to Admiral Carlos Busser, deputy commander of the invasion force. There were no casualties on the British side. Casualties on the Argentine side as reported by the British were five killed (two confirmed, including a captain in the commandos) and seventeen wounded (two confirmed). The British had fired 6,462 rounds of ammunition. Major General Mario Benjamin Menendez, the commander of the invasion force, was named Governor of Islas Malvinas. Port Stanley was renamed Puerto Argentina. Within minutes of the capture of the airfield, the Argentines brought reinforcements in by air, using seven Lockheed C-130 Hercules transports and ten Fokker F-27 aircraft. Thus Operation Rosario was successfully completed by the Argentines.

The Soviet Union launched the Cosmos 1347 reconnaissance spacecraft into a 364- x 181-kilometer orbit inclined at 70.4 degrees. It was thought to have the capability of returning film to earth at intervals during its mission as well as at the end of the mission. At its high inclination it could cover the South Atlantic.

The British logistic landing ship Sir Geraint was reported to have left Plymouth with a cargo of heavy equipment. Sea Harrier aircraft of the No. 800 Naval Air Squadron started to land aboard the HMS Hermes at Portsmouth. Sea King helicopters embarked on the HMS Invincible, also at Plymouth.

Argentine Ambassador to the US, Esteban Takacs, gave a banquet for the US Ambassador to the UN, Jeane Kirkpatrick. Also present were Walter Stoessel, Deputy Secretary of State, and Thomas O. Enders, Assistant Secretary of State for Inter-American Affairs.

April 3

The Argentine frigate Guerrico and the Bahia Paraiso arrived at Grytviken. Argentine Marines were sent ashore in two Alouette helicopters. The Royal Marines directed their fire at a Puma helicopter, which was severely damaged and withdrew. The Guerrico had come into the harbor and the Royal Marines opened fire on it. Three rounds from the Carl Gustav hit home: one expoded against the ship's side, one struck the Exocet launcher, and a third hit the gun turret. According to an Argentine count, the Guerrico was hit with 1,275 rounds of ammunition and beat a hasty retreat. Once out of range of the British weapons, the Guerrico shelled the British position with its 100-mm gun. The British were forced to surrender. Captain Astiz reported the Argentine casualties as four killed and one wounded. One Royal Marine was wounded.

Mrs. Thatcher told the House of Commons that the Falklands remained British territory and the government's objective was to see that the islands were returned to British administration at the earliest possible moment. She also announced that a large Royal Navy task force would sail for the South Atlantic as soon as preparations were complete. The task force would include the HMS Invincible, which would leave port on April 5th.

The unit charged with the recapture of the islands was to be 3 Commando Brigade, composed of three battalions of the Royal Marines and two battalions from the Parachute Regiment. The commando battalions were widely scattered. Forty Commando was at a rifle range near Liverpool, 42 Commando had just returned from participating in Arctic warfare training in the Alloy Express exercise in northern Norway, and 45 Commando was in Scotland, having just returned from service in Northern Ireland.

The UN Security Council adopted Resolution 502 (by a vote of ten to one with four abstentions) that demanded an immediate cessation of hostilities, the withdrawal of all Argentine forces from the islands, and a diplomatic solution to the crisis. It was adopted under Chapter 7 of the UN Charter, which made its terms mandatory and allowed Britain to take measures of self-defense in response to armed attack. Voting for Resolution 502 were Britain,

US, France, Uganda, Jordan, Guyana, Zaire, Togo, Japan, and Ireland. China, the Soviet Union, Spain, and Poland abstained. Only Panama voted no.

President Galtieri gave a speech in which he promised that not one meter would ever be given back to the invaders. Foreign Minister Costa Mendez, feeling that this foreclosed all diplomatic channels, offered to resign. Galtieri told him not to worry.

April 4

Sea Harrier aircraft from No. 801 Naval Air Squadron and No. 899 Naval Air Squadron went aboard the HMS Invincible; 801 Squadron had also been a participant in the Alloy Express exercise. The submarine HMS Conqueror sailed for the South Atlantic.

April 5

The HMS Invincible and the HMS Hermes put to sea from Portsmouth, followed by the support tanker Pearleaf. The Hermes carried twelve Sea Harriers and fifteen helicopters. The first of many merchant ship requisitions were announced. The P&O cruise liner Canberra was to serve as a troop and hospital ship. The P&O ferry Elk and several BP tankers were requisitioned. Rear Admiral John F. Woodward was appointed to command the task force. Governor Rex Hunt arrived in Britain and conferred with leaders of the task force. Foreign and Commonwealth Secretary Lord Carrington resigned and was replaced by Francis Pym.

April 6

The amphibious assault ship HMS Fearless sailed from Portsmouth. The Fearless had also participated in the Alloy Express exercise. The logistic landing ship Sir Galahad sailed from Plymouth carrying Royal Marines, their vehicles, and Gazelle helicopters on the flight deck. Three sea-going tugs were requisitioned from United Towing Co. Two Shorts Belfast aircraft were chartered from the cargo airline TAC Heavylift. The Elk arrived in Southhampton and loaded troops along with their Scorpion and Scimitar vehicles.

Argentina formed a South Atlantic command headquarters at Puerto Belgrano.

April 7

Britain declared a maritime exclusion zone of 200 nautical mile radius centered on a point near the middle of the Falkland Islands, to go into effect at 0400 hours GMT on April 12th. Presumably, one or more British submarines would be in the Falklands area by that time to enforce the declaration.

The P&O liner Canberra arrived in Southhampton for conversion that included the addition of two helicopter landing platforms. The 3 Battalion of the Parachute Regiment and Royal Marines embarked on the Canberra.

Nine technicians from Dessault-Breguet, who were at Bahia Blanca military base to check the airworthiness of the five Super Etendard aircraft that had been delivered to Argentina, were instructed to stop giving technical aid but were allowed to remain in Argentina. The departure from France of a team from Aerospatiale that was to check the fitting of the Exocet missile to the Super Etendard aircraft was canceled.

April 8

Secretary of State Alexander Haig arrived in London for discussions with the British government on the Falklands crisis. With Haig were Thomas O. Enders, Assistant Secretary for Inter-American Affairs; David Gompert, Deputy Assistant Secretary for European Affairs; Robert Funseth, Director of Northern European Affairs; James Rentschler, a National Security Council staffer; Scott Gudgeon, Assistant Legal Advisor, Inter-American Affairs; Dean Fischer, Assistant Secretary for Public Affairs; and General Vernon Walters, Haig's Ambassador-At-Large. They met with Prime Minister Thatcher, Defence Minister John Nott, Foreign Secretary Francis Pym, Sir Antony Acland from the Foreign Office, and Chief of the Defence Staff Sir Terence Lewin. The British position was outlined for Haig's further shuttle diplomacy.

Major General Jeremy Moore discussed the recapture of South Georgia with Major Guy Sheridan, Commander of "M" Company, 42 Commando, and an experienced mountaineer.

The Soviet Union launched the Cosmos 1349 navigation satellite into a 1025- x 984-kilometer orbit inclined at 83 degrees.

April 9, Good Friday

Secretary of State Haig and his team arrived in Buenos Aires. After a preliminary session with Costa Mendez, Haig and Enders saw President Galtieri. Eventually the US team had over twelve hours of discussions with members of the junta. Admiral Anaya took a very hard line while Brigadier Lami Dozo seemed prepared to make concessions. Galtieri seemed to swing between the two positions. Costa Mendez also appeared to take a hard line.

The Canberra sailed with three battalions of troops.

The Elk, carrying arms, munitions, and light-armored vehicles, sailed for the Falklands.

April 10

The ten nations of the European Economic Community agreed to ban all imports from Argentina, thus cutting off about twenty percent of Argentina's export business. Belgium, Denmark, Greece, Luxembourg, and Ireland had agreed the day before. Italy was the last to fall into line. (Italy's ties to Argentina are very close since one-third of the Argentine population is of Italian descent and there are over two million Italian passport-holders in Argentina.)

The composition of the British task force was announced as follows:

Aircraft Carriers

Hermes	23,900 tons
Invincible	19,500 tons

Amphibious Assault Ship

Fearless	11,060 tons

County class Destroyer   5,400 tons

Antrim
Glamorgan

Type 42 Sheffield class Destroyers   3,500 tons

Sheffield
Glasgow
Coventry

Type 22 Broadsword class Destroyers   3,500 tons

Broadsword
Brilliant

Type 21 Amazon class Frigates   2,750 tons

Antelope
Arrow
Alacrity

Type 12 Rothesay class Frigates   2,280 tons

Yarmouth
Plymouth

Fleet Oil Tankers

Bayleaf	40,200 tons
Pearleaf	25,790 tons
Olmeda	36,000 tons
Tidespring	27,400 tons

Supply Ships

Fort Austin	23,600 tons
Resource	22,890 tons
Stormness	16,792 tons

Logistic Landing Ships	3,250 tons

Sir Galahad
Sir Geraint
Sir Bedivere
Sir Percivale
Sir Tristram

Requisitioned Merchant Ships

Canberra	44,807 tons
Elk	5,463 tons

Requisitioned Sea-Going Tugs

Salvageman	1,598 tons
Irishman	686 tons
Yorkshireman	686 tons

April 11, Easter Sunday

Secretary of State Haig and his party left Buenos Aires for London.

April 12

Haig and his party were in London for talks with the British government and left for Washington in the evening rather than return to Buenos Aires.

The 200-nautical mile maritime exclusion zone went into effect around the Falklands.

The Austrian firm Steyr-Daimler-Puch canceled the projected sale of twenty-seven additional Kurassier light tanks to Argentina. Argentina had already purchased fifty-six Kurassiers.

April 13

Four large trawlers and a North Sea oil rig maintenance ship were requisitioned. The trawlers (Junella, Cordella, Northella and Farnella) were owned by J. Marr Ltd., of Hull, and were to be converted for minesweeping operations at Rosyth. The maintenance ship, the 6,061-ton Stena Seaspread, owned by Stena UK, was already fitted with workshops and a helicopter platform. The P&O cruise liner Uganda landed 1,260 passengers at Naples and proceeded to Gibraltar for refitting to a hospital ship.

Four Vulcan bombers and five flight crews were detached from their regular duties with Strike Command and put at the disposal of the task force.

Three British journalists were accused of espionage, arrested in Rio Grande, and spent the war in the world's most southerly jail in the city of Ushuaia on the Beagle Channel. Although they were set free, it was not clear that the charges had been dropped.

April 14

The Cunard container ship Atlantic Conveyor (14,946 tons) was requisitioned to be adapted for sealift of Harrier aircraft. The HMS Intrepid, sister ship of HMS Fearless and the only other amphibious assault ship in the Royal Navy, was put back into commission.

April 15

Written orders were delivered to Major Sheridan and Brian Young, Captain of HMS Antrim, to begin detailed planning for the recapture of South Georgia. Their task force was to consist of HMS Antrim, HMS Endurance, and the tanker Tidespring.
The first Ascension conference was held aboard HMS Fearless to plan Operation Corporate, the retaking of the Falklands Islands.

April 16

Units of the Argentine Navy sailed from Puerto Belgrano; these included the aircraft carrier Veinticinco de Mayo, the cruiser General Belgrano, two destroyers, and "several" (probably three) submarines.
The vanguard of the Royal Navy Task Force began to pass Ascension Island.
The Soviet Union launched the Cosmos 1350 reconnaissance platform into a 380- x 185-kilometer orbit inclined at 67.2 degrees. It was later maneuvered down to a 292- x 163-kilometer orbit, presumably for better resolution.

April 17

The two British aircraft carriers were at Ascension Island. The liner Canberra was some distance behind, having made a fifteen-hour stop at Freetown, Sierra Leone, for fuel and supplies. On the way to Ascension Island, the Invincible developed engine problems and was delayed for twelve hours. A new starboard gear-box coupling was installed after the thirty-five ton unit was flown out to the ship by a Chinook helicopter.
Admiral Sir John Fieldhouse, Commander-in-Chief of the Fleet, flew to Ascension Island to confer with leaders of the task force. Major Ewen Southby-Tailyour, who as Falklands detachment commander in 1978 had mapped every major bay on the islands, was the first to suggest San Carlos Bay as a possible landing site.

April 18

Admiral Woodward ordered the main task force to sail south from Ascension Island. HMS Fearless and the planners stayed behind as did the Canberra and the troops.

April 19

The Argentine Super Etendard aircraft departed Bahia Blanca for a base further south, presumably the Air Base at Rio Gallegos, which is 475 miles from Port Stanley.
Secretary of State Haig left Buenos Aires, having cabled the details of the latest Argentine negotiating position to London. During a stop in Caracas, he received a message from Foreign Minister Francis Pym suggesting that the Haig party not fly to London. Haig returned to Washington instead.

April 20

One thousand more soldiers, including 2 Battalion of the Parachute Regiment, set sail in the Norland from Hull and on the Europic from Southhampton. Mrs. Thatcher said in the House of Commons that the latest Argentine proposals fell short of the government's objectives, but that the negotiating process was to be continued.
The British announced that the Merchant Navy support of the task force had reached thirty-five ships; sixteen requisitioned and nineteen chartered as follows:

Requisitions

Cruise ships
Canberra   44,807 tons P&O
Uganda   16,907 tons P&O

Cargo ships

Elk   5,463 tons P&O
Stena Seaspread   6,061 tons Sterna UK
Norland   12,988 tons P&O
Europic   4,190 tons Townsend Thoresen
Atlantic Conveyor   14,946 tons Cunard
Finnanger   21,267 tons Norwegian

Trawlers

Junella   1,615 tons J. Marr Ltd
Cordella   1,238 tons J. Marr Ltd
Northella   1,238 tons J. Marr Ltd
Farnella   1,207 tons J. Marr Ltd
Pict   1,478 tons Br. United Trawlers

Tugs

Salvageman	1,598 tons	United Towing Co.
Irishman	686 tons	United Towing Co.
Yorkshireman	686 tons	United Towing Co.

Charters

Esk	15,642 tons	BP
Tamar	15,642 tons	BP
Tay	15,560 tons	BP
Test	16,653 tons	BP
Trent	15,650 tons	BP
Dart	15,650 tons	BP
Fawley	11,604 tons	Esso
Wye	15,649 tons	BP
Avon	15,540 tons	BP
G.A. Walker	18,744 tons	Canadian Pacific
Eburna	19,763 tons	Shell
Ivy	13,211 tons	BP
Fern	13,252 tons	BP
Cortina	6,499 tons	Swedish
Luminetta	14,925 tons	Cunard
Orionman	3,623 tons	(Tanker)
Fort Toronto	19,982 tons	Canadian Pacific
Corona	4,899 tons	Swedish
Anco Charger	15,974 tons	Ocean Tpt. & Trading

April 21

The first contact between British and Argentine forces occurred when an Argentine Boeing 707 on a surveillance mission penetrated to within twelve miles of the task force before retreating. It was challenged by Harriers from the Hermes.

The RAF Harrier aircraft slated to go aboard the Atlantic Conveyor were being equipped with Sidewinder missiles in a crash retrofit. Royal Air Force pilots were undergoing training for the ski-jump take-off procedures required for operations from the British aircraft carriers.

HMS Antrim and HMS Endurance arrived at South Georgia Island to reconnoiter the strength of the Argentine forces at Grytviken and Leith Harbour. The main landing force stood 200 miles offshore in the tanker Tidespring. Thirteen members of the British Antarctic survey team had avoided capture by the Argentinian forces and one of them was contacted. The scientist argued against the plan to land thirteen members of the Special Air Service on Fortuna Glacier west of Leith Harbour and about twenty miles from Grytviken. The plan proceeded anyway and the force under the command of Captain John Hamilton was landed from two Wessex 5 helicopters.

The Soviet Union launched Cosmos 1352 from Tyuratam into a 383-x 216-kilometer orbit, presumably for broader coverage. Cosmos 1352 may have returned a limited number of reentry vehicles that carried exposed film prior to the end of its mission.

April 22

The Special Air Service force on Fortuna Glacier suffered from frostbite and hypothermia and required evacuation. A Wessex 3 and two Wessex 5 helicopters were sent to remove them. In the process, both Wessex 5 helicopters crashed. In a second attempt, all seventeen men (thirteen Special Air Service and four helicopter crew members) were squeezed into the five-passenger Wessex 3 and returned to the HMS Antrim.

Foreign Secretary Francis Pym departed for Washington for further discussions.

April 23

Two squads from the Special Boat Squadron were returned to HMS Endurance. They had been set ashore nineteen miles southeast of Grytviken to cross Cumberland East Bay to Grytviken in inflatable Gemini boats. After ice floes punctured their boats, they too had to be rescued by helicopters.

Forces of the Special Air Service went ashore at Stromness Bay between Grytviken and Leith Harbour in five Gemini boats. Only two of the outboard motors would work. Halfway to shore, another motor broke down, leaving a convoy of two boats without power. One drifted to sea and was recovered after a seventeen-hour search. The second landed on the northeast point of Stromness Bay, the last possible landfall before being swept into the Atlantic.

A Sea King helicopter from HMS Hermes ditched in heavy seas with the loss of one crew member.

Foreign Secretary Francis Pym left Washington.

The Soviet Union launched the Cosmos 1353 Earth Resources film return spacecraft from Plesetsk into a 269- x 218-kilometer orbit inclined at 82.3 degrees.

April 25

At 6:30 a.m., a Wessex 3 helicopter from HMS Antrim found the Argentine submarine Santa Fe on the surface about five miles from and proceeding toward Grytviken and dropped depth charges. Later, Lynx helicopters from HMS Brilliant and Wasp helicopters from HMS Endurance renewed the attack. They fired AS12 missiles that apparently passed through the Santa Fe without exploding. The Santa Fe reached King Edward Harbour, near Grytviken, where it beached, listing and leaking oil. The 1,870-ton Santa Fe was commissioned the USS Catfish in 1945 and sold to Argentina in 1971. It carried a normal complement of eighty-three.

Major Sheridan thought that it was now necessary to attack South Georgia Island even though his main landing force was 200 miles away on the tanker Tidespring. He managed to assemble a force of seventy-five men, including Royal Marines, Special Air Service, and Special Boat Squadron forces. They landed at Hestesletten, separated from Grytviken by a 1,000-foot ridge. HMS Antrim and HMS Plymouth bombarded Grytviken with their 4.5-inch guns. Upon reaching the top of the ridge, the British forces found white flags flying. The Argentines had already surrendered. Foreign Minister Costa Mendez arrived in Washington.

April 26

Captain Astiz surrendered his Argentine forces at Leith Harbour. Of 137 prisoners taken, only Captain Astiz was sent to Britain.

The 10,650-ton cruiser General Belgrano sailed from Argentina's southernmost port, Ushuaia.

HMS Intrepid, sister ship to HMS Fearless, sailed for the South Atlantic.

April 27

The British Foreign Office called in the Israeli ambassador to ask for clarification of reports of Israeli arms deliveries to Argentina since the Argentine seizure of the Falklands. In return, the Israeli Foreign Ministry summoned the British Ambassador, Patrick Moberley, to complain that such publicity encouraged unfounded rumors. However, they did not deny that arms had been delivered.

April 28

The British announced that a new blockade of all air and sea routes within the 200-nautical mile exclusion zone around the Falklands would go into effect on April 30th. The blockade would apply to all ships and aircraft, both military and civilian, within the zone without authority from the Ministry of Defence in London.

Four Vulcan bombers were flown to Ascension Island.

The Soviet Union launched the Cosmos 1354 navigation space-craft into a 829- x 759-kilometer orbit inclined at 74 degrees.

April 29

General Galtieri was told by the US of the moves against Argentina that would be announced on April 30th. He agreed to call a meeting of the junta at which he would argue that Argentina should accept UN Resolution 502 and withdraw its troops. He failed to move Admiral Anaya and the junta took no action.

The Soviet Union launched Cosmos 1355 from Tyuratam into a 402- x 128-kilometer orbit, which is a standard orbit for a Soviet ocean-surveillance system that can pinpoint ship locations. The inclination would carry it over the Falkland Islands where recorded data showing positions of the British and Argentine vessels could be played down to Soviet ground stations.

Major General Jeremy Moore flew to Ascension Island to confer with his commanders.

The British warned that all Argentine vessels shadowing the task force were subject to attack.

April 30

The British blockade went into effect. The United States announced its support of the British position and implemented military and economic sanctions against Argentina as well as offering military supplies to Britain.

May 1

In a pre-dawn attack, a single Avro Vulcan bomber dropped twenty-one 1,000-lb bombs on Port Stanley airfield after a nine-hour flight from Wideawake airfield on Ascension Island. The mission required inflight refueling on both the outbound and inbound legs from Handly Page Victor tanker aircraft. Ten Victors were required to support a single Vulcan in this mission because the Victors themselves required refueling in some cases. Limited parking space at Wideawake airfield restricted the British to sixteen Victors. Thus only one Vulcan could be supported at a time.

The Vulcan strike was followed by an attack by Sea Harriers concentrating on the ends of the runway. Sea Harriers also attacked the airstrip at Goose Green about fifty miles west of Port Stanley. Port Stanley airfield was bombarded by frigates of the task force, which in turn were attacked by Argentine aircraft, HMS Arrow being slightly damaged. Argentina admitted the loss of two Dagger fighters (an Israeli-built export version of the Mirage 5). An attack by Argentina using English Electric Canberra bombers resulted in one Canberra being shot down by a Sea Harrier and damage to a second. One bomb apparently cratered Port Stanley runway but did not deny use of the airfield to Argentine Hercules or Pucara aircraft, and the crater was quickly repaired.

Special Air Service and Special Boat Squadron units were put ashore on East and West Falkland Islands by helicopter to reconnoiter possible landing sites. A four-man SBS squad found that there were no Argentine forces in the San Carlos area.

Mr. Francis Pym arrived in Washington for discussions with Secretary Haig and Secretary Weinberger.

Argentine sources said that the submarine San Luis fired a torpedo at a British ship at a range of 1200 meters and escaped from the ensuing hunt by three frigates and two helicopters.

May 2

At 4 p.m., from a range of less than three miles the submarime HMS Conquerer, fired two Mark VIII torpedoes at the cruiser General Belgrano. One torpedo struck the General Belgrano on the port bow; a second hit the stern and the General Belgrano sank within forty minutes. There is a general agreement that the General Belgrano was about thirty-five miles outside the exclusion zone at the time. The British claimed that the General Belgrano and the two accompanying destroyers, Piedra Buena and Hipolito Bouchard, were proceeding toward the exclusion zone and were a threat to the task force; therefore the attack had been ordered by the War Cabinet. The Argentines claimed that the General Belgrano was fifty miles southwest of the exclusion zone and sailing west toward the Argentine mainland with special orders not to enter the zone. The two destroyers mounted an attack on the Conqueror, but the latter escaped. In all, 368 members of the crew of the General Belgrano perished, and some were not rescued for thirty hours after the attack.

The 4,400-ton Conqueror was one of three nuclear attack submarines of the Churchill class and was commissioned in 1971. The General Belgrano was commissioned in 1939 as the USS Phoenix, a Brooklyn class cruiser, and was a survivor of Pearl Harbor. In 1951, this 10,800-ton ship was sold to Argentina for $7.8 million. The two 2,200-ton destroyers (formerly USS Borie and USS Collett of the Allen M. Sumner class) were commissioned in 1944 and transferred to Argentina in 1972.

A Sea King helicopter was fired on by an Argentine patrol ship about ninety miles inside the exclusion zone. It in turn was attacked and destroyed by a Westland Lynx helicopter (from HMS Coventry) firing a salvo of two Sea Skua missiles. The ship, which may have been carrying mines, exploded in a flash visible twenty-five miles away. The ship was thought to be the 689-ton Comodoro Somellera, which was first commissioned the USS Salish in 1945 as an ocean salvage tug. It was acquired by Argentina in 1947 and upgraded to a patrol vessel in the same manner. Although damaged, the second ship--thought to be the Alferez Sobral, a sister ship to the Comodoro Somellera and the former USS Catawba-- reached port at Puerto Belgrano, but the Captain and seven crew members had been killed.

Britain's UN representative, Anthony Parsons, had dinner with Javier Perez de Cuellar, Secretary General of the UN, and Francis Pym, at which time Perez de Cuellar detailed his peace proposal.

May 3

It was announced that the Cunard liner Queen Elizabeth 2 was being requisitioned to take 5 Infantry Brigade to the South Atlantic. This would be a reconstituted unit because two of the battalions of 5 Brigade were already in the South Atlantic (2nd and 3rd Parachute Battalions). Two regular units of 5 Brigade, the 7th Duke of Edinburgh's Own Gurkha Rifles and the 4th Field Regiment, Royal Artillery, would be joined by 2 Battalion Scots Guards, and 1 Battalion, Welsh Guards. The reconstituted unit conducted a major training exercise, code named "Welsh Falcon," as a shakedown in late April. Other ship requisitions announced were the two 6,500-ton Townsend-Thoresen North Sea ferries, Baltic Ferry and Nordic Ferry, and the Cunard container ship Atlantic Causeway, a sister ship to the Atlantic Conveyor. The aircraft carrier HMS Bulwark, which had been waiting for a year to be scrapped, was to be put back into service as a barracks and landing platform for the Falklands garrison.

In the wake of the sinking of the General Belgrano, the Argentines rejected a promising peace proposal drawn up by President Fernando Belaunde Terry of Peru in consultation with Secretary of State Haig.

May 4

The Type 42 destroyer HMS Sheffield, while on radar picket duty southeast of the Falklands and about twenty miles in front of the rest of the fleet, was struck by a single Exocet (AM39) air-to-surface missile launched by an Argentine Navy Super Etendard aircraft from a range of about twenty-three nautical miles. Two Super Etendard aircraft approached the task force and fired two missiles at two separate targets. One target probably was HMS Hermes, which was beyond the missile's range. The Exocet struck the Sheffield about six feet above the waterline amidships and penetrated at an oblique angle to the main engine room and near fuel tanks, where it deflagrated. This instantly cut off most of the electric power, communications equipment, and all pressure to the fire hoses. Within twenty seconds the Sheffield was filled with black suffocating fumes from the PVC coating on the four miles of electrical wiring in the ship. The fire could not be controlled and the order to abandon ship was given about five hours after the attack. Twenty members of the 286-man Sheffield crew were killed and twenty-four injured. The report that the Super Etendard aircraft that had attacked the Sheffield had failed to return to base after running out of fuel was denied by the Argentines, who say that they lost no Super Etendard aircraft during air actions and that these planes returned after being refueled by Hercules aircraft. Reports that the Exocet did not detonate but that damage was caused by unconsumed propellant were denied by the French. Having fired two, the Argentines now had three Exocet missiles remaining.

A single RAF Vulcan again bombed the Port Stanley airfield with twenty-one 1000-lb bombs dropped from an altitude of about 15,000 feet--apparently without damage to the airstrip. Sea Harriers again attacked the Port Stanley airfield; one was shot down by ground fire with the pilot being killed. The term "ground fire" may have meant a Roland missile.

May 5

The task force leaders informed London that the task force could be kept operational for only another month.

The Soviet Union launched Cosmos 1356 into a 684- x 632-kilometer orbit inclined at 81.2 degrees. It was capable of monitoring radio transmissions and would cover the Falkland Islands area.

May 6

Two Sea Harriers disappeared while on patrol in bad weather. It is thought that they may have collided. Rescue operations failed to locate the pilots.

Anthony Parsons informed Perez de Cuellar that the Argentines must drop their demand to have their sovereignty over the Falklands recognized as a precondition to talks.

May 7

The British extended the military exclusion zone around the Falklands to twelve miles off the Argentine coast. Francis Pym, speaking in the House of Commons, stated, "It remains the government's highest priority to achieve an early negotiated settlement of the Falkland Islands dispute if that is humanly possible." A new squadron of Sea King helicopters was commissioned. Britain asked the US for KC-135 tanker aircraft.

The Peruvian government announced that it had decided not to proceed further with a peace plan for fear of prejudicing its relations with the Argentine junta.

May 8

Eight Sea Harriers and six RAF Harriers flew from the United Kingdom to Ascension Island in nine hours with in-flight refueling by RAF Victor tankers. From Ascension the fourteen aircraft were taken to the Falklands aboard the Atlantic Conveyor. In addition, six RAF Harriers were flown by aerial refueling directly from the UK to the Hermes.

May 9

British warships shelled Port Stanley from thirteen miles offshore. An Argentine Puma helicopter was shot down near Port Stanley. Sea Harriers intercepted and attacked the 1,400-ton fishing vessel Narwal, which was being used to gather intelligence (i.e., shadowing the task force). The ship was later secured by a Royal Naval boarding party and found to be seriously damaged.

The United Kingdom failed to secure a commitment from the other European Economic Community countries to renew economic sanctions against Argentina, which were due to expire on May 17th.

May 10

The Narwal foundered in bad weather. The Sheffield sank while under tow outside the military exclusion zone. Argentine C-130 Hercules aircraft, escorted by Mirage fighters, attempted to reach Port Stanley but were turned away by Sea Harriers. Royal Navy ships, standing off the east coast of the islands, again bombarded Port Stanley.

The British imposed a controlled airspace of 100-nautical-mile radius around the Wideawake Airfield on Ascension Island.

Argentine sources said that the submarine San Luis fired several torpedos at two large ships from a range of 5000 meters. One torpedo hit but did not explode.

May 11

British attempts to interdict supply routes between East and West Falkland across Falkland Sound resulted in the sinking of the 3,900-ton transport Islas de Los Estados by gunfire from the Type 21 frigate HMS Alacrity. The ship, carrying fuel and ammunition, exploded when hit by gunfire. An Argentine Puma helicopter was downed. Naval bombardments continued.

Enrique Ros of the Argentine Foreign Ministry told Perez de Cuellar that Argentina would drop its demand for sovereignty.

May 12

Thirty-five hundred troops of 3 Infantry Brigade sailed on the Queen Elizabeth 2. The Baltic Ferry, the Nordic Ferry, and the Atlantic Causeway sailed with the Queen Elizabeth 2. The new Sea King helicopter squadron was embarked on the Atlantic Causeway.

Four Argentine A-4 Skyhawk aircraft attacked two British ships. Two were shot down with Sea Wolf missiles, while a third crashed into the sea while taking evasive action. A second wave of A-4s attacked, striking the HMS Broadsword near the stern with an iron bomb that failed to explode. A third wave of A-4s broke off the attack.

HMS Glasgow was struck by a bomb which failed to explode. Elsewhere a Sea King helicopter was lost without loss of life. The eighty-ton coastal patrol boat Islas Malvinas was damaged by a Sea Harrier attack.

The decision was made, and orders were promulgated, that the landing would be at San Carlos.

The prisoners taken on South Georgia Island arrived at Ascension Island on the tanker Tidespring prior to flying to Montevideo, Uruguay, on a DC-10 chartered by the Red Cross (except for Captain Astiz).

May 13

Addressing the House of Commons, Defence Secretary John Nott said that the military options open to the government ran from a long blockade to the early repossession of the islands by force. He also stated that the government would not be stalled by Argentine procrastination at the UN. Mrs. Thatcher declared that the task force would not be withdrawn until the Argentines had withdrawn from the islands.

May 14

President Galtieri said that Argentina was willing to talk about, but would not give up, sovereignty of the islands.

May 15

Sir Anthony Parsons, the British Ambasssador to the UN, and the UK Ambassador to the US, Sir Nicholas Henderson, flew to London to discuss the peace efforts of Perez de Cuellar with the inner cabinet.

Twelve four-man teams of the Special Air Service carried out a raid on Pebble Island, which is north of West Falkland Island. They blew up an ammunition dump and eleven parked Argentine air-craft, and destroyed a radar installation that guided aircraft to attack the task force; aircraft destroyed were six Pucara twin turboprop counter-insurgency aircraft, several Skyvan light transports, and helicopters. All civilians on board the Canberra, including journalists, were told that they were now under military discipline.

May 16

Sea Harriers attacked two blockade-running ships in Falkland Sound. The Rio Carcarania was abandoned by its crew off Port King. The second vessel that was strafed rather than bombed because of its close proximity to the settlement of Fox Bay was the Navy transport Bahia Buen Suceso, which had taken the scrap-metal workers to South Georgia Island on March 18th. The Special Boat Squadron units were removed from San Carlos.

May 17

The members of the European Economic Community agreed to the renewal of the economic sanctions against Argentina for another seven days. However, Italy and Ireland decided to ignore the embargo.
Talks resumed at the UN. Sir Anthony Parsons, the British Ambassador to the UN, returned to New York with a draft interim agreement setting out the British position in full.

May 18

Perez de Cuellar called Parsons with the Argentine response. The Argentines had retreated from their earlier position. They refused not to prejudge the outcome of the negotiations on sovereignty over the islands, insisted that the agreement cover South Georgia and the South Sandwich Islands, and proposed that forces withdraw to their normal bases (400 nautical miles for the Argentines and 8000 nautical miles for the British).
The Atlantic Conveyor arrived with a cargo of Sea Harriers and RAF Harriers. The aircraft were transferred to the Hermes and the Invincible. A Sea King helicopter was ditched with technical problems. The four-man crew was recovered.

May 19

Radio del Sur, a new Ministry of Defence radio station on Ascension Island, made its first broadcast to the Argentine garrison on the Falklands. A Sea King helicopter was lost while ferrying troops between ships. Nine men were rescued but twenty-one were lost.

May 20

Mr. Muldoon, the Prime Minister of New Zealand, offered the United Kingdom the use of its Leander class frigate Canterbury to allow another British ship to join the task force. Another Sea King helicopter was lost in bad weather.

About 200 miles east of the Falklands, troops were transferred from the Canberra to the Fearless and the Intrepid; this
reduced the danger to the task force if one ship (say, the
Canberra) was sunk.

Several additional ships were said to have been added to the
Falkland Islands task force, as follows:

Warships

Amphibious Assault Ship	
Intrepid	11,060 tons
Type 82 class Light Cruiser	
Bristol	6,100 tons
Type 42 Sheffield class Destroyers	3,500 tons
Exeter	
Southampton	
Cardiff	
Type 21 Amazon class Frigates	2,750 tons
Active	
Avenger	
Type 22 Broadsword class Destroyer	3,500 tons
Battleaxe	
Leander class Frigates	
Minerva	3,200 tons
Penelope	3,200 tons
Andromeda	2,500 tons

Requisitioned and Chartered Ships

Liner		
Queen Elizabeth 2	Cunard	67,000 tons
Cargo Ships		
Atlantic Causeway	Cunard	14,946 tons
Baltic Ferry	Stena Cargo Line	6,455 tons
Geestport	Geest Line	7,730 tons
Lycanon	China Mutual United	
	Steam Navigation Co.	11,804 tons
Nordic Ferry	Stena Cargo Line	6,455 tons
Saxonia	Cunard	8,547 tons
Tankers		
Alvega	Silver Line	33,329 tons
Vinga Polaris	Vinga Tankers	8,000 tons
Cable Ship		
Iris	British Telecom	3,873 tons

```
            Supply Tug
            Wimpey Seahorse    Wimpey Marine         1,599 tons
```

May 21

A series of raids were launched on Port Louis, Goose Green, and Fox Bay. These raids were supported by Harrier strikes and naval bombardment to mask the concentration of forces off San Carlos. Although there had been no Argentine forces at San Carlos as recently as May 16th, a four-man patrol from HMS Brilliant discovered a group of Argentines on Fanning Head, which dominated the north entrance to San Carlos Water. The Special Boat Squadron was given the task of eliminating this Argentine force before the main landing. The Argentines were called upon to surrender and nine of them did so. The remainder of the Argentine force of thirty to forty elected to fight, resulting in twelve Argentine fatalities and the escape of some of the force.

The plan was for 40 Commando and 2 Battalion of the Parachute Regiment to land on either side of San Carlos, 45 Commando to land near Ajax Bay, and 3 Battalion of the Parachute Regiment to land at Port San Carlos. The pump filling the embarkation dock of the HMS Fearless broke down and, at considerable risk, the dock gate was opened to allow the sea to flood in, thus delaying the departure of 40 Commando. The men of 2 Parachute had great trouble climbing off the Norland, which had no dock at all, and then set off in the wrong direction until corrected. The 40 Commando liberated San Carlos and found thirty-one islanders, most of whom had fled Port Stanley. The 2 Paras took Sussex Mountain to protect the beachhead from the south; 45 Commando secured the unused refrigeration plant at Ajax Bay and 3 Parachute occupied Port San Carlos to find evidence that about 40 Argentine soldiers had just left. Thinking that all was clear, a Sea King helicopter lifting Rapier missiles, accompanied by a Gazelle helicopter, took off for Port San Carlos. They were fired upon by the retreating Argentines. The Sea King escaped but the Gazelle was downed, apparently with a Blowpipe missile, and the pilot killed. The same fate met a second Gazelle and both crewmen were killed.

The first air attacks were by Pucara aircraft from Port Stanley. Two were shot down but the frigate HMS Argonaut was damaged. Twenty-one minutes later came the first of the Skyhawks and Mirages that would fly seventy-two sorties against the task force that day. HMS Ardent was hit by two 1000-lb bombs on the aft deck, knocking out all major systems. Ten more bombs were dropped on the helpless Ardent and the order to abandon ship was given. While 178 members of the crew were rescued, twenty-two were missing and presumed dead, and thirty were injured. A Lynx helicopter was lost with the Ardent, which had not previously been listed as a member of the task force. HMS Argonaut was also badly damaged on the flight deck by two bombs, and the Antrim, Brilliant, and Broadsword were all hit by bombs that failed to explode. The Argonaut was immobilized and had to be towed into San Carlos water. The Canberra was not hit and the Argentines claimed that they were not trying to hit it. Sixteen fixed-wing

Argentine aircraft were shot down (nine Mirages, five Skyhawks, and two Pucaras) as well as four of their helicopters. A RAF Harrier was lost away from San Carlos Bay. The British succeeded in landing considerable heavy equipment: 105-mm guns of 29 Commando Brigade, Royal Artillery, armored fighting vehicles (Scimitar and Scorpion), and Rapier air-defence missiles.

A detachment of Sea King helicopters put ashore 520 troops and 912,000 pounds of stores.

President Reagan reaffirmed the US commitment to the UK but emphasized that US personnel would not be involved. Argentina accepted the outline of Peru's peace plan: to establish a cease-fire, withdraw troops, install a UN administration, and begin negotiations.

May 22

Argentine air attacks were limited to a pair of Skyhawks, which were quickly chased off by Harriers. The British took advantage of the lull to land equipment and supplies and establish batteries of Rapier anti-aircraft missiles. By the end of the day, 5,000 British troops were ashore and occupied an area of ten square miles. Under the cover of darkness, the Canberra was removed from Falkland Sound to South Georgia Island. Two Harriers attacked and severely damaged an Argentine patrol craft in Choiseul Sound, about thirty miles southwest of Port Stanley.

May 23

Argentine air attacks resumed. HMS Antelope, sister ship of HMS Ardent, was struck by two 1,000-lb bombs that lodged in the engine room unexploded, killing one crew member. The ship was sailed into San Carlos Water for repairs and to have the bombs defused. One of them exploded, resulting in one killed and seven injured. The ship, engulfed in an uncontrollable fire, was abandoned by the remaining 173 crew members. Five Mirage and one Skyhawk aircraft were shot down. In separate actions, Harriers destroyed one Puma helicopter and one UH-1 Iroquois helicopter and strafed a second Puma which had been forced to land. Harriers attacked the Goose Green landing strip. A Sea Harrier was lost on take-off and the pilot killed.

Emergency debate at the UN adjourned after three days without a resolution.

May 24

HMS Antelope sank. Argentine air attacks were renewed by twenty-four Mirages and Skyhawks. Sea Harrier pilot Commander Nigel "Sharkey" Ward claimed the first double-kill of the conflict, downing two Mirages with two Sidewinder missiles. In all, eight Argentine jet aircraft were claimed downed. The logistic landing ship, HMS Sir Galahad, took an unexploded bomb through the side and had to be evacuated. Her sister ship, HMS Sir Lancelot, was also hit. Since the start of the action at San Carlos, ten British ships had been sunk or hit by bombs that failed to explode. One report stated that overall only twenty percent of the Argentine bombs exploded. A Sea Harrier and pilot from HMS Hermes were lost.

Seven of the nine states of the European Economic Community agreed to continue economic sanctions against Argentina indefinitely. Italy and Ireland declined.

The usually cautious pro-government newspaper Nacion had a front-page report that the Argentine junta was considering a request for military assistance from the Soviet Union to replace losses.

May 25, Argentine national holiday

Argentine reconnaissance revealed that a very large ship was heading west toward Falkland Sound. They decided to attack with Exocet missiles. Between them and their target, which was ten miles north of Pebble Island, were HMS Coventry and HMS Broadsword guarding the entance of Falkland Sound. They were attacked by Skyhawks. The British hoped that the Coventry, a sister ship to the Sheffield, could be protected by the Sea Wolf missiles of the Broadsword. However, the Sea Wolf is a point defense system, and not effective at protecting targets other than itself. Furthermore, both the Broadsword and the Brilliant were hit during the conflict so Sea Wolf was not totally effective even at point defense. HMS Coventry was hit with three 1,000-lb bombs and capsized within twenty minutes. Nineteen men died. HMS Broadsword was hit but suffered no casualties and remained operational. Four Skyhawks were shot down.

With the picket ships neutralized, two Super Etendard aircraft took off from Rio Gallegos. Each fired one Exocet missile. The Atlantic Conveyor was hit and subsequently abandoned with the loss of twelve lives. Also lost were three Chinook helicopters, six Wessex-5 support helicopters, two Lynx helicopters, tents to accommodate 4,000 men, mobile landing strips for the Harriers, and a water-desalination plant. The Chinooks, each capable of carrying up to eighty troops, were to have played a crucial role in the land war.

Major General Richard Trant, calling from the UK, told Brigadier Julian Thompson to press ahead with the land war. The 3 Parachute moved out of San Carlos towards Douglas and Teal Inlet.

South Africa denied reports that they were supplying arms, including the Gabriel sea-skimming missile, and spare parts for Mirages to Argentina. President Qaddafi of Libya supported Argentina's "just cause against the barbaric British invasion."

The Soviet Union launched the film recovery earth resources spacecraft Cosmos 1369 into a 269- x 229-kilometer orbit inclined at 82.3 degrees.

May 27

A RAF Harrier was lost to enemy fire; the pilot was recovered.

May 28

Following pressure from London for some sign of ground action, troops of 2 Battalion, Parachute Regiment, under the command of Lt. Col. Herbert ("H") Jones, launched an attack at 2:30 a.m., in pouring rain, on the Argentine forces holding Goose Green. It is not clear why this was done as the main objective of the campaign was Port Stanley, and Goose Green might have been bypassed without hazard. Intelligence was faulty; therefore, the 450 British troops did not know that they were outnumbered by four to one until the end of the battle. For weapons, they carried fifty-six machine guns, double the normal number, "throwaway" 61-mm antitank rockets, and were supported with 105-mm artillery and Milan guided missiles. They had asked for light tanks but were told that they were required for "other priorities." HMS Antrim was offshore to the west in Brenton Loch for support but had some problems with the 4.5-in guns.

Goose Green and Darwin, about two miles to the north, are on a narrow north-south isthmus that is only 400 yards wide at its narrowest point. Entrenched Argentine troops held the high ground of Boca Hill on the west and Darwin Hill on the east. Three companies of 110 men each moved forward: one to attack each hill and one in the center. By dawn at 6 a.m., neither hill had been taken. Lieutenant Colonel Jones threw the HQ forces into an attack on Darwin Hill but the attack failed and Jones was killed. Major Cris Keeble then assumed command. He brought forward support artillery and moved troops up on Boca Hill, using the cover of an eighteen-inch lip above the beach. Boca Hill was hit from two sides and surrendered in a matter of minutes. The Milan missiles were very effective. At about the same time, Darwin Hill was secured. Major Kebble decided to bypass Darwin village and take the Goose Green airstrip and School House, a strong point between Darwin and Goose Green. This target was assigned to the reserve company. They were attacked by two Pucara aircraft that narrowly missed the troops with napalm. One of the aircraft was shot down with a Blowpipe missile. During the battle for School House three British soldiers were killed when they moved into the open in response to Argentine white flags. Whether this was a trap or the result of confusion will never be known because none of the Argentines defending School House survived.

With clearing conditions, three Harriers dropped anti-personnel cluster bombs on Argentine guns on a narrow split of land east of Goose Green and put them out of action. The Argentines had been holding 112 civilians captive in Goose Green for thirty days. Major Keeble decided, therefore, that negotiations were preferable to further attack. The first conversations effected the surrender of the 150-man Argentine Air Force contingent after the commander called General Menendez. Then the other forces surrendered. The British had lost eighteen killed and thirty-four wounded. Argentine losses were about 250 killed and 120 wounded. One British Scout helicopter and four Argentine Pucara aircraft were shot down.

In a reply to new approaches by the UN Secretary General, Mrs. Thatcher reaffirmed that any ceasefire must be unequivocally linked with a firm unconditional and immediate Argentine with-drawal.

Pope John Paul II arrived in Britain for a six-day visit.

The Soviet Union launched the imaging reconnaissance satellite Cosmos 1370 into a 290- x 203-kilometer orbit inclined at 62.8 degrees.

May 29

The liner Canberra returned to San Carlos Water with the troops of 5 Infantry Brigade (Scots Guards, Welsh Guards, and Gurkhas). They had been transferred from the Queen Elizabeth 2, which had ventured no closer to the action than Cumberland Sound, South Georgia Island. Also on board was Major General Jeremy J. Moore, commander of the land forces of the task force.

The 3 Battalion, Parachute Regiment, had completed a twenty-six mile march in full kit and in total darkness to Teal Inlet. The 45 Commando had left for Douglas. Elements of 42 Commando attempted a helicopter landing on Mount Kent (near Port Stanley) that nearly ended in disaster when the sole surviving Chinook helicopter inadvertently touched down in water in a storm and lost a wheel and a door before returning to Port San Carlos.

Major General Menendez sent a message to Buenos Aires warning that his forces would not win.

An Argentine Air Force Hercules aircraft attacked the BP tanker Wye north of South Georgia Island with eight 500-lb bombs. One bomb struck the deck but failed to explode; the Wye was then carrying 21,000 tons of fuel.

A flight of two Super Etendard and four A-4 Skyhawk aircraft attacked a target about ninety miles east of the Falklands. The target was struck by two 500-lb bombs and the last of the Argentine air-launched Exocet missiles. The Argentines reported that they had identified and hit the aircraft carrier Invincible. The British claimed that they hit the Atlantic Conveyor. Two A-4 aircraft were reported to have been shot down. The final tally for the AM30 Exocet missiles was five firings, two ships sunk (40%), and four hits on the primary target (80%). The Argentines, and more particularly the French, denied the British claim that the Exocet was fooled by chaff and that the Atlantic Conveyor was not the primary target during the attack of May 25th. Nonetheless, the British continued to insist that only one Exocet hit the primary target (Sheffield) and the Argentines continued to insist that they hit the Invincible.

A Sea Harrier was lost without loss of life.

May 30

The 45 Commando and 3 Parachute secured Douglas Settlement and Teal Inlet on the north side of East Falkland Island.

Elements of 42 Commando and units of the Special Air Service succeeded in landing on Mount Kent and Mount Challenger. Mount Kent, 1,504 feet high, is only ten miles from Port Stanley. British warships bombarded positions around Port Stanley. Major General Moore assumed command of all land operations. An RAF

Harrier was lost to enemy fire, but the pilot was recovered. There were reports that Argentina was seeking military assistance from abroad and Israel was thought to have responded.

June 1

President Galtieri sent two envoys to New York with a new Argentine peace proposal that went further toward a compromise, accepting temporary United Nations' trusteeship of the islands.

The Soviet Union launched an intelligence spacecraft, Cosmos 1371, into a 833- x 793-kilometer orbit inclined at 74.1 degrees.

5 Infantry Brigade came ashore at San Carlos.

June 2

A Sea Harrier was lost to enemy fire but the pilot was recovered.

June 4

Forces of "B" Company, 2 Battalion, Parachute Regiment, were landed by helicopter at the undefended settlements of Fitzroy and Bluff Cove, thirty-six miles from Goose Green. The story of Brigadier Tony Wilson, commander of 5 Brigade, calling Reg Binney, the farm manager at Fitzroy from a pay phone at Swan Inlet to ascertain the absence of Argentines was apparently not true, there being no pay phones at Swan Inlet or anywhere else on the Falklands. However, Major John Crossland, the company commander, did call from a private house.

Britain vetoed a United Nations Security Council motion calling for a ceasefire. Although the US joined Britain in the veto, instructions directing the US to abstain arrived five minutes later. US Ambassador Kirkpatrick made these new instructions known.

June 5

The problem now was to get 1,200 members of the Scots and Welsh Guards to the Fitzroy-Bluff Cove area. The Scots Guards were taken to Lively Island near the mouth of Choiseul Sound aboard HMS Intrepid. They could not go further for fear of attack by land-based Exocet missiles that had been deployed at Port Stanley. From there they proceeded to Bluff Cove in landing craft. Due to the atrocious weather, it took five hours to reach Bluff Cove; the trip was further lengthened by a challenge from HMS Cardiff, which must not have known of their presence.

Five Harriers (two Sea Harriers and three RAF Harriers) landed at the forward operating base at San Carlos.

June 6

The Captain of HMS Fearless, Jeremy Larken, agreed to take his ship beyond Lively Island to Direction Island to rendezvous with the landing craft then at Bluff Cove. The Welsh Guards were embarked on the Fearless but the weather was still so bad that the landing craft could not get out of Bluff Cove. The two landing craft on the Fearless were filled with troops and sent ashore. The remaining troops returned with the Fearless to San Carlos water.

The landing of 5 Brigade had been completed. The British now had about 8,000 troops ashore.

At ten each morning Captain Roderick Bell commenced daily broadcasts to the Argentine garrison at Port Stanley.

A British Gazelle helicopter was lost to enemy fire.

June 7

It was decided not to risk HMS Fearless again and the remaining guardsmen were embarked on the landing ship HMS Sir Galahad, which would go all the way to Bluff Cove. Most of the spare cabins on the Sir Galahad had been wrecked by an unexploded bomb on the morning of the San Carlos landings. The Sir Galahad would have no escort and therefore no protection. (Logistic landing ships normally carry no guns though they are fitted for two 40-mm guns.)

June 8

Morning found the Sir Galahad heading up Port Pleasant, a finger of water leading to Fitzroy and not Bluff Cove. The passage to Bluff Cove was too shallow for the Sir Galahad. At Fitzroy, the Sir Galahad joined her sister ship HMS Sir Tristram that had earlier brought supplies and equipment. The unloading of the two ships took much longer than expected because the beach at Fitzroy settlement is very narrow. In addition, the Welsh Guards were not anxious to disembark since getting to Bluff Cove involved a twelve-mile march that might be avoided if they waited for the landing craft to come for them. Although Fitzroy and Bluff Cove are only four miles apart, the bridge across the inlet that separated them had been blown up by the Argentines. At 2:10 p.m., the Sir Galahad and Sir Tristram were attacked by two Skyhawks and two Mirages. The ships were within range of the Argentine radar atop Sapper Hill near Port Stanley. The British suffered fifty-one killed and forty-six injured. The attacks occurred before the Rapier surface-to-air missile defenses were fully established. In fact, it is said that helicopters were in the process of ferrying Rapier equipment ashore at the time of the attack.

The frigate HMS Plymouth was attacked by five Mirage aircraft of San Carlos and struck by four bombs, none of which exploded. One passed through the ship's funnel and another set off a depth charge, starting a fire that was put out after an hour. The Plymouth suffered one casualty and remained operational. During the day, seven Argentine aircraft were shot down.

One RAF Harrier was lost.

June 10

Captain Astiz was flown back to Argentina.

Captain John Hamilton was killed in the only combat action on West Falkland Island when his observation post was overrun by Argentine forces. British 105-mm guns commenced bombardment of Port Stanley from positions high on Mount Kent. Each of the five batteries (six guns each) was given 1,200 shells.

June 11

The Queen Elizabeth 2 arrived back in the United Kingdom with 700 survivors of the Royal Navy warships Coventry, Antelope, and Ardent. The only civilian fatalities in the attack on Port Stanley occurred when a British naval shell struck a house that was thought to be unoccupied. Three women were killed.
Pope John Paul II arrived in Argentina.

June 12

Following three days of artillery bombardment, the British launched the first phase of the attack on Port Stanley. The 3 Parachute Battalion was assigned to take 600-foot Mount Longdon, five miles west of Port Stanley, while 2 Paras, the Welsh Guards, and two companies of 40 Commando were held in reserve. The fighting was very sharp and on many occasions the British advance was only made possible by very close naval gun support from HMS Avenger. The Argentine forces were found to be equipped with effective night sights (passive night goggles). While the British forces had a few dozen pairs, the Argentines had hundreds. The British losses were twenty-three killed and forty-seven wounded. The Argentines lost more than fifty killed and ten wounded as well as thirty-nine taken prisoner. The 42 Commando were ordered to take 900-foot Mount Harriet and 750-foot Goat Ridge, with naval gun support from HMS Yarmouth; the Scots Guard and Gurkhas were in reserve. They achieved this objective with the loss of only one man. Argentine losses were unspecified but heavy. About 200 prisoners were taken. They found the Milan missile to be a very effective way of dislodging entrenched troops (but expensive at $35,000 each). The 45 Commando attacked the Two Sisters range just west or Port Stanley, with naval gun support from HMS Glamorgan. They achieved the goal with the loss of four men.
The HMS Glamorgan was struck by a land-launched Exocet missile. The Argentines did not possess any of the land-launched version of the Exocet but removed one of their shipboard Exocets and mounted it on a flatbed trailer. The Glamorgan attempted to shoot down the Exocet with a Sea Cat missile but failed. The missile exploded in the area of the helicopter hangar, destroying a Wessex 3 helicopter and resulting in thirteen killed and seventeen injured. The ship remained operational.
The Argentine Air Force launched its final air attacks, losing one aircraft to a Sea Dart Missile.

June 14

The second phase of the attack on Port Stanley was launched before dawn. The 2 Battalion, Parachute Regiment, took Wireless Ridge with little opposition but considerable difficulty caused by 155-mm Argentine artillery fire. For the first time, light tanks (Scimitars and Scorpions) were used in support of the advance. The Scots Guards attacked Tumbledown Mountain and found it defended by an elite Argentine Marine battalion. The Scots Guards were supported by Harriers using cluster and laser-guided bombs. They took Tumbledown Mountain with a loss of nine killed and forty-one wounded. Argentine losses were estimated at thirty killed. The Gurkhas took Mount Williams with little resistance. The Welsh Guards took Sapper Hill with little resistance, but had to make a six-hour crossing of a minefield under artillery fire to reach it.

After an expression of willingness, Captain Roderick Bell and SAS Colonel Michael Ross arrived in Port Stanley in a Gazelle helicopter for conversations with General Menendez. Captain Bell, raised in Costa Rica, was fluent in Spanish. The talks were stiff and formal and at first Menendez refused to surrender West Falkland Island. Three hours later, Major General Moore arrived in a Sea King helicopter (after flying through a snow storm) with a surrender document in hand. In a final gesture, General Menendez struck the word "unconditional" but did surrender all Argentine forces in East and West Falkland together with their equipment to General Moore.

As proof that the British never closed the Port Stanley airfield, the last departure of an Argentine C-130 aircraft took place on this day.

June 18

The liner Canberra with 4,200 prisoners and the ferry Norland with 2,000 prisoners sailed from Port Stanley for Puerto Madrym. The British took a total of 11,400 prisoners.

June 20

The Argentine scientific base on Thule Island, one of the South Sandwich Islands which stretch from 250 to 500 miles southeast of South Georgia Island, surrendered to the HMS Endurance and its warship escort.

June 21

The burnt hulk of the logistic landing ship Sir Galahad was towed from Fitzroy and sunk at sea. The Port Stanley airstrip was opened for operations by British Hercules transport aircraft.

June 25

Governor Hunt returned to Port Stanley.

July 1

General Reynaldo Bignone was inaugurated as the new President of Argentina.

July 9

Four hundred forty men of 45 Commando arrived at their home base of Arbroath in Scotland after flying on four VC-10 sorties from Ascension Island.

July 10

The County class destroyer HMS Glamorgan arrived in Portsmouth.

July 11

The liner Canberra returned to Southampton with about 2,500 Royal Marines aboard. The BP tanker Wye arrived in Portland.

July 12

The Falkland Islands conflict technically ended with the announcement that Britain was satisfied that active hostilities were ended. The total exclusion zone and the economic sanctions remained in effect. The P&O cargo ferry Elk and the tanker Olmeda arrived at Devonport.

July 13

It was announced that Britain would not sell the HMS Invincible to Australia. Australia would get a new carrier of the Invincible class and was offered the lease of HMS Hermes while the new carrier was being built. The Type 22 frigate HMS Brilliant arrived at Devonport. Sea King helicopters from HMS Fearless and HMS Intrepid flew from their ships to Yeovilton, along with two captured Augusta A109 helicopters.

July 14

The remaining 593 Argentine prisoners, including General Menendez, arrived back in Argentina aboard the ferry St. Edmund. The two Royal Navy amphibious assault ships, HMS Fearless and HMS Intrepid, arrived at Portsmouth. The Rothesay class frigate HMS Plymouth arrived at Rosyth showing the scars made by four unexploded bombs.

July 17

The Tribal class frigate HMS Tartar was recommissioned at Devonport.

July 19

Six Sea Harriers arrived at Yeovilton after flying off the

HMS Hermes while the carrier was en route to Portsmouth.

July 21

HMS Hermes arrived in Portsmouth.

July 22

Britain lifted the total exclusion zone but warned Argentina to keep military ships and aircraft away from the Falklands.

August 2

The newly commissioned carrier HMS Illustrious, sister ship of the Invincible, departed for the Falklands.

August 5

The Ministry of Defence issued an "Interim Commentary of Equipment Matters" that serves as a kind of scorecard of performance and losses in the Falklands conflict. It is interesting to put these MOD statements in counterpoint with unofficial statements by sources in the Argentine Air Force (the only Argentine service that has been willing to talk) and other sources, mostly British.

Initial deployment. The MOD stated that twenty-two Sea Harriers were pitted against 120 Argentine fast jet aircraft. The Argentine Air Force said that they employed eighty-one aircraft of this class (Mirage III, Mirage V or Dagger, and A-4). However, the Argentine Navy supplied some planes: five Super Etendards and perhaps fifteen A-4Q Skyhawks. If one then throws in eight Macchi MB-326 and about eight Macchi 329 aircraft that were probably based on the islands, one can come up with 117 Argentine jet aircraft, near the MOD figure of 120. The Argentines also had an estimated forty-five Pucara aircraft.

Final deployment. The MOD stated that twenty-eight Sea Harriers and fourteen RAF Harrier GR-3 aircraft were deployed. They were close to exhausting the inventory of Sea Harriers because the Royal Navy possessed only thirty-four such aircraft. Sea Harriers flew about 1,500 sorties, and the RAF Harriers about 150. The MOD stated that no Harriers of either type were lost in air-to-air combat and that five were lost to ground fire. There is a raging debate between British and French arms makers as to the meaning of the term "ground fire." The French claim that several were shot down by the Roland missile while the British admit to only one, with the others lost to gunfire. The MOD statement also omitted non-combat losses. Other sources quote seven Sea Harriers lost, plus four Harriers lost in accidents.

Argentine losses. The MOD quoted Argentine losses as 109 aircraft of all kinds, including thirty-one A-4 Skyhawks and twenty-six Mirage aircraft. This has been broken down by the International Defence Review as follows:

Skyhawk   31

Mirage	26
Pucara	23[a]
Helicopters	18[a]
Attack trainers	5[b]
Light aircraft	3
Skyvan	1
Canberra	1
C-130 Hercules	1

---

a
An approximate number. It includes those aircraft wrecked or captured on the ground.

b
Probably Macchi aircraft

As to how these losses were inflicted, the MOD gave the following partial breakdown: air-to-air combat (mainly Sea Harrier/Sidewinder), twenty; Sea Wolf, five; Sea Dart, eight; Sea Cat, eight; Blowpipe, nine; Rapier, fourteen; and eight by other missiles. This only totals seventy-two. The International Defence Review gave a breakdown of kills that totaled 109, as follows: Harrier thirty-one (twenty-four by Sidewinder and seven by guns); SAM forty-one; destroyed on the ground or captured thirty; "other" seven (includes small arms fire, planes shot down by the Argentines by mistake, and one shot down by a naval 4.5-inch gun). They also broke down the thirty-one Harrier kills as follows:

Mirage	19
Skyhawk	5
Pucara	2
Canberra	1
C-130 Hercules	1
Helicopters	3

On the other hand, the Argentine Air Force admitted the loss of thirty-four Mirage and Skyhawk aircraft (forty-two percent of their deployed force). Other figures given by the Argentine Air Force included: 505 sorties planned, 445 actually executed, and 302 (with 2,782 flying hours) reached their objectives. There were also 446 search and rescue missions. After May 1st, 435 tons of cargo were supplied to Port Stanley and 264 wounded were evacuated. They estimate British losses as twelve to fourteen aircraft, twelve helicopters (MOD is silent about helicopter losses but there were many non-combat losses that the Argentines did not know about), six ships sunk, ten damaged, and seven probably damaged.

Air support. The MOD stated that 5,600 troops and 7,500 tons of cargo were flown to Ascension Island using over 17,000 flying hours by RAF C-130 and VC-10 aircraft. Nimrods also flew about 150 sorties from Ascension Island to monitor activity along the

Argentine coast, and there were thirty-five air drops from Hercules onto the islands.

Artillery support. About 8,000 rounds were fired from naval guns in support of ground operations. The 105-mm artillery delivered fire support at rates up to 500 rounds in twenty-four hours.

Ship support. Noting that the average sailing time from the UK to the Falklands was twenty-one days, the MOD said that over fifty ships, totaling 673,000 tons, were requisitioned from private companies. These ships transported 100,000 tons of freight, 9,000 men, and ninety-five assorted aircraft to the South Atlantic. These figures apparently did not include ships in the Royal Fleet Auxiliary. A complete listing of ships known to be with the task force from unclassified sources showed 675,038 tons of merchant shipping and 398,958 tons from the Royal Fleet Auxiliary broken down as shown in the table below. The tonnage of the tankers was very impressive indeed.

The Rothesay class frigate HMS Berwick was recommissioned after 1-1½ years on the disposal list at Chatham.

	Private	Royal Fleet Auxiliary	Totals
Troop Transports and Equipment Ferries	13 ships of 215,339 tons		13 ships of 215,339 tons
Supply Ships	4 ships of 35,615 tons	5 ships of 109,772 tons	9 ships of 145,387 tons
Support Ships	15 ships of 49,912 tons	5 ships of 20,832 tons[a]	20 ships of 70,744 tons
Tankers	23 ships of 374,172 tons	10 ships of 271,954 tons	33 ships of 646,126 tons

[a]Includes HMS Endurance.

August 7

Brigadier Lami Dozo was replaced by Brigadier Augusto Hughes as head of the Argentine Air Force.

August 10

The hospital ship Uganda returned to England.

August 11

The requisitioned trawler Pict, which had been converted to a minesweeper, returned to Rosyth. The Pict was the first British ship to enter Port Stanley after the cessation of hostilities.

August 13

A high-ranking Soviet mission began a week-long visit to Argentina.

August 17

Operation Tin Lion was started by 50 Squadron, Royal Engineers, to strengthen and lengthen the Port Stanley airfield to take F-4 Phantom fighters.

August 18

Shells which contained toxic chemicals similar to nerve gas were found near Port Stanley.

August 28

HMS Illustrious relieved HMS Invincible on station in the South Atlantic.

August 31

The Leander class frigate HMS Bacchante returned to England from the Falklands. The ship, which had been sold to New Zealand, was transferred to that country in October.

September 1

Flight operation statistics during Operation Corporate were issued by the Office of the Flag Officer, Naval Air Command. They show a total of 12,757 sorties and 23,724 flying hours for Royal Navy aircraft. A breakdown by aircraft is as follows.

	Flying Time (hours)	Sorties
Sea Harrier	2,675	2,376
Sea King	11,922	5,552
Wessex	5,090	2,054
Lynx	3,043	1,863
Wasp	994	912

September 11

HMS Avenger, HMS Andromeda, and HMS Penelope returned to Devonport.

September 13

HMS Fearless landed Dutch marines in Denmark as a part of the NATO exercise "Bold Guard."

September 14

Britain and Argentina lifted their financial sanctions. The trade sanctions remain in place, however.

September 17

HMS Invincible arrived at Portsmouth.

October 1

Admiral Jorge Isaac Anaya retired as head of the Argentine Navy.

October 2

Juan Lanari, Argentine Foreign Minister, told the UN General Assembly that hostilities in the Malvinas had officially ceased. They would take no action to alter this situation.

October 9

Lieutenant Colonel H. Jones and Sergeant Ian McKay were awarded posthumous Victoria Crosses, Britain's highest decoration for valor.

October 17

The first F-4 Phantoms of 29 Squadron landed on the 6,100-foot runway at Port Stanley after a flight of eight hours and forty five minutes from Ascension Island; this flight involved seven inflight refuelings.

October 22

John Nott arrived in the Falklands for a visit.

October 26

Mr. Nott was present for the reburial of the dead in a new cemetery overlooking Port San Carlos. In all, the British suffered 255 killed and 777 wounded. Argentine losses were 712 killed and less than 1,000 injured. The Prime Minister reported to the House of Commons that the cost of repossessing the Falkland Islands, South Georgia and Thule was 700 million pounds.

About the Contributors

F. Clifton Berry, Jr. is Editor in Chief of Air Force Magazine, published by the Air Force Association in Washington, D.C. He served in the Air Force on the Berlin Airlift, and then in the U.S. Army in airborne units. Mr. Berry has been writing feature articles on military topics for more than fifteen years, was co-editor of Armed Forces Journal from 1975 until 1978, and was appointed to his current position with Air Force Magazine in 1980.

Peter M. Dunn, Colonel, U.S. Air Force, is Assistant Provost for Research, Defense Intelligence College. Colonel Dunn is a veteran of three tours of duty in Vietnam, and flew well over one hundred and fifty combat missions over North Vietnam and Laos. Dr. Dunn's ground-breaking work on the beginnings of the Indochina conflicts, The First Vietnam War: The Allied Occupation of South Vietnam 1945-1946, will be published in 1984. He is currently writing about the U.S. Army in Vietnam for a book on counter-insurgency to be published in 1984 by the Royal Military Academy, Sandhurst, and is researching his next book, which will deal with revolutionary war in the twentieth century.

Norman Friedman is a theoretical physicist and strategist at the Hudson Institute, where he specializes in naval and military technological analysis. Dr. Friedman is a prolific author. His recent books include Battleship Design and Development, 1905-1945, Modern Warship Design and Development, Carrier Air Power, Naval Radar, U.S. Destroyers: An Illustrated Design History, and U.S. Aircraft Carriers: An Illustrated Design History.

James L. George is Assistant Director, Multilateral Affairs Bureau, U.S. Arms Control and Disarmament Agency. Prior to this assignment, Dr. George served as a Public Affairs Fellow at the Hoover Institution on War, Revolution and Peace, as a Professional Staff Member for Senator William Brock, and then as a Professional Staff Member for National Security Affairs, Committee on Government Operations, United States House of Representatives. Until recently, Dr. George served as Acting Director, U.S. Arms Control and Disarmament Agency pending the approval of Ambassador Kenneth Adelman by Congress. Dr. George is a frequent contributor to the U.S. Naval Institute Proceedings. He has edited a book, Problems of Sea Power as We Approach the Twenty-First Century, and is coauthoring a book entitled The New Caribbean Triangle: Soviet, Cuban and American Interests in the Region with Bruce W. Watson.

Lawrence S. Germain is a staff member on the Weapons Program, Los Alamos National Laboratory, where he is researching the history of nuclear weapons technology. Dr. Germain is most concerned with the history of nuclear policy. He is well published, and his Falklands chronology is a result of his extensive analysis of the Falklands War.

Gerald W. Hopple is the Distinguished Visiting Professor, Defense Intelligence College. Previously, he has served on the faculty of the University of Maryland, and as a research scientist in the National Security and Foreign Policy Study Centre of the Washington, D.C. Human Affairs Research Centre of the Battelle Memorial Institute. Dr. Hopple is a specialist in crisis analysis, political psychology, analytical methodology, and comparative foreign policy. He is a prolific writer, and his books include, Political Psychology and Biopolitics: Assessing and Predicting Elite Behavior in Foreign Policy Crises, Expert Generated Data: Applications in International Affairs (co-author and co-editor), Foreign Policy Behavior: The Interstate Behavior Analysis Model (co-author), and Biopolitics, Political Psychology and International Politics: Towards a New Discipline (editor). He is currently editing a book entitled The Military Intelligence Community with Bruce W. Watson.

Brad Roberts is Executive Assistant to the President of the Georgetown University Center for Strategic and International Studies. Prior to joining the Center, Mr. Roberts was an analyst in defense policy and arms control at the Congressional Research Service of the U.S. Library of Congress. He has published on a variety of political-military subjects.

William J. Ruhe, Captain, U.S. Navy (Retired), is the editor of The Submarine Review, the quarterly journal of the Submarine League. He was a submarine commander in World War II and later commanded a division of submarines. His surface ship commands included the division which had the first U.S. guided missile destroyer. Upon retirement, Captain Ruhe was appointed to the staff of the President's Commission for Marine Science, Engineering and Research. For the past fifteen years, he has been the General Dynamics Corporate Director of Marine Program Development and Manager of Warfare Analysis. He is presently a consultant for General Dynamics in the same areas.

Harry G. Summers, Jr., Colonel, U.S. Army, is an infantry veteran of the Korean and Vietnam wars. He has served on the faculty of the U.S. Army Command and General Staff College, as a political-military staff officer on the Army General Staff, and as a strategic analyst for three successive Army Chiefs of Staff. He currently serves on the faculty of the U.S. Army War College. His book, On Strategy: A Critical Analysis of the Vietnam War, is a major contribution to our understanding of that conflict.

William J. Taylor, Jr., Colonel, U.S. Army (Retired), is Director, Political-Military Studies and Chief Operating Officer at Georgetown University's Center for Strategic and International Studies. Prior to his retirement from the Army, Dr. Taylor served in command and staff positions in tank and rifle battalions in Germany, Korea, and Vietnam, as the Director of National Security Studies at West Point, and as a visiting professor at the U.S. National War College. Dr. Taylor has written extensively. His most recent works include, American National Security: Policy and Process (co-author), Defense Manpower Planning: Issues for the 1980s (co-author), and The Future of Conflict: U.S. Interests.

Earl H. Tilford, Jr., Major, U.S. Air Force, is Associate Editor of Air University Review. Major Tilford is a frequent contributor to military journals and has written a book entitled Search and Rescue in Southeast Asia. Prior to joining the Air University Review, Major Tilford taught at the U.S. Air Force Academy, and served as a historian at the Office of Air Force History. Major Tilford is a frequent contributor to Air Force Magazine and other professional journals, in which he discusses national subjects pertaining to air power.

Frank Uhlig, Jr. is Editor of Naval War College Press and Naval War College Review. He is also assistant director at the War College's Center for Naval Warfare Studies. Prior to assuming these positions, Mr. Uhlig served as editor and then senior editor at the U.S. Naval Institute, and was founding editor of the Institute's annual Naval Review. A prominent commentator on naval matters, he has written for a wide variety of magazines, newspapers and books. In 1970 he was awarded the Navy League's Alfred Thayer Mahan Award for Literary Achievement.

Bruce W. Watson, Commander, U.S. Navy, is Director of Research at the Defense Intelligence College and is an Adjunct Professor in the Russian Area Studies Program, Georgetown University, where he lectures on the Soviet Navy. Dr. Watson is a frequent contributor to military journals and is the author of Red Navy at Sea: Soviet Naval Operations on the High Seas, 1956-1980. He is currently co-editing a book entitled The Soviet Navy: Strengths and Liabilities (with Susan Watson), a second book with Gerald Hopple on the military intelligence community, and is co-authoring a book on the Caribbean basin with James George.

Index

175